Healing Addiction

An Integrated
Pharmacopsychosocial
Approach to Treatment

PETER R. MARTIN, M.D.
BENNETT ALAN WEINBERG, Esq.
and BONNIE K. BEALER

BICENTENNIAL
1807
WILEY
2007
BICENTENNIAL

John Wiley & Sons, Inc.

This book is dedicated to my cherished wife, Barbara Bradford Martin, and my son Alec, my pride and joy, both of whom continue to teach me how to love and live a balanced life, and also to my parents Eva and Nicholas Martin, who provided my foundation.

—Peter R. Martin, M.D.

Our work on this book is dedicated to Bennett's aunt, Miriam W. Shore, DO, a physician who, recognizing the meaning and value of our work, met with us repeatedly to provide advice and encouragement and supported our efforts in every possible way.

—Bennett Alan Weinberg, Esq., and Bonnie K. Bealer

Contents

Part II The Integrated Approach: Pharmacopsychosocial Treatment of Addiction as a Bona Fide Mental Illness

Part III Gaining Understanding: Treating Drug Addictions

Part V Recovery as an Ongoing Process: Control Is Never Complete

Foreword

I HAD BEEN asked to be present at "grand rounds" at Vanderbilt University on the topic of sex addiction. Within teaching hospitals, this is an occasion for colleagues to share expertise, recent research, or new technology. For me it was a very different challenge. To start, I am a psychologist and not a physician. Second, I was not on the Vanderbilt faculty so in effect was an outsider. And, most important, sex addiction, of all the addictions, is one of the hardest to understand. This challenge is not because the mechanisms are very different. Rather the difficulty arises in talking about sex including some of the dark ways human sexuality is expressed. Finally, physicians are a difficult audience because they are not well prepared usually to understand either addictive behavior or sexual behavior. Plus their scientific training always demands evidence. I knew it would be a challenging audience. With physicians, I always start with data because without that the attention span would be short. I also used case examples of physicians because doctors always like to learn about the problems of other doctors.

Just before we started Peter Martin breezed through the door. He clearly was a man on a mission and, like so many other talented physicians, the demands of his day were showing. My intuition was that he would be in and out and not spend the time to learn about how human sexuality could go awry. Not only did he stay, but he became deeply engaged in the discussion. He was clearly skeptical. He asked tough questions. But he listened. And there began a dialogue that has gone on now for almost a decade. He is a rare talent. His ability to formulate significant research has been helpful to the whole field of addiction medicine. As a clinician, he has helped many, as any reader of this book discovers. It is very unusual to have someone do both. All of which brings us to the significance of this book.

To have a physician of Dr. Martin's stature write a book that acknowledges the threads of addiction beyond drugs and alcohol is a testimony first to his vision and second to the maturation of addiction medicine as a field. To look at the common characteristics across behavioral addictions and chemical addictions helps profoundly to make sense of the distorted world addiction creates. Most addicts have more than one addiction. We are finally filling the empty spaces the average addict knew were there but did not know why or what to do about it. That this book is designed for both the entire therapeutic community and for the people who have the problem is also very important. Peter and his collaborators have written an easy-to-read yet thorough book for the person who really wants to understand addiction and what can be done about it.

In follow-up conversations I would meet Peter and other faculty members to talk about various projects. I remember standing at the blackboard one day with them and we took turns with a piece of chalk. I had to push very hard to get them to really understand the inner world of a sex addict. Peter pushed me on how memory and learning work in the human brain. The passing around of the chalk was symbolic to me in how we started to make progress in understanding one another. Out of that came many good things. Peter and his colleagues are credited with breakthrough initiatives of using very sophisticated ways of looking at how the addict's brain operates. Also, the first course in teaching physicians about sexual boundaries was piloted there at Vanderbilt University and is now taught throughout North America. Eventually Peter and I would go on to present together, and I appreciated having his competence on my side.

The truth is that we all have come to understand that addiction is a brain disease with a definite biological basis. To think in only moral terms brings us up a dead-end street that has only led to more misery. Human beings do lose control. It is our number-one medical cost and our number-one problem in schools. Most child abuse and domestic violence involve addiction. Most crime is committed under the influence. And even though it should be our number-one priority, almost four million people need help for drug addiction every year—and cannot get it. Until we as a country deeply understand this, we are destined to see the same headlines every day—which never look at the deeper issues of addiction.

No disease entity has ever received the research support or the treatment necessary until those with the problem stood up and said there was a problem. Diabetes, Alzheimer's, AIDS, cancer—the list is endless. Once the people with the problem and their family members united and demanded action, we made progress. Addiction has been filled with so much shame and misunderstanding that we cannot face the obvious. The irony is that it is the community of recovering addicts and family members who through self-help have created a model of being good consumers of health information. Though the misunderstanding and pain persist, we are now in a position scientifically, clinically, and socially to make a difference. *Healing Addiction* draws deeply on all of these roots and provides a significant vision to help make that happen.

Patrick J. Carnes
Author of *Out of the Shadows*
Executive Director, Gentle Path Program
Pine Grove Behavioral Health Center

Hattiesburg, Mississippi
August 2006

Preface

PETER R. MARTIN, M.D.

EVERY DAY, IN my clinical work as an addiction psychiatrist, I encounter the personal tragedies of patients suffering from addictive disorders. The medical histories of my patients are representative of the enormous health care and societal costs of alcohol, drug, and tobacco use—estimated as well above $500 billion annually in the United States alone, according to a 2004 study (Uhl & Grow, 2004). This figure includes health care and law enforcement expenditures and lost productivity, but it cannot begin to meaningfully quantify the associated human suffering. How does one determine the monetary value of the loss parents experience after their adolescent daughter dies in an automobile accident while driving home from the senior prom with her intoxicated boyfriend? How does one tabulate the consequences for a young woman of growing up in a disintegrating family in which she did not learn to parent and love effectively? How can one forget seeing one's favorite brother in a pool of blood after he has shot himself in the head as a result of a cocaine binge or calculate in dollars the suffering this inflicts in the survivor for years thereafter? Nevertheless, these faces of addiction, though compelling, represent but the tip of the iceberg.

The last decade has seen a *bona fide* paradigm shift in our understanding of addiction. Until the mid-1990s, the realm of addiction psychiatry strictly comprised the diagnosis and treatment of "substance use disorders" and "substance-induced disorders" as defined by the fourth edition of the *Diagnostic and Statistical Manual* (*DSM-IV*) of the American Psychiatric Association, namely substance abuse and dependence and its complications and consequences. Scientific rigor prohibited the consideration under the rubric of abuse or dependence of many other behaviors, such as pathological gambling, problematic hypersexuality, or obesity, behaviors clearly as self-destructive and out-of-control as drug use disorders. Rather, these nondrug "addictive behaviors" were elsewhere classified in the *DSM* as obsessive, compulsive, or impulse control disorders. However, lay therapists, counselors, and those who were "in recovery" from out-of-control behaviors had recognized for years that a self-help and mutual support treatment approach similar to the 12 steps of Alcoholics Anonymous could provide significant relief for these other problematic behaviors. Interestingly, clinical psychologists also observed that behavior therapy techniques used for the treatment of alcoholism and drug addiction were useful in management of various out-of-control behaviors.

I, along with many of my medical colleagues, was one of the last to seriously consider this unitary perspective of addiction, in which out-of-control behaviors and drug use disorders were viewed as mechanistically similar. In retrospect, some of the counselors and psychologists with whom I worked over the years would say that I only came to this realization "kicking and screaming." I started to appreciate that my "12-step" colleagues were on to something significant when we first began conducting brain functional magnetic resonance imaging studies of sexual arousal and humor in healthy men. Interestingly, reward pathways of the brain overlapping with those activated in addicts by exposure to drug-related stimuli were activated in healthy men when they viewed sexually explicit videotape segments. These findings were quite relevant to the many patients whose sexual behavior is out of control and self-destructive, which some call "sexual addiction" or "sexual compulsivity." The *DSM* has not classified this disorder at all, in spite of the facts that there are examples of individuals with out-of-control sexuality in the daily news and experts are convinced that such cases are very prevalent in our society. I have chosen to use the term "problematic hypersexuality," instead of "sexual addiction," to describe such patients, so as not to jump to a conclusion about the cause of the disorder before the appropriate research is done. (Nevertheless, this term does not preclude our seeking to understand and treat the problem from the perspective of an addiction.) I am grateful to Patrick Carnes, Ph.D., David Dodd, M.D., and Reid Finlayson, M.D., who were instrumental in persuading me that, in spite of my intuitive resistance, examining sexuality in the same framework as drug addiction was a worthwhile research undertaking.

During the past decade, many imaging studies have been carried out to map the regions of the brain that are activated by other drives besides out-of-control behaviors. Also, studies of co-occurring mental illnesses have demonstrated how various addictive behaviors tend to cluster and interact with each other and within the same families. Finally, advances in medications for treatment of these disorders have supported shared underpinnings of drug and behavioral addictions. The results of this research has made even the purists among psychiatrists open to considering, if not accepting, that the similarities among addiction disorders are more common than heretofore thought (Martin & Petry, 2005). This paradigmatic shift has opened the field of addiction psychiatry to new scientifically based questions that will help our patients. For example: What is the role of sexual or other behaviors in relapse to drugs? Are there underlying neurochemical mechanisms underpinning obesity and cocaine dependence? What is the role of early losses or trauma in all addictive disorders? How do medicines that affect learning and memory affect addictions of different forms? How can we prevent these devastating illnesses in the next generation?

Earlier I mentioned the devastation of addiction. However, the longer I am in clinical practice, the more I have become encouraged by the success stories of my patients. For example, in my Wednesday afternoon clinic, I see patients in follow-up whom I first saw in crisis on the inpatient unit of the addiction center at Vanderbilt University Medical Center. These patients are now generally doing well coping with their addiction. Some I see relatively frequently to help them cope with the ups and downs of their chronic illnesses; others I have been following for more than 15 years and see only once or twice yearly. All are living productive, fulfilling, and healthy lives. They typically come to see me to check in, discuss milestones in their lives, and obtain prescriptions that have become a reliable way to manage their mental illness. If you looked at them in the hallway outside my office, you might not think that they were patients at all; rather, they look much like the faculty, students, or staff. It is remarkable how good I feel after seeing these patients.

Why then is there such stigma associated with addiction in our society? Why is it that most people find it so difficult, even shameful, to admit that they have an addict in their family? The clearest consequence of this stigma is that most people who are close to addicts or are addicts themselves live lives of quiet desperation, suffering without the relief that can be available should they seek out treatment. If they choose to enter treatment, they often have to struggle to have their health insurance policies cover treatment costs. Many people consider addiction as a sin to be punished by society rather than an illness that merits the attention of the medical profession. Why do major programs of research, education, and patient care at major academic medical centers for cancer, heart disease, or diabetes receive so much funding while addiction programs receive so little? Considering the role of addiction in many of the most common illnesses that affect humankind, the many scientific advances in our understanding of addiction in recent years, and the prevalence of addiction in our country, this disparity seems unjustified. The truth is that affluent families readily identify with and fund programs that deal with cancer, heart disease, or diabetes as a public service to their communities but have difficulty having their names associated with addiction research or treatment, even if some of their family members suffer from these disorders.

It is easier to admit to cancer or heart disease in your family than to the addictive behaviors that played a vital role in causing these diseases. Understanding the out-of-control brain that underlies all addictions might be the last medical frontier, but we already know enough to stop blaming people for not being able to stop the self-destructive behaviors that are the consequences. People who are addicted no longer enjoy alcohol, drugs, or their dysfunctional behaviors. Their lives actually lack the day-to-day pleasures that we all live for. They no longer enjoy a beautiful flower, the smile of a loved one, or seeing their children grow to adulthood. Isn't that sad? Why can't we, as a society, understand they are suffering rather than blame them for their illness? I hope this book contributes to helping us as a society overcome some of these mistaken attitudes and allows us to assist those suffering from addictive disorders feel better about themselves as they seek treatment. I have long wanted to synthesize over 30 years' worth of clinical and scientific experience in the addiction field for the broad range of treatment professionals. With this book I am hoping to provide the wisdom I have learned over the years from so many of my patients, each of whom deserves my thanks.

It was indeed fortunate when I encountered Bennett Weinberg and Bonnie Bealer rather serendipitously. Because I had done research on the neurobiology of coffee constituents, Bennett and Bonnie sent me their book, *The World of Caffeine: The Science and Culture of the World's Most Popular Drug*. I found their writing succinct and scientifically descriptive and with a popular flair that I realized I could not hope to capture— hence began a very interesting and fruitful collaboration. This book is, in reality, the product of three people who each offer different skills. When combined, we hope it is greater than the sum of its parts.

Finally, I wish to acknowledge others who taught me more than they will ever realize, who had critical input in my development as an addiction psychiatrist. This book is a tribute to my colleagues, teachers, and friends. To W. Anderson Spickard, Jr., M.D., I owe a debt of gratitude for taking a rather green physician who came to Vanderbilt from the ivory towers of the National Institutes of Health (NIH) and allowing him to see some "real doctoring" in the trenches—watching how Andy treated his patients taught me practical things you can never learn in books. To Thomas A. Ban, M.D., I owe my understanding of *clinical* psychiatry research—Tom took me under his wing when I came to Vanderbilt and gave me the wise counsel to "go see a lot of patients" in order to determine what questions were most important to pursue in the laboratory. Pietro Castelnuevo-Tedesco, M.D., taught me that classical psychiatry and its emphasis on human relationships, especially as they relate to one's love and work, is fundamental to every human pursuit. Karen Starr, R.N., M.S.N., allowed me to recognize the usefulness of the right versus left brain in healing addiction. Howard Roback, Ph.D., helped me laugh at some of life's travails and revert to playful adolescence in the security of friendship. Michael J. Eckardt, Ph.D., my early collaborator at NIH, taught me that consistency among different scientific perspectives is the real test of validity. Markku Linnoila, M.D., Ph.D., another collaborator at NIH, stimulated me to understand how addiction and other co-occurring psychiatric illnesses may have the same neurobiological underpinnings. Edward M. Sellers, M.D., Ph.D., my supervisor at the Addiction Research Foundation at the University of Toronto, helped me begin to understand interindividual differences in human responses to drugs of abuse, and Harold Kalant, M.D., Ph.D., inspired me with his logic and scholarly approach to addiction. Finally, the inspiration of Donald Olding Hebb, Ph.D., who taught my introductory psychology course at McGill University, is even now apparent as I reread this book.

Most important, my dear wife Barbara B. Martin, M.S.W., the best psychotherapist I know, was tolerant of the many hours I spent toiling on this manuscript. She was the person who taught me how important psychiatry is to human health and helped me in my transition from internal medicine to psychiatry—a journey I began alone, but one I could not have completed without her support and love. My son, Alec, makes me happy and proud by showing me every day how exciting and important the next generation is to us all. Through him I see how wonderful and stimulating life can be. My mother, Eva Martin, was also an important motivating factor by asking so often during our phone calls about the status of the book. My father, Nicholas M. Martin, a very wise man, continues to inspire me even after his death. They both deserve my thanks.

Nashville, April 2006

Preface

Bennett Alan Weinberg, Esq.
Bonnie K. Bealer

After reading our book *The World of Caffeine: The Science and Culture of the World's Most Popular Drug* (Routledge, 2001), Dr. Martin contacted us and proposed that we collaborate to create a book that would present his new theories of addiction treatment in a format accessible to the entire spectrum of the treatment community. Addiction was a new subject for us. But, after speaking with Dr. Martin, we quickly came to understand both its major effect on the health of Americans and the dramatic improvements in therapeutic outcomes that could be expected if Dr. Martin's theories were widely applied. We became delighted to be playing a part in such a socially worthwhile undertaking.

The publication of this book by John Wiley & Sons marks a breakthrough in the treatment of the most damaging and costly health problem in the United States today. The two of us coined the term "pharmacopsychosocial" to designate Dr. Martin's integrated treatment approach, which combines pharmacological therapy with psychological counseling and social support.

Dr. Martin's pharmacopsychosocial approach to addiction therapy is the first to advocate the full use of the powerful, effective medicines, recently developed to treat both primary and secondary addiction, and to combine this pharmacological treatment with the established treatments offered by psychiatrists and members of social support groups. This holistic approach offers new hope to addicts, giving them the same chance for recovery as is enjoyed by the sufferers from other chronic illnesses, such as diabetes and heart disease.

In the past, the efforts to overcome addiction have fallen into one of two schools of thought. The first, promulgated by a professional community of psychiatrists and psychologists, regarded addiction as a failure of willpower with no real medical treatment, unless sufferers had co-occurring psychiatric illness such as depression or anxiety. The second, advanced by self-help groups such as the 12-step programs, regarded addiction as a disease, a failure that can be overcome by relying on the social support offered by the recovering addict's peers.

Both groups, physicians and professional therapists and the lay leaders of self-help communities, offer useful ways of helping addicts to cope with addiction. Unfortunately, however, these groups not only do not work together as much as they might to help addicts, they frequently regard each other's work with suspicion and believe it does more harm than good. Worse still, neither of these groups has recognized the proper place of pharmacological therapy in the armamentarium of treatments for addiction.

It is with pride and hope that we present *Healing Addiction*, a book we are convinced can enable doctors and therapists to help recovering addicts to take back their lives and learn to live free.

Philadelphia, Pennsylvania
June 24, 2006

Acknowledgments

Peter R. Martin, M.D. is supported by research funding from the National Institute on Alcohol Abuse and Alcoholism and the National Institute on Drug Abuse of the National Institutes of Health.

PART I

Out of Control: The Biopsychosocial Model of the Causes of Addiction

CHAPTER 1

The Many Faces of Addiction

ADDICTION IS THE nation's number-one health problem today. Perhaps you thought that distinction belonged to cancer or cardiovascular conditions. But in part because it provides the behavioral underpinnings for so many of the common "lifestyle-related" diseases, addiction is the most widespread and costly of all illnesses. Over the course of a lifetime, at least 20 percent of Americans suffer from substance use disorders, and many of them die as a direct or indirect consequence of these disorders. As commonly recognized, substance use disorders include alcoholism, cigarette smoking, marijuana smoking, and the abuse of cocaine, heroin, and amphetamines. However, newer research findings indicate that the mechanisms of addiction are shared with other problematic and repetitive behaviors that interfere with a balanced lifestyle, such as out-of-control gambling, exercise, computer gaming and viewing pornography on the Internet, and problematic hypersexuality. For example, the current epidemic of obesity, affecting the health of both young and old, can be attributed to similar addictive brain processes that in the past were considered unique to drug abuse and addiction.

Addiction is defined as a persistent, repetitive, and often irresistible self-destructive activity that, at least in the beginning, is perceived as rewarding by individuals, but that robs them of time, resources, or the motivation to do the things that are part of a balanced life and may well have been part of their lives before becoming addicted.

When these behavioral disorders are included in the definition, the

3

percentage of people afflicted with addiction-related disorders is far greater than the 20 percent suffering from substance abuse disorders. Because these afflictions frequently have catastrophic consequences, not only for the addicts but also for family members, friends, and coworkers, it is fair to say that the overwhelming majority of Americans—and indeed of the population of the entire world—will suffer adverse consequences from addiction at some point during their lives.

In this book, we advocate and teach you about the *pharmacopsychosocial* approach to addiction treatment. Pharmacopsychosocial therapy is a breakthrough treatment that uses the latest nonaddictive pharmaceuticals to treat addiction while integrating the psychological and social support necessary to enable the medications to help addicts gain control of their disease.

Contrary to the common myth that addictions are untreatable, we believe that addictions *are* treatable. The prognosis is similar to that of other chronic, life-threatening conditions, such as emphysema, heart attacks, hypertension, and diabetes. Many addicts, if given medical and psychological treatment and social support, can recover their health and lead normal, productive lives. In fact, the goal for the treatment of addiction is recovery, whereas preventing complications may be all that is possible for those suffering from the other chronic disorders just mentioned.

In *The Diseasing of America* (Free Press, 1989), Stanton Peele proposes ways of understanding and coping with addiction that recent research has seriously called into question. During its ascendancy, this title and follow-up titles, such as *The Truth About Addiction and Recovery* (Simon & Schuster, 1991), sold hundreds of thousands of copies. The main idea of these books is that addiction can be overcome through willpower and mentoring by other recovering addicts. These books emphasize that addiction is not a disease that can be treated with pharmaceuticals or should be covered by medical insurance policies. But recent studies of brain activity using functional brain imaging tools, such as functional magnetic resonance imaging (fMRI), have shown that these treatment ideas are wrong. In particular, neuroscientists have shown that addiction alters the neurochemical operations of the brain. Today there are dozens of books about *particular* addictions, such as alcoholism, gambling addiction, cigarette smoking, and even overeating and problematic hypersexuality. In this book, we provide the reader with an authoritative, up-to-date guide to understanding and treating *addiction as a whole*. To this end, we discuss addictions in the context of commonly associated mental and physical conditions. We also show patients, physicians, and counselors how to communicate more effectively and thus increase chances of successful treatment. To do so, we employ the newer integrative perspectives on treatment stemming from the latest findings of neuroscience.

The bad news is that although *some* addicts can recover on their own or with 12-step programs, those who don't seek and receive professional treatment are probably destined to see their condition worsen until it eventually destroys their health and their life. The good news is that medical science now recognizes that addiction is treatable, and, as we have said, success rates are similar to the success rates for other long-term chronic diseases.

So what can people do if they are suffering from addiction? First, they must decide that their behavior represents a significant problem to themselves and to those they hold dear *and* that they are ready to accept treatment. If people are ready for the changes that come with treatment, they must make a commitment to persevere until their addiction is under control and they can lead a productive life. This perseverance must include a commitment to relationships with others with whom they engage in the journey of recovery. Addiction is a lonely state focused on an illness; recovery involves broadening patients' horizons, including developing relationships with others that allow them to grow beyond the myopic concerns of repetitive harmful behaviors. Once addicts have made this commitment, they must learn what medical science can teach us about their disease. Equally important, they must come to appreciate which components of recovery require personal growth beyond the scope of medical understanding. This aspect of recovery is commonly referred to as spirituality, but, in essence, it represents a level of comfort with the uncertainties of life over which none of us has much control. To live life successfully, addicts must come to grips with a delicate balance of relative certainties and uncertainties. The mastery of this skill can save their lives.

Each type of addiction may have unique features that set it apart from other types. However, we wish to emphasize the similarities shared by people who suffer from *all* addictive disorders. In addition to certain similarities in the causes and life courses of addictive disorders, the aspects of addictions that relate to their treatment are, in fact, the most important features they have in common. All addictions are disorders of brain circuitry that result in uncontrolled and repetitive behavior. Addicts may not recognize how harmful these behaviors may be, until the behaviors progressively disrupt their lives. If allowed to run their course, the behaviors will eventually displace all other pursuits.

About half of all addicts are born with genetic markers that predispose them to become addicted. But despite an important genetic component, addiction is *learned behavior*. It is important to understand, therefore, that *genetic risk does not preordain that you will be an addict*. In fact, part of what we are trying to do in this book is to help those with a significant family history of addiction *prevent* the development of addiction in themselves and their children. Our learning is modulated by our emotions and our experience of the world. Addicts learn over time to become numb to the joy they had previously derived from life's normal activities, as these activities are progressively supplanted by repetitive, out-of-control behaviors. Although initially perceived as beneficial and pleasurable, the behaviors become overwhelming and all-consuming and eventually brain chemistry is modified in such a way that these behaviors become "hard-wired" in the brain. Recognizing that you are at significant risk to become an addict because of your family history may enable you to make choices that steer you away from this outcome.

WHO IS THE ADDICT?

People who suffer from the disease of addiction and those who love them are looking for a way out: a treatment that can cure the disease and allow formerly addicted people to live normal, productive, happy lives. But before you can understand how to treat addiction successfully, it is vital that you understand just what addiction is.

Maybe you think you know what addiction is and that you can recognize an addicted person when you see one. Studies by hundreds of researchers, however, reveal that addiction is a complex disease, manifesting itself in many different and, at first sight, confusing ways. It is not only addicts and their families who are confused by this baffling disorder. Many excellent physicians are uncomfortable making this diagnosis, either because they lack appropriate training or have difficulty in accepting addiction as other than a "bad habit" that will go away if left alone.

Do you think you know what an addict "looks like"? In your mind, are addicts people sitting in ramshackle apartments, shooting heroin into their veins? Or do you also regard alcoholics—people from any walk of life who drink excessively without being able to stop—as typical addicts? Would you include the people who use their ingenuity to run methamphetamine labs and abandon their children in order to attain the potent, long-lasting high engendered by this drug? Or the "mellow," unmotivated potheads who grow marijuana and do little else but smoke it? Or the college students who need three or four extra years to complete their education or drop out as a result of excessive "partying"? As we shall see, all these are, in fact, examples of people suffering from the disease of addiction. However, as we shall also see, addiction has many other faces. People with this disease may be addicted not to one drug alone but to many drugs, drugs with a range of diverse pharmacological profiles that interact to heighten the confusion in their lives.

Moreover, addiction is not limited to "substance" abuse. Behavioral addictions can be as destructive to your well-being as substance abuse. Therefore, people who gamble, eat, surf the Internet, or are consumed by work at the expense of other aspects of their lives engage in these behaviors in the same "addictive" manner as those who are addicted to drugs. In fact, brain imaging studies substantiate this understanding of the commonality between substance abuse and behavioral addictions. These studies demonstrate that many of the same areas of the brain are activated during the anticipation of a reward, whether the reward arises from a drug or a behavior to which the individual is addicted. People frequently engage in destructive, out-of-control—or "addictive"—activities to assuage their emotional suffering from other psychiatric illnesses. The intense mental focus required by these activities corresponds with the "high" or "altered" or "numbed" mental states experienced by substance abusers.

Is addiction simply a sign of a weak character, the inability to "say no"? Certainly not! Addiction is a disease. It is a brain disease, contracted when something goes wrong with the biochemistry or physiology of the brain. It is also a disease of the mind, contracted when a person has the necessary emotional disposition or vulnerability to succumb to it. Finally, it is a social disease, because addictive behavior occurs in a social context that not only makes it possible but actually fosters its development. Thus, regardless of the face an addiction presents—regardless of whether drug abuse or other behaviors are involved—treating the disease of addiction successfully requires a therapy that addresses the neurochemical, psychological, and social components of the illness.

As we have said, neuroscientists have shown that addiction is a disease of brain circuitry, not a "bad habit" or character defect. Further, they have shown that it is a disease that can be treated successfully. Addictions are best understood in terms of the neuroadaptive factors (related to memory and learning) that they have in common instead of in terms of their differences. A holistic approach that uses psychological counseling, social intervention, and psychiatric treatments with pharmacological agents offers the best hope for treating the disease of addiction in its many faces.

SYMPTOMS OF ADDICTION

What are the symptoms that all the people suffering from the disease of addiction have in common? In addicts, we find out-of-control behavior that is self-destructive. These two symptoms are always present.

First, the disease manifests itself in behavior that is *out of control*. If a person's conduct is under his or her control, then the person is not properly considered an addict. For example, a person who uses heroin once or visits a casino to gamble on one occasion would not be considered a heroin or gambling addict. What about a person who uses heroin twice? Three times? Many dozens of times? How about someone who visits the casinos to gamble every week for several years? Would such repeated users of heroin and regular gamblers be properly called "addicts"? Again, the answer is that simply engaging in the activities that can support addictions repeatedly does not, in and of itself, make a person an addict. An addicted person is someone who is overcome by forces that are beyond his or her ability to manage. Whatever else addicts may be, they are people who are being driven or compelled to engage in certain conduct. Although this conduct seems desirable at first blush, it quickly loses this attraction for addicts, as their control over their use of drugs or engaging in addictive behaviors diminishes.

This brings us to the second sign or symptom of addiction: behavior that is *self-destructive*. You might wonder how a given behavior can be desirable and self-destructive at the same time. In fact, any behavior, no matter how innocuous it may appear, becomes problematic and ultimately self-destructive if it disturbs a balanced life. The *loss of control* over the behavior and the *destructive consequences* it causes is what renders a particular behavior harmful. For example, eating ice cream can be quite pleasant. However, eating nothing except ice cream and eating ice cream incessantly would soon become both boring and unhealthy, resulting in obesity, diabetes, and other illnesses related to gaining weight. The onset of obesity and related health problems is likely to diminish the person's ability to get around and fend for himself, thereby reducing his self-esteem and making him depressed and causing him to eat more. Complications of diabetes could cause the person's vision to become disturbed, and he could begin to experience burning pains from his nerves. Ultimately, he may become unable to carry out his responsibilities as a member of his family and at the workplace. Life is too complex, varied, and exciting to be restricted by focusing on eating ice cream! As organisms we were designed by evolution to enlist a range of behaviors to enable us to survive and thrive. However, addiction impairs our capacity to adapt to life's challenges. Addicts function in a rut.

Therefore, the two symptoms of addiction—the inability to control a behavior and the self-destructive consequences of a behavior—are really two sides of the same coin. We know this because the clearest evidence that a behavior is really out of control is that a person continues to engage in that behavior, even when it has markedly adverse effects on his life.

When we encounter people who persist in behavior that is impairing or even destroying the fabric of their lives, and who are incapable, despite every effort on their part, to stop engaging in this behavior, we have very probably found people suffering from the disease of addiction.

STAGES OF ADDICTION

Addiction to drugs or alcohol is not an all-or-nothing condition. In the early stages, before the onset of a full-blown addiction, people toying with drugs or alcohol often say they are just "partying." Partying (sometimes called "chipping") is the intermittent use of an addictive drug—for example, alcohol, marijuana, heroin, or cocaine—presumably to make life more "fun," make human interactions more enjoyable, to loosen inhibitions, and so on. Intermittent use, also called "abuse," supports a low-level addiction during which a person can carry on a relatively normal life. People suffer "hangovers" and other mild withdrawal symptoms, often no more than a feeling of unease or disturbed sleep, when they skip using the drug. People with the time and money to keep partying can continue the process of abusing drugs for years. People who party with drugs often sniff them or take them orally, which are less addictive modes of ingestion than injecting or smoking. However, abusing drugs is an unstable condition. Eventually, people who party excessively almost always cross the line, by starting to use the drug every day, and graduate into full-blown addiction.

The disease of brain circuitry that characterizes addiction makes it a mental illness like many others, including thought disorders, dementia, and mood disorders. Schizophrenia, or psychosis, is primarily a thought disorder. Dementia is primarily a disorder characterized by impaired cognitive abilities and memory in a person who was previously functioning normally. Depression is primarily a mood disorder. Addiction is primarily a drive disorder; however, problems with mood, cognitive capacity, and thought can also complicate addiction. In addiction, normal drives go awry, leading to a problematic imbalance of biological, psychological, or social functioning, an imbalance of so-called biopsychosocial components. Drive disorders are also present in other psychiatric disorders, and understanding addiction may therefore help us to understand several psychiatric disorders.

PRIMARY AND SECONDARY ADDICTION

Addiction may be a person's *primary* problem, or it may be a *secondary* problem, resulting from a person's efforts to cope with a deep-seated mental or emotional disorder. Primary addiction, like all psychiatric illnesses, arises directly from a combination of biological, psychological, and social factors. Secondary addiction results from an attempt by someone afflicted with another psychiatric disorder, such as a thought or mood disorder, or a physical incapacity, to relieve suffering by self-medication. Therefore, addiction bears a complex relationship with other mental illnesses. In order to discover the best treatment strategy for each patient, we must unravel this relationship in him or her.

To better understand the important phenomenon of secondary addiction, consider a few examples of this condition.

- Bill W., a U.S. soldier, returns from military duty in Iraq suffering from post-traumatic stress disorder. He finds that he is unable to cope with normal responsibilities and relationships outside the military. He is haunted by memories, shrinks from loud noises, becomes withdrawn, and is beset by severe nightmares. To help counteract his depression and block his memories, he starts to smoke marijuana and to drink alcohol heavily. As time goes on, his life seems to have come to a standstill. His wife has been patient, and she has encouraged Bill to get counseling. But he ignores her. He has even lashed out at her several times and thrown a vase at her once, so that she is now frightened to stay in the same apartment with him. He feels that he is a failure because he cannot recover from his problems, but he refuses to seek help. Finally he commits suicide.
- Ellen B. cannot stand to have her husband touch her unless she is drunk or high on drugs. She is despondent, has very poor self-esteem, and has gained a great deal of weight. During therapy with her psychiatrist, she reveals that her mother spent very little time with her and was very promiscuous. Ellen was also sexually abused by more than one of her mother's live-in boyfriends, and her mother did nothing to protect her. In her early teens, Ellen began smoking marijuana, which she got from her older friends, in an attempt to dissociate or "numb out" during episodes of sexual abuse. As she began to understand that her mother would never protect her, she coped

with her unhappiness by initiating and increasing her use of a variety of drugs. Ellen also became promiscuous, getting a "charge" out of the sense of power she experienced by controlling men with one-night stands. However, except for the time when she was high on drugs, she would experience flashbacks that made her panicky and nightmares and would avoid sexual contact with men. Ellen began to use opiates, such as prescription painkillers, and benzodiazepines, such as Valium or Ativan, regularly and continued the use of marijuana to help her forget her past and medicate her anxiety and various physical pains. She starts visiting doctors with vague complaints for which she can get prescriptions to "help" her. For example, her family doctor has prescribed narcotic pain pills for her chronic back pain. The doctor has been unable to identify an anatomically based cause for the back pain, but he continues to prescribe the pills, because she claims they make her feel better. Her back pain is exacerbated by the fact that she continues to gain weight and fails to exercise, because escalating drug abuse has made her increasingly lethargic and withdrawn. She wants to stay married, but as her husband pressures her to get help, she responds by increasing her drug use.

• Dennis R. was successful in everything he tried. He was the high school quarterback and received a football scholarship to an excellent school. Although he partied all through college, he still won multiple honors in football. He was headed for the pros. He painted the town red during an incredibly successful career, surviving several "career-ending" injuries, always to return better than ever. He hated when his pro career ended, but he began to thrive in the business world. In his early forties, the multiple injuries from his football days began to cause him pain. Eventually, chronic back pain made it very difficult for Dennis to get started in the morning, and sometimes it was hard to get through the day without a good stiff drink. Although he retained his ability to drink heavily from his earlier life, he had avoided it because he was building his many businesses and did not want to compromise his success. However, since drinking helped him tolerate his pain, he stepped it up a notch. Not liking the hangovers and the effects on decision making, he decided to visit his family doctor, who suggested a number of lifestyle changes: Take more care of his physical health, begin exercising again with support from a nutritionist and physical therapist, cut back from his breakneck business traveling, and so on. Dennis was honest with his doctor: He wanted a "quick fix" because he was about to take his corporation public, and he couldn't risk starting to slack off. Since Dennis had had previous surgeries related to sport injuries, his doctor suggested a visit to a pain clinic. The pain doctor reviewed his history and his wishes and felt that chronic low-dose OxyContin might do the trick. The drug worked great and allowed Dennis to carry on. However, after a few months, the OxyContin stopped working for him. The pain doctor recommended that Dennis increase his dose of OxyContin, which helped a lot. During his second year of using OxyContin, Dennis started feeling low and noticed that his energy was waning. He started making mistakes in the business. His frustration led him to start drinking again, and his wife became quite concerned, as there was not much he could do to alleviate his recurring back pain. Dennis became withdrawn and distant from his wife and friends. The business suffered, and he became less responsive to his wife. Her concern turned to anger, and she threatened divorce unless he changed his ways.

We could tell many other stories—the physically abusive and rigid father who produces an antisocial son who becomes an addict; avoidant children who become socially phobic and can relieve their loneliness only with drinking; the young man who was in an automobile accident and was given opioids for pain and found they gave him energy; the head injury patient whose consequent irritability and impulsiveness led to sexual and other acting out that he cannot discontinue; the prostitute or exotic dancer who can work only while high; people who become nervous in intimate situations and so have many meaningless one-night stands.

When addiction is a person's only psychological, emotional, or behavioral problem, he or she is said to be suffering from a *primary addiction*. If people suffer from psychological, emotional, and behavioral problems that began before the onset of their addiction and were the cause of their becoming addicts, they are said to be suffering from a *secondary addiction*.

This book will explain how treatment with addiction-specific medicines, such as methadone, naltrexone, buprenorphine, or acamprosate, among others, may be indicated to help overcome primary addictions. (See Appendices D and E for a complete list and description of these medicines.) However, people with other primary psychopathologies—for example, depression, anxiety, or psychosis—frequently develop a secondary addiction to drugs or alcohol. (In fact, secondary addiction is probably more prevalent than primary addiction.) When addiction is the secondary problem and another disorder is the primary problem, pharmacopsychosocial treatment for the underlying condition must come first. For example, say a woman who suffers from long-standing depression uses heroin to attempt to feel better; it is essential to treat the underlying depression in order to help her stop using heroin.

In order to provide enlightened treatment, doctors and therapists must be able to grapple with the complex relationship of addiction with other mental and physical illnesses. Unfortunately, many addiction treatment programs are poorly equipped to address those other disorders, and psychiatric treatment facilities usually want to avoid or fail to address the needs of addicted patients, even though they suffer from bona fide psychiatric illnesses. And the pharmaceutical industry often excludes from clinical trials of antidepressants, mood stabilizers, and other psychiatric medications patients with alcoholism or drug addictions, even though by doing so they are leaving out a large group of people who suffer from the primary disorders for which these medications are being developed. Only recently have pharmaceutical companies started taking an interest in this enormous addicted patient population, by developing medications specifically for addiction treatment and by evaluating their medications in patients with co-occurring addiction and other psychiatric disorders. Comorbidity, the presence of a psychiatric illness co-occurring with addiction, is widespread for all psychiatric illnesses but is particularly marked in cases of mood disorders, such as bipolar disorder, and in certain personality types. For example, 30 to 50 percent of the addiction patients treated at the Vanderbilt Addiction Center at Vanderbilt University in Nashville, Tennessee, meet criteria for bipolar disorder or post-traumatic stress disorders.

Throughout this book we will consider the place of psychotherapeutic support and how important it is to understanding and grappling with the underlying causes of addiction. The most common areas needing this support involve psychological trauma, life experiences, and developmental processes. And because addiction is a social phenomenon as well, and because it cannot be understood or managed without considering the situation of the addicted person in society, we will also explore the social factors that give rise to addiction and the critical role family, friends, and work experience play in recovery. Psychological and social interventions can both help addicts to learn to cope with and change maladaptive behaviors and actually modify the activity and structure of the brain on a molecular level.

Finally, we will focus on resilience of the human spirit, an ephemeral trait that allows addicts to recover and is not easily defined using the "scientific method." Empathy expressed by other addicts, for example, in the context of self-help groups, can help those who, because of drugs and alcohol, are on the precipice of self-destruction turn toward a better life, a life that is not one of quiet desperation but imbued with zest, healthy relationships, and fulfillment. The cost of the alternative is to re-create the turmoil of addiction in the generation that follows, and no addict, no matter how ill, wants to do that.

CHAPTER 2

The Historical Development of Drug Addiction

SINCE THE BEGINNING of recorded history, people of almost every society have used psychoactive substances for medical purposes. Equally ancient is the self-administration of psychoactive agents to "feel good" or otherwise to alter one's subjective state and experience of the world. The socially acceptable amount used varied from place to place, but some people always consumed more than was generally considered acceptable within social norms. Inhabitants of Sumerian city-states drank beer before 3000 B.C. Opium was used in Greek and Roman medicine and was widely available in Egypt, Persia, and India prior to the Christian era. South American Indians ingested cocaine by chewing the leaves of the coca plant. Marijuana, the flowering tops of the weed *Cannabis sativa*, has long been smoked to treat pain, convulsions, glaucoma, muscle spasms, bronchial asthma, and nausea and vomiting. Tobacco, the source of nicotine, was introduced into European culture by the sixteenth-century Spanish explorers of the New World, where Native Americans commonly smoked the plant. From Spain, tobacco use spread throughout the world.

Recently, pharmaceutical science has created a wide range of new central nervous system (CNS) depressants and stimulants, hallucinogens, and dissociative anesthetics, such as phencyclidine (PCP), as well as variations of traditional psychoactive compounds. Technological advances in preparation (e.g., distillation processes for ethanol, purification of cocaine, synthesis of heroin from morphine, "cooking" recipes to turn the cold medicine pseudoephedrine into methamphetamine) and drug delivery (the hypodermic needle) have allowed the self-administration of increasingly greater doses of the drugs found in nature or their synthesized derivatives.

CHANGING ATTITUDES ABOUT PSYCHOACTIVE SUBSTANCES

Whenever people take "inappropriate" or "excessive" amounts of a psychoactive substance, they are regarded as having a "disorder," and society's response has been to regard such people as addicts. In the 1960s, because the term "addiction" was considered pejorative, the term "dependence" became widely used by doctors. "Dependence" is still the preferred term, according to the *Diagnostic and Statistical Manual of the American Psychiatric Association* (*DSM*), although, since the 1990s, the terms "addiction" and "addict" resurfaced in the scientific and clinical literature, either interchangeably with "dependence" or "dependent person" or as a particularly severe form of dependence. We have chosen to use both terms interchangeably in this book.

Addicts are, in turn, seen as either patients or criminals and, hence, as moral or immoral, innocent or guilty, victims or perpetrators. Accordingly, the task of rehabilitation is assigned to medicine or the criminal justice system. Only in recent years have these two extreme views been reconciled in the forum of drug courts, specializing in prosecuting drug cases. These courts are a compassionate and effective way to deal with severely addicted criminals who require incarceration but have not perpetrated violent crimes. In our culture, there is no straightforward correspondence between a drug's effects on health and whether it is classified as licit or illicit within criminal law. For example, the use of alcohol, which poses a great health and safety risk, is not illegal, while the use of far less toxic drugs, such as marijuana, is severely sanctioned by the law.

The ever-changing drug laws in the United States document cyclical shifts in our attitudes toward and ways of dealing with drug use. These cycles include, in sequence: permissiveness, criminal prohibition, enforcement, nonenforcement, and noncriminal regulation. Today there is a concept known as *nonpredatory behaviors*. These are culturally accepted offenses that involve voluntary participation with no perceived *direct* victim. Most scientists and doctors would classify psychoactive drug use in this category.

At different times during the twentieth century, the legal system focused its suppression efforts on, in turn, alcohol, heroin, marijuana, cocaine, and methamphetamine. The rational basis for these efforts at legal control is subject to question. The prohibition of the production and sale of alcohol in the United States from 1919 to 1933 had its impetus in the moral pressure of temperance ideology rather than a concern for health. Drinking had been a concern of the churches in America since the beginning of the nineteenth century. During Prohibition, alcohol continued to be consumed; in fact, use actually became much riskier, since the manufacture of alcoholic beverages was unregulated and the alcohol produced was often tainted.

With the criminalization of opiates by the Harrison Act of 1914, opiate addicts became socioeconomically marginalized. The cost of heroin skyrocketed, making it impossible for addicts to purchase the drug without recourse to crime. Heroin addicts were forced into a particularly damaging lifestyle, characterized by predatory crime and self-neglect, including malnutrition and infectious diseases, even though it is clear that well-controlled opiate use is less physically dangerous than the equivalent use of certain other psychoactive agents, such as alcohol, that are not illegal.

One of the most controversial legal sanctions has resulted in the enormous financial and social costs of the large-scale criminalization of marijuana, even though the drug has arguably few demonstrable adverse effects on health. These costs increased dramatically as millions of mainly young people began using the drug in the 1960s and 1970s. Harsh legal controls have been mostly ineffective in reducing the prevalence of cannabis use. It became increasingly stylish among college students in the 1980s and 1990s to "smoke pot." Many of these smokers are responsible legal, political, and medical professionals today. There are also many advocates for the legalization of marijuana in the legal and medical community.

In the late 1980s, in response to alarm over the devastating consequences of cocaine use by rich and poor alike, the government launched a "War on Drugs," appointed a "drug czar," and enacted legislation focused on the reduction of the supply of cocaine. Nevertheless, many contend that the reduction of cocaine use that followed was not attributable to stricter legal controls but instead reflected the changing fashions in preferences among users of psychoactive drugs.

The highly addictive drug methamphetamine (meth) is probably the biggest concern today. Manufacturing methamphetamine is both easy and cheap. Further, users become addicted quickly, and their downward slide is faster than is seen with other addictive drugs. According to a review conducted by the federal government's Mental Health and Substance Abuse Administration, the number of meth users seen in drug abuse clinics quadrupled during the 10-year period from 1993 to 2003. Currently, in response to widespread press coverage of the damage to lives caused by methamphetamine, several governmental jurisdictions are launching major offensives on this gargantuan and growing problem. New government initiatives on meth are discussed at http://methresources.gov.

Even though our policymakers focus on the actual drugs involved, drugs are not so much the problem as is the predisposition of some people to cope with stress through many forms of addictive behaviors. Addictive behavior is one way people cope with the human condition, and prohibition of a drug will only make it appear more compelling to those who wish to be different and cannot fit in well with mainstream society. There seems to be a cycle of about 20 to 30 years during which attention and concern shifts from one addictive drug or addictive behavior to another. For example, marijuana and cocaine were partially remediated in the late 1970s but then became "demonized" again in the late 1980s. The "War on Meth," so recently declared by the government, is eerily reminiscent of the earlier clamor against cocaine. The fact is, despite the changing focus of attention and concern, human nature is *not* changing. The question of which drug is being used is actually somewhat incidental in the context of social disapproval and criminalization. At the end of the day, drugs are just one form of addictive behaviors—behaviors that include gambling, overeating, and hypersexuality. The recent development of addictive Internet activity clearly shows that behavioral addictions are also influenced by technological advances.

EPIDEMIOLOGY: THE PREVALENCE OF DRUG USE

It has long been noted that the popularity of specific psychoactive drugs of abuse varies widely over time. In the late 1960s, the techniques of epidemiology—the science that studies the distribution of diseases and their effect on society—was finally applied to drug use. Epidemiological findings are important, for example, in helping public health officials to plan how to allocate public funds to most efficiently help people with problems associated with drug and behavioral addictions.

Epidemiologic surveys in the United States objectively document the changing fashions of drug abuse. There were epidemics of marijuana abuse in the 1960s, of heroin in the 1970s, and of cocaine in the 1980s. These studies occurred against a background of an upward trend in the usage of all drugs, including alcohol, during the 1970s, followed by a downward trend in the 1980s. Most recently there has been a return to the use of heroin and other opioids, particularly prescription pain medications, such as MS-Contin (morphine sulfate) and OxyContin (oxycodone). There has also been an increasing interest in so-called club or designer drugs. Most dangerous of all, methamphetamine has become a scourge in our communities over the past few years (see www.drugabuse.gov/DrugPages/Methamphetamine.html). All this is taking place at a time during which research funded by the National Institute on Drug Abuse has documented declining drug use by teenagers.

The somewhat irrational demonizing of individual drugs has occurred repeatedly in history: Consider the slogans "demon rum," "reefer madness," and "speed kills." The recurrent theme is to blame most of the evils of society on expanding abuse of a particular drug. The disease of addiction is blamed on the drug rather than on the problems of the drug user. Even the most benign of drugs, caffeine, has been castigated, without weighing the fact that the relative risks associated with caffeine consumption are not in the same ballpark as those from alcohol, marijuana, cocaine, or heroin. Also, coffee and tea and other caffeinated products have been consumed for centuries, with no documented harmful or out-of-control behavior resulting from their use.

It is often assumed that there is specificity between an individual's brain biology and the particular drug of abuse chosen, making the person more vulnerable to a given drug and less so to others. Although, as will be shown, there certainly are significant differences in dependence liabilities of various drugs when assessed in laboratory models, all drugs of abuse are potentially problematic to individuals who are addiction prone. Apparently, instead of harboring a specific weakness for or susceptibility to a given drug, most drug abusers use whatever drug is most "fashionable" or most readily available. This seeming interchangeability among various drugs of abuse suggests that the neurobiological bases of addiction are not the results of the particular chemical effects of a specific drug, as previously thought. Rather, the basis of addiction lies in the more general effects of all addictive drugs on fundamental drives or motivations of the people inclined to try them and continue to use them.

More Americans use alcohol than any other drug. The most commonly used illicit substance is marijuana. Younger people tend to combine alcohol with illegal drugs to which they have access; older people generally use alcohol alone or together with prescribed medications. National studies have consistently shown that use and abuse of alcohol and other drugs is most widespread among young people ages 18 to 34. However, the current preoccupation with perpetuating youth has spread beyond the clothes people wear and the increasing demand for plastic surgery to encompass drug use patterns; the "youth" pattern of drug use also has extended to those in their forties and even fifties. The highest rates of drug use and abuse are observed for young men, but, as in so many other areas of life today, the genders are becoming more and more alike in their proclivities for drugs.

Contrary to some popular myths, drug abuse and drug dependence are not problems confined to a small sector of the population. In fact, drug and alcohol abuse and dependence are among the most widespread of all mental illnesses, affecting nearly 15 percent of all people in the United States, over 18 years old. Alcohol abuse and drug abuse independently afflict nearly 13 percent and 8 percent of the population, respectively. In 1990, according to Regier and associates, the prevalence rates for abuse of and dependence on other psychoactive substances were:

Marijuana	4.3%
Amphetamines	1.7%
Barbiturates	1.2%
Opiates	0.7%
Hallucinogens	0.3%
Cocaine	0.2%

Year-to-year fluctuations in these values likely represent differences in the pattern of use and the populations surveyed as well as changes in diagnostic criteria and the study methods employed. Statistics are updated as they are gathered on www.drugabuse.gov/infofacts/nation trends.html and www.niaaa.nih.gov/databases/qf.htm.

As we have stated, alcohol and drug use have a profound relationship with other mental problems. In fact, the odds of suffering from a mental disorder are nearly three times greater for those who abuse alcohol or other drugs and nearly five times greater for those with alcohol or other drug dependence. Approximately half of those in the U.S. National Co-morbidity Survey with lifetime alcohol or drug abuse or dependence also had at least one lifetime mental disorder. Conversely, half of the respondents with a mental disorder met criteria for either alcohol or drug abuse or dependence. Furthermore, the use of alcohol and other addictive drugs seems to go hand in hand, and many addicts use more than one psychoactive substance at a time. For example, over 20 percent of alcohol users suffer from other drug abuse problems, compared with less than 4 percent among the general population.

Among psychiatric illnesses, the so-called "externalizing disorders," relating to interactions with other people, which include antisocial personality and attention deficit/hyperactivity, are more likely to be associated with substance use disorders than the "internalizing disorders," which include anxiety and mood problems. Of the internalizing disorders, bipolar disorder is the one most commonly associated with substance abuse. The extensive overlap between substance use disorders and other mental disorders has led to theories that many of the same problems that give rise to alcohol and drug abuse also engender certain other mental disorders. Behavioral genetic studies suggest that the same genetic factors may contribute to both the externalizing disorders and to substance use disorders. Doctors and counselors should be alert to these facts when confronted with new patients with mental disorders, and doctors should be very cautious about prescribing medications that have the potential for abuse or dependence.

CHAPTER 3

Addiction as a Disease

THE BIOPSYCHOSOCIAL MODEL of the causes of addiction provides the basis for the pharmacopsychosocial treatment of addiction. The perspective offered by the biopsychosocial model is very different from the traditional medical model, which regards drug use as merely a bad habit, until organ damage occurs. It also is very different from the traditional social learning model, which denies that addiction is an illness, even when organ damage or other physical problems develop. In contrast, the biopsychosocial model shifts our focus from the drug itself to understanding drug use as a disease whose course depends on the interactions of the addictive drug or compulsive behavior, the biogenetic and psychological susceptibilities of the individual, and the social context in which drug use or other out-of-control behavior occurs.

The effects of a psychoactive drug are determined by its pharmacologic actions, the dose and the route of administration, and a host of individual factors. Descriptive terms, such as "excessive use," "abuse," "misuse," and "addiction," which are generally used to express the magnitude and consequences of psychoactive drug use, depend on difficult and often changing value judgments.

However, medical diagnoses, which are called for in dealing with the disease of addiction, must stand on more objective ground. The effort to develop diagnostic criteria is guided by an attempt to define maladaptive patterns of drug use in terms of their objective consequences.

The direct consequences of acute intoxication are predictable from the *pharmacological actions* of the drug. For example, central nervous system (CNS) stimulants enhance arousal, attention, and performance at low doses but can lead to psychomotor agitation, psychotic confusion, and convulsions at higher doses.

The *route of drug administration* can influence the medical complications of drug use as well as the intensity with which people pursue the use of drugs. For example, intravenous administration results in rapid entry of the drug into the brain with intense but relatively short-lived euphoria; compulsive, bingelike use; increased likelihood of death from an overdose; and medical complications from infections related to neglect of sterile technique and cross-contamination of blood that occurs when different people use the same injection equipment without adequate cleansing. In contrast, a drug that is taken orally affects the brain relatively slowly. The oral route of administration poses its own dangers, however. These dangers can be seen in alcohol consumption, which is often associated with damage to the gastrointestinal tract, including gastritis, ulcers, and cancers.

The many *individual factors* particular to each person greatly complicate an understanding of any drug's pharmacological effects. These effects include variables such as a person's previous experience with the drug, the social context in which the drug is used, and the presence of genetic susceptibilities or medical disorders that affect the central nervous system (CNS) or other organ systems that influence brain sensitivity to drug action or how concentrated the drug will become in the brain.

THE DRIVE TO USE DRUGS

The biopsyschosocial perspective provides a framework for understanding the entire spectrum of drug use, from its initiation to its progression to addictive use, as well as the acquisition of tolerance and physical dependence. Biopsychosocial processes that initiate, maintain, and regulate a person's drug-seeking behavior include the positive reinforcing effects of drugs—that is, their rewarding effects—environmental stimuli associated with drug effects, and the aversive effects of drugs. All of these processes are modified, to some extent, by a person's biology, especially his or her genetic makeup; by psychological factors, including the person's previous drug use; and by social factors, such as the influence of a person's family and friends and environment on his or her choices.

The biopsychosocial model of the causes of addiction has led scientists to recognize the central role of conditioning and learning in drug addiction. The brain mechanisms underlying addiction can be explored by studying the neuropharmacolgy and neuroanatomy of the brain systems that control the experience of reward.

Drugs that can give rise to addictions are "positive reinforcers." That is, laboratory animals (and, by inference, people) that are given the opportunity to self-administer the drug will tend to do so.

Drugs that prompt self-administration include stimulants (e.g., cocaine and amphetamine), opiate analgesics (e.g., morphine and heroin), dissociative anesthetics (e.g., phencyclidine [PCP]), CNS depressants (barbiturates, benzodiazepines, and ethanol), nicotine, and some volatile solvents (e.g., glue). Interestingly, in animal models, hallucinogens such as LSD (lysergic acid diethylamide) and the cannabinoid that is the active component of marijuana do not initiate positive reinforcement leading to self-administration. This evidence underlines the fact that animal models are only partially generalizable to humans and suggests that reward is not the full story.

The characteristic effects of most drugs of abuse—the subjective responses of a person taking them—are obviously major factors in why people use them. However, these stimulus properties are complex and multifaceted, because they encompass both favorable and aversive effects.

The favorable effects include the feelings of euphoria and well-being that follow the administration of a drug, the relief of anxiety or depression, and improved physical and mental performance. Favorable effects also include the alleviation of withdrawal symptoms.

The aversive effects take many different forms. The initial exposure to nicotine in the form of smoking cigarettes often results in distressing symptoms such as coughing, nausea, and light-headedness. The initial exposure to alcohol is likely to result in unpleasant hangovers, and chronic alcohol use often results in severe gastritis. Such aversive effects can lead users to terminate smoking cigarettes or reduce or limit their alcohol consumption. What is so intriguing is the fact that drug use often continues in spite of these adverse effects—either because all your friends are starting to smoke when you are a young teenager and you want to be like them, or because you are so addicted to alcohol that you tolerate the pain of gastritis just so that you can attain the "benefits" of drinking.

The combination of favorable and aversive effects underscores that the drive to use drugs is not simply pleasure-seeking, as the popular media commonly represents it to be. Drug use is, rather, a means of changing one's experience of the world, whatever that experience may be for a particular individual. Such changes can also be accomplished by engaging in behavior that does not involve the use of drugs: gambling, for instance. It therefore must be recognized that some individuals use drugs or engage in addictive behaviors not because it makes them *feel good*, but because it makes them *feel less bad* or, perhaps, *not feel at all*. For this reason, a punitive attitude in treatment is doomed to failure. The constructive approach to treatment is to help addicted individuals understand what they are running from by using drugs or numbing out in other ways and what they aim to accomplish in treatment.

If an addictive drug or behavior is repeatedly administered in the same set of circumstances—a certain situation, time, or place—the accompanying environmental stimuli may become associated with the drug or behavioral effects. This effect is the result of so-called Pavlovian conditioning processes, named after Ivan Pavlov, a Soviet behavioral scientist who discovered that dogs could be conditioned to react physically to auditory stimuli. For example, a dog can be trained to salivate when hearing a certain bell, even though no food is present. This acquired link between a stimulus and a reaction is the result of the formation of neural connections within existing brain circuits. When people are placed in the circumstances in which they previously used an addictive drug, the stimuli they experience often triggers either reexperiencing aspects of the drug use or cravings to use the drug. For example, patients who haven't injected heroin for many years can experience a desire to use heroin when they return to the location where they previously used it or even when they view a film portraying people injecting drugs. This phenomenon is closely related to such common experiences as having one's mouth water when one smells a favorite food or becoming sexually aroused when one's partner wears a seductive outfit or fragrance. (A patient of Dr. Martin who had been sober for several months while receiving buprenorphine—a medicine used to treat opiate addiction—and was doing very well, indeed, described how he was disturbed by recollective triggers of cravings when he saw the protagonist in a movie inject morphine. The man had to leave the theater.)

In general, the way drugs affect a person is shaped by psychological factors and social context, including the presence of psychopathology, such as anxiety, depression, attention deficits, or thought disorders, and previous exposure to psychoactive drugs.

DRUGS AND THE CHEMICAL SYSTEMS OF THE BRAIN

The powerful favorable effects of drugs, especially the euphoria they produce, involve several neurotransmitter systems of the brain. These brain systems have been identified by scientists as mainly the dopamine, opioid, and gamma-amino butyric acid (GABA), and glutamate systems (although the brain is so complex that other systems yet to be discovered also likely play a role). The regions of the brain that are governed by these neurotransmitters, including the nucleus accumbens, are often called "pleasure centers" by the popular press. For the reasons just given, the term "reinforcement centers" might be more appropriate. It is the reinforcement centers of the nervous system that steer people through the challenges of life and prompt them to approach or avoid a particular stimulus or situation.

Current thinking is that all addictive drugs are "dopaminergic" to some degree: that is, they generate the release of the neurotransmitter dopamine, which results in psychostimulant actions in nerve cells within the "reward" circuits of the brain and reinforces continued drug use. For example, studies confirm that dopamine is released from dopamine neurons in the nucleus accumbens when cocaine reaches the brain after a person introduces the drug into the bloodstream. Conversely, when dopamine signals in the nervous system are blocked, the desire to continue using cocaine is extinguished. These phenomena confirm the idea that the dopamine system is a critical component of the reward pathways of the brain.

However, attributing the reward effects of drugs and out-of-control behaviors, such as gambling, to the operations of the dopamine system alone is probably an oversimplification. This is because the effects of drugs and addictive behaviors on dopamine transmission are altered by other neurotransmitters, especially norepinephrine, serotonin, GABA, glutamate, and opioids that are naturally produced by the brain. These neurotransmitters also play a part in reinforcing the use of stimulants, opiates, alcohol, and other CNS depressants.

NEUROADAPTATION

TOLERANCE

After repeated exposure to many of the drugs that affect the brain, a greater dose is required to produce the level of intoxication that was experienced when the person started using the drug. Hardened users are scarcely affected by doses of the drug that at first were sufficient to cause intoxication. This phenomenon, called "tolerance," is a pharmacological characteristic shared by many psychoactive substances of abuse, particularly CNS depressants and opioids, that enables and encourages the use of progressively greater doses. (Note that tolerance to all pharmacological actions of a given drug or within all organ systems of the body may not develop at the same time or to the same degree.) A common related phenomenon is so-called cross-tolerance. For example, tolerance to one CNS depressant, such as a barbiturate, usually results in some cross-tolerance to other (even chemically unrelated) CNS depressants, such as alcohol, which suggests that they share certain mechanisms of pharmacological action.

DEPENDENCE

Dependence is defined by the presence of tolerance, the emergence of a withdrawal syndrome when drug use is discontinued, or the accompanying "craving" for the drug. Scientists use the term "neuroadaptation" to designate the neuronal changes and symptoms that occur as a result of repeated drug administration, encompassing both biological tolerance and "physical" (as opposed to "psychological") dependence. The term "dependence syndrome" refers to the elements of psychological dependence, including drug-seeking and psychological and social consequences of drug use. Repeated cycles of drug administration and withdrawal cause both tolerance and physical dependence to re-emerge more quickly. Once again, this phenomenon suggests similarities between tolerance and physical dependence and learning and memory.

WITHDRAWAL

When addicts abruptly discontinue using drugs or engaging in addictive behaviors, a *withdrawal syndrome* emerges. The symptoms of withdrawal are generally the opposite of the effects of intoxication with the drug or the effects produced by the behavior. For example, withdrawal from CNS depressants causes hyperexcitability, whereas withdrawal from stimulants causes depression. In addition to effects like these, which are associated with specific drugs, the withdrawal syndrome for all drugs of abuse also causes a stress reaction, in which the brain attempts to reverse the neuroadaptive changes that occur as a result of long-term drug administration. The severity of withdrawal symptoms is correlated with the dose addicts had been using and the duration of their use.

The initial concern in treating addicts is to grapple with the consequences of physical dependence and to treat the effects of the withdrawal syndrome, which lasts up to one week after last drug use and which is often accompanied by medical problems. The long-term treatment is directed at resolving the so-called protracted abstinence syndrome, which includes longer-term physiological problems, lasting weeks to months, such as sleep and hormonal disturbances, and psychiatric problems, such as anxiety, depression, and difficulty in concentrating and thinking clearly. This protracted abstinence syndrome is what increases the risk of relapse during the first six months following the discontinuation of drug use.

DEPENDENCE SYNDROME

The concept of a dependence syndrome derives from the biopsychosocial model of the causes of addiction. This model frames, for the first time, the interactions among the pharmacological actions of the drug, individual biogenetic characteristics, including psychological problems, and the effects of the environment that are generalizable to all drugs of abuse. Behavioral addictions also follow this pattern. The dependence syndrome should be clearly distinguished from what are merely the physical responses to drug administration. For example, a patient who has been receiving morphine for acute pain relief following surgery clearly exhibits neuroadaptation, that is, she experiences changes in her brain in response to morphine administration. But she is not likely to develop a dependence syndrome once she has recovered from the pain associated with the surgery and is discharged from the hospital. Fundamental to the concept of the dependence syndrome is that *drug-seeking behavior*, not mere neuroadaptation, is the critical factor in sustaining drug addiction. Focusing on drug-seeking behavior avoids the need to draw a line between so-called psychological and physical dependence. Regarding the mind (psyche) and the body (soma) as two sides of the same coin is a seminal concept in modern psychiatry and medicine.

ADDICTION AS DEFINED BY THE AMERICAN PSYCHIATRIC ASSOCIATION

The criteria for diagnosis of drug and alcohol addiction, as presented by the American Psychiatric Association in its *Diagnostic and Statistical Manual of Mental Disorders*, 4th edition (*DSM-IV*) are based on the concept of the dependence syndrome.

The presence of one or more of three clusters of symptoms is required for the diagnosis of psychoactive substance dependence:

1. *Loss of control:* The substance is taken in larger amounts or over a longer period than intended, or there are unsuccessful efforts to reduce use.

2. *Importance of drug use in the person's life:* The person spends a great deal of time in drug-related activities at the expense of important social, occupational, or recreational activities, which are reduced or given up, or the person continues abusing substances despite knowing that he has a persistent or recurrent physical or psychological problem that likely has been caused or exacerbated by the substance.
3. *Neuroadaption:* The presence of tolerance or withdrawal.

In the *DSM-IV*, dependence syndromes are associated with all commonly abused psychoactive drugs, specifically alcohol, amphetamine, cannabis, cocaine, hallucinogens, inhalants, nicotine, heroin and other opioids, PCP and related substances, sedatives and hypnotics, as well as miscellaneous drugs, including anabolic steroids, nitrous oxide, and various over-the-counter and prescription drugs that do not readily fall into other categories.

The *DSM-IV* defines "substance abuse" as "clinically significant impairment or distress" in life-functioning as a result of substance use that has not risen to the level of a full dependence syndrome. However, it must be recognized that the line between where abuse ends and dependence begins is somewhat arbitrary. The treatment goal is to differentiate between pathological alcohol or drug users who lose control of the amount of drugs or alcohol they use from those who do not. Then the assessment can be made of the degree these patients suffer associated problems while continuing substance use. Presumably not all people abusing drugs progress to dependence. But once a person is diagnosed with dependence, there is no way back to abuse.

COMPLICATIONS OF DRUG ABUSE

There is a stigma associated with being an addict. Because of this stigma, patients resist admitting that they have a drug problem. Most people grow up believing that discussing physical problems, such as a broken leg or a heart attack, is more acceptable than discussing emotional distress. For these reasons, physicians are most likely to confront the problem of addiction when addicts come for treatment of another physical or psychological condition. The limitations on physicians' time imposed by the strictures of managed care cause many to confine their treatment response to the immediate problem presented to them, instead of inquiring into its root causes. Out of frustration over seeing the same patients returning with the same problems, physicians may simply reach for their prescription pad to prescribe a remedy (e.g., Valium or Xanax). The drugs may pacify the patients, but, unfortunately, they do nothing to address their underlying problems. In addition, many of these prescribed drugs are themselves addictive, and, if physicians recognize a pattern of misuse, they frequently refuse to write patients more prescriptions. Thus the patients have acquired a further problem in the course of these doctor visits: They now have another addiction to cope with. Patients try to manage this prescription-drug addiction by finding another doctor who will prescribe the drug for them or by seeking out illicit "street" sources.

The medical and psychiatric complications of drug abuse of which physicians should be aware encompass both *direct* and *indirect* effects of drug abuse. Direct effects include:

- Overdose
- Organ damage
- Metabolic problems

Indirect effects or consequences include:

- Inappropriate use of prescribed medicines, such as painkillers and tranquilizers
- Failure to comply with the prescribed treatment of coexisting illnesses
- Malnutrition
- Trauma
- Infection
- General neglect

Obviously, treatment of severe medical complications must take precedence when these complications are life threatening. However, such initial treatments usually fail to resolve the underlying problem of drug abuse, which must be recognized and addressed if patients are to recover from the disease of addiction itself.

One of the most difficult problems in making a diagnosis and initiating treatment is the tricky question of whether a drug addict's psychological problems are a consequence of drug use or are caused by a separate psychiatric condition. Clearly, mental disorders associated with substance abuse and other mental disorders overlap. For example, delirium, psychotic, mood and anxiety disorders, sexual dysfunction, and sleep disorders can have their origins in intoxication or withdrawal. Alternatively, these may be separate problems, requiring their own treatment. It is not easy to distinguish if a complicating psychiatric disorder is the primary (separate) problem or whether it is secondary to substance dependence (i.e., caused by drug addiction). This is particularly true if both disorders started early in life or if they arose around the same time in a person's life. It is critical, however, that this distinction be drawn. Physicians who do not recognize the underlying primary disorder of drug addiction may prescribe medications that can cause dependence (e.g., benzodiazepines [Ativan or Valium] or stimulants) to treat secondary psychiatric disorders, to the detriment of the patient.

CHAPTER 4

Biopsychosocial Factors in Addiction

WHEN WE LOOK at a group of people suffering from the disease of addiction, one thing we notice right away is the many differences among them. They have varying levels of intelligence, education, and income; the onset of their addictions began at different ages; they are of both sexes; and some look hale and hardy, while others look extremely ill. So, whatever addiction is, it doesn't strike only at one group within society.

In this chapter, we approach the question of what addiction is by examining what physical, social, and psychological problems cause people to initiate and persist in behavior that seriously hurts them.

There is no single explanation of why, although alcohol and other psychoactive drugs and outlets for addictive behaviors, such as compulsive gambling, are widely available, some people develop an addiction while others do not. Psychoactive substance use disorders are complex and multifaceted, and they take different forms in different people. The life situations of people that give rise to drug use vary widely. In some people, using drugs seems to continue inexorably until they die as a result of the drugs' damaging effects; other people can decrease or stop using drugs completely. Because of the diversity in the ways drug use manifests itself, drug addiction is best understood as a result of many different factors interacting over time.

The fact that many people who take drugs when they are young do not become addicted has led to the search for the factors that make some people vulnerable to addiction. A variety of biological and psychological factors probably predispose a person to become an addict. These factors include:

- Genetically based resistance (low susceptibility) or sensitivity to the immediate intoxicating effects of a given drug or behavior
- The way the person metabolizes the drug
- The usually rapid adaptation of the brain to regular exposure to the drug or behavior
- Personality traits that incline a person to use the drug or engage in compulsive behaviors (e.g., thrill seeking or antisocial traits)
- High susceptibility to the neurological and emotional damage caused by regular drug use

BIOLOGICAL FACTORS: BRAIN CHEMISTRY

While, as we shall see, addiction is more than simply a function of brain chemistry, recognizing and understanding the many ways the addicted person's brain is different from the brain of a healthy, nonaddicted person is one of the keys to understanding the nature of addiction. The most critical discovery in addiction treatment in recent years is the way in which abstinence from addictive drugs or addictive behaviors can help to restore the normal function of an addicted person's brain. However, recovery of the brain may take a long time: a year or even longer, and some brain functions may never fully recover.

One of the most exciting areas of research is determining the ways in which safe, effective pharmaceutical therapies enhance the capacity of addicts to maintain abstinence, thus allowing the brain circuitry to mend itself. Moreover, in individuals with addiction that is secondary to other psychiatric or medical conditions, addressing these conditions appropriately with the help of pharmaceutical therapies will also facilitate abstinence and brain recovery from the ravages of drug dependence. Once the brain circuitry has been repaired and underlying psychiatric disorders are brought under control, patients are able to begin breaking the pattern of their previously out-of-control, self-destructive behavior. There is more to the story of addiction than a breakdown in brain function, but repairing the breakdown that does occur and teaching addicts to cope with deficits that cannot be reversed are absolutely necessary for additional therapeutic efforts to be effective.

PSYCHOLOGICAL FACTORS

Although the psychological profiles of the addicted people whose stories we tell throughout this book are very different from each other, studies have demonstrated that certain common psychological factors can predispose or even drive a person to become an addict. A single example illustrates this process. People who suffer from depression naturally seek relief from the profound sadness and worry or self-doubt that their depression causes. One way of coping with the effects of depression is to use drugs or alcohol to alleviate depressive moods. The problem with this way of coping with depression is that it does not address the underlying causes of the depression, which means, of course, that it will not help the person to feel better in the long run. Therefore, the underlying depression persists, and the sufferer continues to self-administer increasing amounts of drugs and alcohol with little success controlling the depression. Unfortunately, the regular use of substantial amounts of potentially addictive substances has psychiatric, medical, and social consequences that in themselves can encourage the onset of addiction. Once addiction has set in, its destructive effects are so devastating that the original depression may be misconstrued as just another of the many components of addiction. Nevertheless, the depression remains the underlying problem that must be addressed if the addiction is to be treated successfully and overcome. The good news is that depression, anxiety, or phobias often can be alleviated with psychotherapy, counseling, and the use of pharmaceuticals. When the emotional problems that gave rise to an addiction are relieved, addicts finally have a chance of being successfully treated for the addiction.

Certain emotional hardships have also been seen as increasing a person's vulnerability to becoming addicted to drugs. These include mental disorders, such as bipolar disorder, attention deficit/hyperactivity disorder, and psychosis; medical illnesses and physical injuries, such as those that cause chronic pain or other disabilities; and severe stress, such as follows a crime, a military battle, a sexual assault, or financial disaster. The problem is that certain people become addicted to drugs when they attempt to "self-medicate" these chronic problems. However, the tendency to experience heightened stress when faced with extreme challenges may arise from the same brain chemistry as drug addiction itself. Therefore, heightened stress may not, in fact, be the reason a person becomes an addict. For example, not everyone who is involved in a major external upheaval, such as 9/11 or Hurricane Katrina, is affected in the same way or to the same degree or is left with equally disturbing memories, such as flashbacks or nightmares.

SOCIAL FACTORS

We've all heard of "peer pressure"—the inclination, especially as experienced by young people, to join in with the activities of their crowd, even when doing so means compromising standards of conduct or safety they had previously respected. Peer pressure is definitely one example of social factors that create the setting for addictions to develop. A seemingly paradoxical example of this phenomenon arises from the fact that psychoactive drugs are illegal. The attempt to control the use of these drugs, by making them illegal, bonds drug users into a subculture of lawbreakers, tending to isolate them from the rest of society and, frequently, serving to intensify their preoccupation with drugs. The illegality of drugs also serves to put people beyond the pale of legitimate treatment options. Many people fear that they have become "criminals" simply because they are using illegal drugs. They fear admitting their condition to doctors or hospital staff because they want to avoid being stigmatized as lawbreakers or even being prosecuted and imprisoned.

While poverty, another social condition, certainly does not invariably lead to addiction, it creates a constellation of factors that help predispose a person to contracting the disease of addiction. Obviously, not all of the social factors that contribute to creating and sustaining addiction can be overcome. Parents who cannot properly care for their children are an example of an intractable problem, and one that makes children vulnerable to becoming addicts as they grow up. Or parents who drink or who use drugs and then offer them to their children create a high probability that the children will develop a substance abuse problem. However, by identifying the social causes, we can formulate ways to intervene on the behalf of patients—for instance, by helping them to find a decent job or put a roof over their heads—and thereby enable them to recover. Teachers can present drug and alcohol education in schools and direct vulnerable children to speak with school counselors.

Social relationships also contribute to a person's vulnerability to developing an addiction to drugs. The favorable attitudes of friends about drug use and how they influence each other, the lack of availability of alternatives to drug use, such as educational, recreational, and occupational opportunities, and the availability of drugs during a person's early development also lead to drug use and, ultimately, to drug addiction. To give a single example: Growing up in a family in which all adversity or causes for celebration are seen as excuses or opportunities to "get high" can teach young people that alcohol and drug use is a normal and desirable coping mechanism.

The essence of social interventions is to help addicted people to find out what help is available, to understand what is keeping them from availing themselves of help, and to motivate them to seek and accept help. On one hand, shame about needing help is a powerful barrier to asking for assistance. On the other hand, a sense of entitlement that some addicts evince can be a turn-off to social workers and others who are attempting to provide help. Clearly, what works best is a balanced approach in which help is sought, provided, and actively used, rather than taken for granted. As a result of this approach, addicts, instead of continuing to feel as if they are blowing aimlessly in the wind, begin to feel that they have some control over their lives.

BIOPSYCHOSOCIAL FACTORS AND THE TYPICAL COURSE OF ADDICTION

The typical course of addiction begins with *exposure* of a vulnerable individual to a given psychopharmacological agent in a certain social context; *dependence* follows, characterized by compulsive drug use; and eventually *medical*, *psychiatric*, and *social complications* develop. At each stage, the interactions among the drugs, the user, and the environment are altered. For example, social drinking on a date by a teenager differs dramatically from drinking alcohol to prevent morning "shakes" or from drinking after discharge from the hospital following treatment of liver failure. Similarly, "snorting" a line of cocaine obtained from a friend at a party on the weekend is different from working as a prostitute to earn money to buy cocaine and using a needle shared with an HIV-positive partner to inject the drug intravenously.

The stages in the development of drug and behavioral addictions are strikingly similar. However, the *speed* of both progression and the severity of the problem varies widely among different drugs and among different behaviors. Factors affecting the speed and severity of addiction to drugs include how available a drug is (e.g., its cost and purity), its route of administration, and its reinforcing effects, especially the power of the drug to promote craving for the drug. Often months or years can pass between initial exposure to alcohol and people becoming compulsive users. In contrast, only weeks or months may be required for casual cocaine use to become a full-blown cocaine addiction. Similarly, the serious complications caused by drinking alcohol typically occur 10 to 15 years after initial exposure to alcohol. Serious problems with cocaine usually begin in less than 1 or 2 years.

People often use several addictive drugs simultaneously or use different drugs serially, switching from one to another. Such multiple drug use indicates that the similarities in the use of various drugs are more important than their differences. In addition, it is common for people using addictive drugs to also engage in addictive behaviors, such as gambling or compulsive overeating. It is not uncommon for problematic hypersexuality, so-called sexual addiction, pathological gambling, or drug addiction to trigger each other.

Youngsters usually use legal, easily available drugs, such as tobacco and alcohol, before they begin using illegal drugs, such as marijuana, heroin, and cocaine. For this reason, these readily obtainable drugs are called "gateway drugs." It is believed, but it has not been proven, that preventing the use of these "softer" drugs will reduce the likelihood that youngsters will abuse "harder" drugs. Of course, people don't always follow the usual pattern of starting with softer drugs and moving on to using more serious ones. For example, in inner cities, where crack co-caine or heroin is often available to preadolescents, drug use may begin with these drugs. More recently, in rural communities, the ready avail-ability of methamphetamine from local meth labs has created a similar shortcut to highly addictive "hard" drugs.

The typical pattern of progressing from softer drugs to harder drugs, however, suggests that the same factors that make people vulnerable to becoming addicted to one drug also make them vulnerable to the use of others. This pattern also suggests that similar diagnostic criteria and treatment strategies should be applied to the abuse of *all* drugs.

As young people are developing into adults, some are also becoming full-blown addicts. All adolescents are confronted with the challenges of learning about human intimacy and sexuality, beginning productive work, and, in general, exploring and facing the challenges of life. Drug use plays a part in determining whether they will be able to meet these challenges or whether they will be overwhelmed by the problems that addiction creates. Addictive behaviors, such as sexual addiction, com-pulsive thrill seeking, and becoming a workaholic, interfere with suc-cessfully meeting these life challenges in ways that are similar to the interference created by substance abuse. Sadly, these young people, whose behavior is no longer under their control, often miss the chance to initiate fulfilling relationships, establish intimacy and a healthy fam-ily life, and obtain a college or professional degree.

PART II

The Integrated Approach: Pharmacopsychosocial Treatment of Addiction as a Bona Fide Mental Illness

CHAPTER 5

The Players: Psychiatrists and Other Physicians, Therapists, Social Workers, Clergy, Family and Friends, and Support Groups

THE FACE OF addiction therapy is changing. Discoveries about the brain mechanisms that underlie addiction and a wider recognition of the prevalence of co-occurring psychiatric problems have established the need to incorporate pharmaceutical agents into an integrated, pharmacopsychosocial approach to addiction treatment. The opportunity is ripe for advancing the message that nonaddictive pharmaceutical products, by alleviating the emotional distress that often drives people to self-medicate with drugs or alcohol and by rectifying the brain chemistry that supports destructive, out-of-control behaviors, can play a vital role in helping addicts to recover from addiction.

This new era of integrated addiction treatment raises new challenges. Because addiction is more than a social or psychological problem, achieving recovery requires more than talk therapy, social support, and criminal sanctions. However, we must remain wary of a simplistic "scientizing" of addiction—that is, believing that addiction treatment can be limited to administering appropriate medication alone. Such a gross oversimplification overlooks the humanistic and spiritual components of healing, which experience has shown should definitely be included in any effective "prescription" for recovery.

Treatment with medications works best when it is combined with counseling or therapy and a network of social support from family members, friends, or self-help groups. This integrated approach is not so different from the established approach to other devastating illnesses, in which the physician, physical therapist, and other medical professionals, along with family and friends, provide help that is accepted as essential for the healing.

In the past, leaders of 12-step programs and many counselors and other members of the addiction treatment community minimized the part that pharmaceuticals could play in addiction treatment. Many even believed that the use of *any* psychopharmacological agents was fundamentally inimical and in opposition to the purposes of a recovery program. However, new research has proven that we can vastly improve addiction treatment outcomes by incorporating appropriate pharmaceutical agents into an integrated pharmacopsychosocial treatment plan. In this section, we discuss the major and not widely recognized benefits of pharmacological agents for treating primary addiction and the many co-occurring psychiatric conditions that give rise to secondary addiction.

For years taxpayers have funded studies that have proven the value of pharmaceuticals in addiction therapy. The time has come to get this message out to the addiction treatment community and pass the results of this

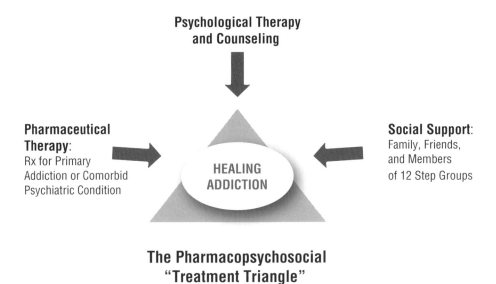

Figure 5.1   Pharmacopsychosocial Treatment Triangle

research on to help the people who need help the most. Some members of the addiction treatment community regard pharmaceutical companies with suspicion; they are against the idea of treating drug addiction and other addictions, such as gambling, with pharmacological interventions. It is critical that these skeptics come to recognize that new pharmacological interventions offer extremely powerful adjuncts to the successful treatment of addiction. The latest research findings have shown the vital role pharmaceutical agents can play in an integrated pharmacopsychosocial approach to addiction therapy, an approach that combines pharmaceutical agents with the best aspects of therapy and counseling. The conjunction of therapeutic modalities is illustrated in Figure 5.1.

ADDICTION AND CO-OCCURRING PSYCHIATRIC CONDITIONS

It is common for addicts to suffer from both substance or behavioral addictions and other psychiatric disorders. It is necessary to treat all the psychiatric problems, including the addiction, in order to cure addicts and enable them to lead normal lives. Unfortunately, no area of addiction treatment is subject to more confusion than the treatment of these so-called dual-diagnosis patients.

Decades ago, psychiatrists and mental health counselors, who evolved in a professional, academic environment, had little success in treating addicted patients and were uncomfortable working with them, largely because addicts tend to "lie," to relapse, and to adopt an adversarial posture toward those who are trying to help them. To find help, people suffering from addictions developed self-help organizations, such as Alcoholics Anonymous (AA), and the field of addiction treatment eventually evolved from these groups. To this day, mental health counselors and addiction counselors are trained separately, and the two groups of counselors have little or no experience with the others' field.

The members of each group frequently harbor suspicions about the quality and integrity of the other. For instance, psychiatrists and other mental health professionals often think that self-help groups help patients to avoid confronting or seeking treatment for their psychiatric problems. And self-help groups generally reject the psychiatric perspective, wherein the focus of treatment tends to be on depression or anxiety rather than on the addiction *per se*. Usually, self-help groups condemn the concomitant use of medications, believing them to be intrinsically harmful to addicts and even a potentially addictive "crutch" that impairs *real* recovery. As a reflection of this fragmentation within the treatment community, the National Institutes of Health artificially separates biomedical research related to psychiatric disorders into three institutes: for drug addiction—the National Institute on Drug Abuse (NIDA); for alcoholism—the National Institute on Alcohol Abuse and Alcoholism (NIAAA); and for mental disorders—the National Institute of Mental Health (NIMH).

The reality, as we have noted, is that addicts actually need help for *all* their mental health problems, which include, of course, their addictions to drugs, alcohol, or other self-destructive behaviors. For example, anxious people often begin using drugs or alcohol as a way of self-medicating their fears. They find that drugs or alcohol help them to feel better or numb their painful emotions. However, the use of drugs or alcohol obviously does nothing to address the underlying conflicts driving their use and, typically, deepens people's anxiety. The use of drugs or alcohol continues and tends to increase as a result, eventually giving rise to an addiction. Once this occurs, people suffer intertwined problems that are difficult to disentangle. However, all the problems of patients must be treated if they are to recover their health.

Typically, a dual-diagnosis patient—suffering, for example, from alcoholism and depression—is treated for one condition or the other. It is not surprising that such a treatment approach is not very successful. After one aspect of the illness is addressed with little benefit, the patient is shunted back and forth between mental health counselors and addiction counselors, who are poorly informed about what happens in the other camp and may even offer the patient conflicting advice. Nothing is more unfortunate than when the patient receives an addictive medicine to treat pain or anxiety; this medicine will actually compound problems arising from heavy alcohol use. Instead of improving, the patient may get worse and even give up treatment.

A history of childhood abuse may result in a plethora of problems later in life, including addiction, depression, anxiety, nightmares, difficulties with relationships, troubles with one's own children, and poor work performance. Often it may not be possible for patients to determine where to begin to get help. But not all people who are abused become depressed or use drugs or become sexually promiscuous. Not all who are depressed abuse drugs or alcohol. And not all addicts have been abused in childhood. That is why it is so important for treatment to be orchestrated by those who have a broad understanding of the biopsychosocial model of addiction and the capacity to apply a pharmacopsychosocial treatment approach: in other words, by doctors who can treat the entire patient.

Only psychiatrists experienced in the treatment of addiction can determine the appropriate combination of treatment modalities. For example, there are now very effective pharmaceutical treatments for depression (these include Pamelor and Tofranil, or their newer versions, Prozac, Zoloft, Paxil, Celexa, Effexor, and Cymbalta), which clearly work better when combined with talk therapies. Indeed, the benefits of talk therapies, even when used without medications, may be more lasting for some patients than use of medication alone. Some depressed alcoholics may do better and others may do worse with antidepressants—so the indiscriminant administration of antidepressants to depressed alcoholics is not justified. For some alcoholics, 12-step programs can be very effective alone, without medications, but others relapse repeatedly in spite of having a "black belt" in AA. They may not recover until their depression is treated or certain conflicts are confronted in talk therapy. Still others may have such a severe dependence on alcohol that the disruptive effects of stopping their alcohol use must be mitigated by a medicine that helps reduce their craving and helps them to avoid relapse. Only with abstinence supported by pharmacotherapy will these patients become open to talk therapy or 12-step support groups.

On the one hand, psychiatric medications have risks and should never be given unless needed. For example, giving a depressed alcoholic an antidepressant while not monitoring him either in a hospital psychiatric unit or with regular follow-up visits may lead to death by an overdose, whether intentional or not. On the other hand, not providing a suicidal addict the correct pharmaceutical treatment for his depression, insisting instead that he join a recovery group and follow its discipline and self-control, is a formula for calamity.

Older antidepressants, such as Pamelor, Tofranil, and Anafranil, or the newer selective serotonin reuptake inhibitors (SSRIs), such as Prozac, Zoloft, Paxil, and Celexa, and the newer combined norepinephrine/ serotonergic agents, Effexor and Cymbalta, are among the most powerful agents for the treatment of primary depression and of the many associated forms of anxiety, such as obsessions and compulsions, panic attacks, post-traumatic stress disorder (PTSD), and agoraphobia, that often lead to secondary drug or alcohol addiction. These medications can help prevent relapses in the large subgroup of addiction patients who suffer from clinical depression and obsessive-compulsive disorder. Taking the appropriately chosen medication decreases patients' inclination to resort to drugs or alcohol to self-medicate their depression or anxiety, which means that they are more successful at remaining drug and alcohol free. Fortunately, the outstanding safety profiles of these medications make them ideal for maintenance therapy.

IMPORTANCE OF PHARMACEUTICALS IN TREATMENT

Prominently displayed in the physician work areas of the psychiatric hospital at Vanderbilt University, where Dr. Martin is director of the addiction center, are laminated cards that list "The Guiding Principles of Pharmacological Treatment for Psychiatric Disorders." These principles were formalized by the members of the Medication Utilization Committee of the Vanderbilt Psychiatric Hospital because of concern that hospital psychiatrists sometimes prescribed more psychotropic, or mood-altering, medications to their patients than necessary. (These principles will be reviewed later in this chapter.) The committee believed that *additional* medications are not likely to be as helpful as the *appropriate* medication thoughtfully selected; in fact, additional medications can actually harm patients. Also, of course, in the interests of cost containment in the treatment of disease, using the fewest medications possible makes eminent sense.

One might expect that inexperienced resident physicians would be responsible for most cases of prescribing several psychotropic medications simultaneously, so-called polypharmacy. But this problem is relatively common and is not restricted to trainees. In fact, established doctors with inadequate academic training or experience may do even more poorly than young physicians in managing simultaneous use of several pharmaceuticals. Polypharmacy has many causes. It results from both doctors' and patients' frustration with inadequate time and resources available for treatment. Often the problem is the fault of managed care organizations; we can only hope that, in time, they will change their policies when they realize that spending time and money to help patients in the early treatment of addiction is a very efficient way of containing costs. The problem with polypharmacy also results from a trend among some doctors to idealize the value of drug treatment for psychiatric illnesses, compared with talk therapy and other forms of counseling; therefore, they tend to overprescribe medications. Finally, some doctors treat psychiatric symptoms in piecemeal fashion—one medicine to promote sleep, one to reduce anxiety, one to lift depressed mood, and one to combat the voices the patient is hearing telling him that he is worthless. Instead, doctors must see the big picture: If a patient is suffering from depression—which can, and often does, include each of these symptoms—prescribing an appropriate antidepressant will address the problem. Pharmaceutical companies foster this piecemeal approach, as they tend to market medications for specific indications and focus on symptoms rather than diagnoses. And many physicians have an inadequate understanding of the potential harmful effects of the interactions among multiple medications.

Reviews of doctors' drug prescribing patterns reveal that there is often little relationship between the patient's diagnosis and the medications ordered. For example, a common trend throughout the country is for doctors to prescribe antianxiety medications for depression, post-traumatic stress disorder, bipolar disorder, and psychosis. This fact suggests that the reduced time available to doctors to spend with patients may cause diagnostic precision to suffer. Another possible reason that the medication may not strictly fit the diagnosis is that psychiatric medications are used for purposes in addition to those recommended by their manufacturers or by the Food and Drug Administration (FDA), which approves their use for specific indications. Psychiatrists must play an important role in selecting the most appropriate treatment based on a thoughtful diagnosis and must carefully monitor the effects every drug has on patients.

Psychiatric patients are especially vulnerable to improperly prescribed multiple medications and need more protection than patients without emotional problems, whose higher brain functions may be more intact. Incorrectly prescribed psychiatric medications can further compromise patients' capacity to come to terms with their illness, to render normal judgments, and to question the doctor's choice of treatment. Because addicted patients often present multifarious problems, they are easily misdiagnosed, are less likely to comply with the doctor's recommendations, and are particularly difficult to monitor. The fact that addiction is the "great masquerader" of psychiatric disorders—that is, it can resemble each of the major psychiatric syndromes—the choice of medications is especially difficult. The difficulty in selecting the appropriate drug is increased when one considers the fact that many medications that are liable to be abused are contraindicated for this population.

Psychiatry is the medical specialty in which treatment without medications is most highly developed, is often preferred, and in which the effectiveness of medications is largely dependent on the therapeutic relationship between the physician and the patient. The accepted treatment for bacterial pneumonia is an antibiotic. The effectiveness of the antibiotic does not depend in any way on the personal relationship between the doctor and patient. However, the effectiveness of the treatment for psychiatric problems does, in great part, depend on the quality of the interactions between the doctor and patient. For example, the treatment of moderate depression may employ cognitive behavioral therapy, an antidepressant, or both together. Obviously, the psychiatrist's experience and skill in performing psychotherapy, the amount of time the doctor has available to spend with the patient, and the patient's readiness to accept psychotherapy can affect the outcome. Too often, psychiatric medications are prescribed to help compensate for the doctor's lack of time and skill. Even experienced psychiatrists often fall into the trap of thinking that, if one medicine is helpful, a second will be even more helpful. A typical example is prescribing a second antidepressant to a depressed patient who had been experiencing some benefits from the first antidepressant he had been taking, but at an insufficient dose or for an inadequate trial period.

The pharmaceutical industry and the government tacitly support prescribing two or more medicines, even for patients for whom only one medication is clinically justified. The FDA does not mandate that pharmaceutical companies conduct research to determine if combinations of medications are superior to single medications. Unfortunately, the cost of evaluating the potential benefits of using several medications at the same time is extremely high. Thus, psychiatrists are tempted to add another medication to the one they have previously prescribed without the kind of scientific justification that could have come from research trials of the combinations in question. Of course, adding a second medication to a patient's treatment regimen may be less beneficial than simply changing to another, perhaps more effective medicine.

Increasing the number of medicines a person takes almost always poses hazards. With each additional medication prescribed, there is a significant increase in the likelihood of adverse side effects resulting from drug interactions. The need to take large numbers of pills daily— some addiction patients are prescribed more than 20 different pills a day—can be a source of confusion. Also, psychiatric patients are not always reliable sources of information about their experiences with medications and may be seeing more than one doctor. Each of the doctors involved in the patient's treatment may be prescribing medications and may not be aware of other medications being prescribed for the same patient. Sometimes patients deliberately visit several different doctors and manipulate these doctors into prescribing medications that they then abuse or sell on the black market.

ADVICE TO CAREGIVERS: "ABOVE ALL, DO NO HARM!"

"The Guiding Principles of Pharmacological Treatment for Psychiatric Disorders," referred to earlier, were formulated to help psychiatrists and trainees follow the most fundamental maxim for guiding medical practice: "Above all, do no harm." We include these principles so professionals will be aware of them and can judge the quality of treatment they are providing and ask the right questions. Making patients and their families aware of these four guiding principles will help patients and their families to be proactive in the therapeutic process.

1. LESS IS MORE—SIMPLIFICATION OF PHARMACOTHERAPY

If one medication will do, the psychiatrist should not prescribe two. If two are necessary, the psychiatrist should not prescribe three. And he should think very carefully when considering prescribing more than three different medicines for essentially the same problem. If a medication does not seem to be working well, the psychiatrist should discontinue using it and try prescribing a new medication by itself, instead of adding the new medication to the first one. The "simplification" principle also requires that, when a patient is referred to a psychiatrist by another doctor, the psychiatrist who is just coming aboard should make a careful inventory of the drugs that the patient is using and begin discontinuing medications that are unnecessary or even hazardous. The patient may start to feel better simply as a result of paring down the number of medications being taken. This is particularly true for addicts whose major problem is taking too many addictive medications that are not indicated.

For their own protection, patients should play a proactive role in this process. They should ask their doctor to change medications when they are not working. If patients feel better after adding a new medication, they should ask if they still should be taking the previously prescribed and ineffective medication. No competent psychiatrist will object to questions from a patient, and all competent psychiatrists should understand that responding to those questions is a critical part of a healthy therapeutic alliance between doctor and patient.

2. IMPORTANCE OF AN ACCURATE DIAGNOSIS
AS THE BASIS FOR TREATMENT

General practitioners and even psychiatrists too often fail to see the "big picture," to recognize that there is a single disorder, the diagnosis of which can explain all or most of the patient's symptoms. Instead, there is an ill-advised trend in present-day American psychiatry to treat patients' problems as if they are simply a "shopping list" on which one checks off the appropriate symptom. As we have noted, the pharmaceutical industry supports the piecemeal approach to psychiatric treatment. Advertisements, company-financed research, and industry-supported presentations at scientific meetings all encourage the separate treatment of individual symptoms. In promotional literature, medications are targeted for treatment of individual symptoms instead of for the treatment of the single psychiatric disorder that may underlie all of these symptoms. This is a classic example of the old saying, "You can't see the forest for the trees." Doctors who have not spent enough time with patients to diagnose the underlying disorder, which should be the focus of treatment, are especially vulnerable to falling into the temptation of treating multiple symptoms. Again, to protect themselves, patients should ask their physician: "What is my diagnosis, and how is my diagnosis determining your choice of treatment for me?" Physicians should be concerned if they cannot answer these questions; patients should be on guard if a clear answer is not forthcoming.

3. COORDINATION ACROSS THE CONTINUUM OF CARE

Good doctors recognize the importance of finding out what treatment a patient had been receiving before he or she entered their care. And the best specialists maintain contact with the physicians or other healthcare providers with whom patients will be working during treatment and throughout recovery and aftercare. This communication can be accomplished by telephone, correspondence, or contact by members of the treatment team. Essential information includes:

- Diagnosis
- Medications prescribed
- Precautions for each medication
- When the specialist should be called in again

A good example of the value of these communications is a young woman who was very depressed. After a nasty ski injury, she started to take excessive amounts of narcotic painkillers prescribed by the orthopedic surgeon who set her fracture. She felt that the pain pills not only relieved the postsurgical pain but also gave her energy and relieved her depression. As her injury healed, pain was no longer a serious problem. But the narcotic painkillers helped her in so many other ways, she told the surgeon that her leg had not healed properly and that her pain continued. This charade went on for some time; for the busy surgeon, calling in prescriptions was preferable to arguing with an insistent patient. When the surgeon eventually put his foot down and said that he would no longer prescribe the narcotics, the patient recognized that she had a serious problem with drugs. She initially tried "doctor shopping," going from one doctor to another in the attempt to renew her supply of narcotics, but soon realized she needed help for what had become an addiction.

The first duty of a good addiction psychiatrist is to become familiar with the patient's history. In this case, the psychiatrist will address her depression and the chronic pain syndrome, interwoven with it for a time, that has developed. The psychiatrist will communicate with the physician who will be taking care of the patient subsequently and encourage the woman to be open with all the doctors she consults in the future about her problem with narcotic painkillers. Finally, the psychiatrist should ensure that, if the patient ever needs surgery again, she will be aware of the risks of becoming addicted to painkillers.

We strongly believe that an addict should not have to suffer unnecessary pain and should not be denied the benefits of painkillers when they are needed. However, a proactive strategy should be in place for stopping the pain pills when the pain is longer severe. It is probably wiser for recovering addicts to endure modest pain by stopping pain pills after the acute pain of surgery has passed than to risk getting back on the addiction roller coaster.

4. MAXIMIZATION OF NONPHARMACOLOGICAL STRATEGIES

This area is particularly important in the practice of addiction psychiatry. The self-help movement is a good guide to how much benefit can be obtained using nonpharmacological treatments. If psychiatric pharmacotherapy—that is, the use of medications to treat psychiatric conditions—is to be helpful rather than harmful, it must not lose sight of its role as an *adjunct* to psychological and social therapy. It is very unlikely that we will ever discover medications that will totally prevent relapses or craving by themselves. Medications will always need to be combined with the powerful support provided by psychosocial therapy, whether this therapy is being provided by professionals or by self-help groups.

Psychiatrists must not forget their roots—they are physicians whose primary charge is to provide personal treatment for emotional problems, in the context of a therapeutic alliance with their patients. Fortunately, the best medical schools are beginning to emphasize this approach in training not only psychiatrists but all physicians. As a result of this training, and if corrupting financial pressures can be overcome, the quality of the interactions between doctors and patients will be substantially enhanced and the health and well-being of addicts will improve.

CHAPTER 6

Identification and Diagnosis: Why Is It Difficult to Recognize Addiction?

PEOPLE ARE UNLIKELY to go to their physicians complaining that they have a problem with addiction. Instead, they visit the doctor's office seeking treatment for problems that are *caused* by their addictions, that is, for the *complications* arising from addiction to drugs or from addictive, out-of-control behavior, such as gambling. Most patients are unlikely to mention to their doctor that they use drugs or alcohol, and, unless the doctor questions them directly, they are even less likely to admit that they abuse drugs or alcohol. Even if their doctor poses pointed questions, many patients deny that a problem exists, not because they are dishonest or "bad people," but because poor insight into their situation is one of the main characteristics of addiction. This characteristic of addiction is often called "denial." But, contrary to what this term seems to suggest, the failure to acknowledge addictions is not malicious. Instead, it is a psychological defense mechanism that arises to protect the self-esteem of the addict.

Society so stigmatizes being "out of control" that it is difficult for someone who is experiencing a loss of control to believe that he is a worthwhile person, one who is ill and needs medical help. It is therefore easier and more comfortable for addicted people simply to deny that they have any problem.

Other factors also distort addicts' ability to appreciate the severity of their out-of-control behavior. If a person was brought up in a family in which alcohol or drug abuse was an acceptable means of dealing with problems, he may unconsciously regard the abuse of drugs as a "normal" part of life. Further, a person may have so much resentment toward these family members, because of childhood neglect or abuse related to addiction, that it is very painful for him to admit to suffering from the same problem. Despite having vowed never to become like them, the person regards herself as just as "bad" as these other members of his family. Finally, acknowledging the fear in his children's eyes as they encounter the same behavior that the addict encountered in his own parents may be more painful than the addict can bear.

In addition to the confusion caused by patients' unreliable and fragmentary accounts of their condition, the diagnosis of addiction is difficult because the disease displays a wide variety of symptoms that are not *specific* to addiction. It can be difficult to arrive at the correct diagnosis for the diverse problems that addicted patients complain of, especially when the patients suffer from another physical or emotional illness in addition to addiction. These other illnesses, which may be medical or psychiatric, or both, commonly complicate or influence the course of the addiction itself. Therefore, when a patient comes to the doctor's office presenting signs and symptoms that are consistent with drug or behavioral addictions, the doctor should strongly suspect that an addiction is present.

Physicians must remain open to making this diagnosis, because most addicts can easily be diagnosed with something other than addiction. For example, a patient can complain of symptoms that suggest major depression. When additional questions are posed, the fatigue and poor concentration the patient complains of may be seen to have been caused by hepatitis or cirrhosis of the liver. Of course, alcoholism may eventually be recognized as the cause of the liver disease. Nothing is more futile than treating cirrhosis and eventual liver failure with a liver transplant, without recognizing that the original cause might have been treated successfully with far less heroic and costly treatments. Obviously, "overlooking" the underlying diagnosis of addiction can also result in considerable suffering for patients and stress for their families.

Why do excellent physicians sometimes overlook the possibility that their patients may be suffering from an addiction? The most important reason is that physicians have a psychological tendency to recognize those illnesses for which they have a potential solution—either by providing a treatment themselves or by referring the patient to the "right" specialist. If physicians feel that treatments for addictions are probably hopeless, it may seem reasonable to them to focus their diagnoses on the symptoms of problems they think they *will* be able to treat successfully. This "therapeutic nihilism" is usually the result of the fact that medical schools have traditionally not done a good job teaching medical students about effective treatments for drug or behavioral addictions.

Another cause for skepticism about the value of treatments for addiction may arise from a physician's personal experiences with an addicted parent or loved one, whose illness caused great pain for all who were involved and made the physician feel powerless. Physicians are only human and are vulnerable to the same emotional weaknesses that afflict other people. Therefore, it may be very difficult for physicians to deal rationally with a patient who reminds them of an addicted person from their past. Addictive disorders are so common in the United States that it is not far-fetched to think that many doctors will have been closely involved with an addict. In fact, perhaps a child from such a troubled background chose a helping profession in order to come to terms with his past. A physician with this background might unconsciously avoid recognizing the signs and symptoms of addiction for what they are. He may prefer to understand a patient's complaints as arising from an illness other than addiction, one that he thinks is more amenable to treatment. Unfortunately, addressing the complications of addiction rather than addiction's root cause will never make patients healthy. Such an effort merely results in frustration for the physician and in years of suffering for patients and those who love them.

CHAPTER 7

Initiating Treatment

ONCE THE DOCTOR has made a preliminary diagnosis that a patient is suffering from a drug or other addiction, he must determine the underlying cause of the visit and identify any drug or drugs that are creating the problem. Then the doctor must decide whether patients are currently high on the drugs or feeling the symptoms of withdrawal. This determination is difficult to make; withdrawal from some drugs looks like intoxication with others, and emotional turmoil can resemble either intoxication or withdrawal. But this determination is vital, because treatment approaches used to manage intoxication are completely different from those used to manage withdrawal, and still other approaches are used to manage emotional instability.

Often doctors cannot determine what drugs patients have taken just prior to presenting themselves for care. Unless this portion of the history is gained, however, misdiagnosis can result. In general, it is very difficult to get an accurate history from patients who are high on drugs or in other tumult, not necessarily because the patients are lying or being evasive but because their thought processes and memory may have been compromised by the drugs themselves. When dealing with polysubstance abuse—the simultaneous use of more than two different addictive drugs—an accurate determination of what drugs patients have been taking is critical. This determination will dictate the choices the doctor makes in managing patient treatment.

The doctor's work thus begins with a careful history and physical examination, one purpose of which is to confirm which drugs patients have been using. This examination should focus on the amount of the drug used and when it was last used. The doctor's examination may also provide a clue about how long patients have suffered from addiction, because, over time, addicts tend to develop complications, such as liver disease, brain damage, and depression. The exam may also help the doctor to understand whether drugs are the major problem or whether other psychiatric problems are of overwhelming importance. In fact, discovering which other medical or psychiatric illnesses coexist with the disease of addiction can help guide the doctor in deciding how to treat patients.

At this stage of the investigation, the doctor has to play detective. Family members or friends can be helpful in supplying information, even though their knowledge may be incomplete because drug addicts are often secretive about their drug use. Empty medicine bottles found at home can provide clues about problems for which patients were being treated. Fortunately, a laboratory test for the presence of drugs, so-called urine drug screening, enables the doctor to determine what drugs patients have been taking during the few days before seeking treatment. Blood tests can also be used to determine the severity of patients' dependence on the drug or drugs they are using. For example, blood alcohol concentration can be considered together with how drunk a patient seems to be at the time the blood test is taken. If he has a high blood alcohol concentration, then the less intoxicated he appears to be, the more severely he is addicted to alcohol. These additional tests should be made as soon as possible after patients present for treatment, because it may require several hours to get the results of the urine drug screening, and patients suffering from a severe overdose may need immediate medical intervention.

Unfortunately, once patients feel better because an overdose, acute withdrawal symptoms, or other psychiatric crisis has been alleviated, they often decide that they do not have a problem and that they do not need further treatment. Such patients typically say that the problem that brought them to seek medical treatment on this occasion was a "one-time occurrence" and promise to "stop using" and "become healthy again." Tears of regret, shame, and guilt are followed by seeking forgiveness from loved ones, and on the surface, everything becomes "right" again. Such patients then return home and reenter the *identical* social circumstances in which their addictions began.

It is not hard to guess what usually happens next. Because the underlying causes of the addiction have not been changed in any way, patients often find themselves returning to the doctor for treatment of the same or similar problem.

As these problems recur, over the course of months or years, addicts' families are forced to consider if anything can be done to put an end to this revolving door process. Family members wonder if they have the power to force the patient to undergo treatment. They also wonder if threats can be effective at stopping drug use or changing concomitant behaviors.

However, unless patients are legally committed to a facility in which they are forced to undergo treatment—which can happen only if addicts prove to be a threat to themselves or to others or have committed a crime for which they are sent to drug court—no one can make them do what they don't want to do. Unfortunately, addiction and the impaired judgment of an intoxicated person are not, in themselves, legal grounds for committal except in a few jurisdictions.

In any case, most families are inclined to shelter addicts, welcoming them back to the "safety" of their homes. Family members also attempt to conceal addicts' problem from children and employers. Doctors are often asked to write a letter to the employer providing a medical excuse for the patient's absence from work. "Doctor," the patient will say, "please don't say in your letter what kind of treatment I received, just that I was in the hospital. I cannot afford to lose my job, and if I go into active treatment, I'm out." Such appeals are grounded in reality. Addiction is stigmatized in our society, largely because of the misconception that an addiction is simply a bad habit that can be broken if the person simply has "enough willpower." Overcoming such stigmas is one of the primary advances that will occur once the biopsychosocial model of the causes of addiction is more widely understood.

An additional reality of life in America today is that it is illegal to fire someone from a job purely for a disability that is accountable by a medical illness. A United States Department of Justice web site that explains the Americans with Disabilities Act is: www.usdoj.gov/crt/ada /adahom1.htm. However, addicts sometimes have such low self-esteem that they do not recognize or assert their legal rights. Classifying addiction among these disabilities has clear advantages in the fight against the stigma of addiction. However, if addicts propose to wage a legal war on their employers instead of getting treatment for their addiction, the effort to protect their "rights" can be more harmful than helpful. Experienced attorneys often work with the family and the addict's physician and employer to encourage the patient to get help. Larger companies also assist their employees to cope with addiction through employee assistance programs (EAPs). The goal of these programs is to prevent the need to discharge previously effective employees from their positions by allowing or even mandating that they take a medical leave of absence to address their illness. Ultimately, this is a win-win situation. After treatment, valuable and well-trained employees can return to their positions and function effectively. However, some workplaces are either too small or financially unstable to have an EAP or a sophisticated policy to assist their employees in this way. In addition, often addicts have already burned many bridges with their employers by the time it is recognized that addiction is the real problem. To be given additional time off from work may no longer be an option.

Because the decision of whether to accept treatment is the patient's to make, the challenge for the physician, therapist, family members, and perhaps employer is to enable patients to recognize the self-destructive path they are following and that there are better alternatives available. Gaining awareness of just how powerless they are in their efforts to end the downward spiral of addiction helps patients to understand that they have a problem. Without this awareness, patients often return to the same situations that contributed to their addiction after being treated for acute problems arising from drug abuse. The family must understand that, even though patients seem pleased to be restored to their homes, the long-term prognosis is not good. At this stage, the family and the doctor must become allies, working together to try to raise addicts' awareness of their problem; otherwise the downhill course will almost certainly continue.

WHAT CAN THE FAMILY DO, AND WHY IS THE FAMILY INVALUABLE IN RECOVERY?

Drug and behavioral addictions affect the entire family. In fact, addictive disorders are one of the major reasons families dissolve. Early on, young children tend not to recognize that any problem exists; they may even idealize the father who is suffering from addiction as "the best of parents." If the man becomes abusive when drunk, children frequently blame themselves, thinking "If only I were better, Daddy wouldn't get so angry." If the father abandons the family for binges of drinking, gambling, and womanizing, the children pray he will be back soon. When he is sober again, the addicted parent is often loving and affectionate, as if nothing untoward is going on in his life. He will simply ignore or forget that, the night before, before passing out, he terrorized the entire family by throwing furniture and beating his wife. When he returns from his "flights" from his family, they are all grateful that he has not left them for good.

As children grow up and have contact with other families, they become aware that something is different about their own family and, in fact, that something is seriously wrong at home. The level of behavior abnormalities displayed by the addicted parent can range from subtle sarcasm ("I can never please him"), to violent outbursts and physical abuse ("I fear him"), to sexual abuse ("I cannot trust him").

Of course, the father is not always the addicted parent. The mother may have an addiction, which causes the same fundamental elements of uncontrolled anger and, for children, the fear of abandonment. Worse still, it is becoming relatively common for children to be raised in families in which both parents and even older brothers or sisters are suffering from drug addiction or other related destructive behavior.

When both parents are addicts, they often lead separate lives and engage in extramarital relations. This may lead to exploitation of the children by live-in boyfriends or exposure to experiences in which young children should not partake. Most important, addicted parents don't do much planning for their children's lives or even express much consideration for their well-being. In such dysfunctional families, in the context of tumult, hostility, and confusion, parents may introduce their children to drugs or to inappropriate sexual activities. Addicted parents may rationalize that they are not hurting their children but are actually helping them learn about the world. More cynical or mentally disturbed addicted parents may give children a few drinks to help them to sleep, so the parents can "party" undisturbed or enjoy the "fun" of seeing an intoxicated child stumble about; some even use drugs as a numbing part of a seduction ritual, so that child will not report abuse to the authorities.

It is not surprising that the underlying pervasive emotions experienced by many children who are brought up by addicted parents are uncertainty, fear, anger, fluctuating or out-of-control moods, and a lack of trust. The decision by these children to use addictive drugs themselves to cope with such unpleasant feelings seems natural and useful. Fortunately, significant numbers of children from these disintegrating families are resilient enough to not follow in their parents' footsteps. More research must be done to understand how they do this, so therapists can apply their behaviors to help the children of addicts who are not succeeding at school or in life.

The relationships we experience in childhood set the pattern for future relationships. The emotions experienced in childhood have probably created the foundation for the enabling behaviors that are seen in the adult members of an addict's family. Members of an addict's family often feel that they are "damaged goods." The thought patterns attending this feeling include: "How can anyone love me if my parents did not and could abandon me by putting me up for adoption?" "No one will want to marry me," "I will pass the affliction down to my children," and "I am ashamed of myself and my family."

Family members fear that if outsiders find out about the addict's problem, this discovery will reflect badly on everyone. Thoughts accompanying this fear follow the lines of, "What if Dad is fired from his job because of drinking, what will happen to us?" or, "Other kids won't want to play with me or invite me to a party." Even when the addiction has gotten so out of control that it has erupted in physical violence or sexual abuse, family members continue to fear family dissolution. A child, for example, may think, "If I report what Dad did, Dad will be put in jail, I'll be sent to foster care, and I'll never see my family again." A passive mother, fearing the dissolution of her marriage, may refuse to acknowledge, even to herself, that the father has sexually abused her daughters. Of course, that makes the daughters feel empty for two reasons: "I cannot trust my own father—men are bad," and "My mother would protect me if she loved me—women are weak and I cannot be strong because I am a woman like my mother." The worst-case scenario is when family members completely overlook their own needs out of fear that the addict will leave if he does not get his own way. These emotions and thought patterns help maintain family secrets, and thus the denial, which is so characteristic of the addicted person, infects the entire family.

Nevertheless, healthy family members, especially if they recognize how much they also suffer from the addicted family member's disease, can play an active, important part in helping their loved one follow through with treatment. They have significant power to facilitate the process of healing and recovery. To do so, however, these healthy family members must overcome the guilt they may be feeling for not taking the addicted person back into the family home or for "going against his wishes." It is easier for healthy family members to recognize just how incapacitated the addict has actually become.

Mobilizing a family's emotional resources to encourage or pressure an addicted family member to enter treatment is called "intervention." Interventions can be either formal or informal, but they are invariably accompanied by an incredibly powerful outpouring of emotions of hurt, anger, and fear that have been pent up for years, perhaps for generations. During this process, the demonstration of love and caring has potentially rejuvenating effects for all who participate. The goal is to help addicts recognize how much their behavior is hurting the people they love, that they are not "bad persons," but suffer from an illness, and to pressure the patients to enter treatment. In interventions, threats that the family will abandon addicts if they do not seek treatment are joined with the promise of a better tomorrow if they do so. In common parlance, this combination is called "tough love."

Members of an addict's family cannot always accomplish an intervention without professional guidance. However, the potential benefit for the entire family is so great that working with a doctor, a family therapist, or an addiction counselor to help steer the addict to enter treatment is a wise investment of time and effort. Professionals can often help the process along by identifying the ambivalent and conflicting emotions that everyone in the family is feeling. Most important, by showing addicts, in an unbiased way, all they will lose if they do not follow through with treatment, while also helping the family to stand firm in the conviction that there is only one way to escape the addiction, the professional can help motivate addicts to make the choice to enter treatment that they would not have been comfortable with initially.

HOW SHOULD TREATMENT CONTINUE AFTER DETOXIFICATION OR STABILIZATION?

Addicts who have decided or have been persuaded by family members or friends to enter treatment often feel tremendously relieved. The burden of continuing their secret life has been lifted. Now that they have found a place in a hospital or other treatment facility, they embrace the opportunity to gain control over their problem. Family members feel relief as well. They finally have a reprieve from the day-to-day uncertainty of not knowing where the self-destructive course of their loved one will end up.

However, initiating treatment itself becomes a new source of stress. Addicts can no longer resort to drugs or addictive behavior to help them cope with the pain and uncertainty of their lives. Worse still, the onset of withdrawal symptoms, a necessary step in readaptation to a drug-free life, usually brings a combination of fear, stress, and discomfort that can feel overwhelming, especially because addicts cannot cope with these feelings in the way that they did prior to admission: by taking a drug or engaging in some other type of addictive behavior.

For example, it is not unusual for patients going through withdrawal to say that unless the doctor alleviates their suffering completely, they will leave the hospital. "I can stop using drugs at home myself," the patient argues, "if all you are going to do is just let me suffer!" Thus, patients exhibit substantial drug-seeking behavior to alleviate distress, aches and pains, and temper outbursts. Veiled threats usually accompany these behaviors: "Doc, I just need something to numb me," or "I'm about to lose it, and you don't want to see what will happen!" The addicts' resolve to become abstinent can melt like ice on a warm day. At times like these, the psychiatrist and nursing staff need to empathically and firmly remind patients why they decided to enter the hospital and why they wish to change their lives. Also, they need to advise the family not to take the addict home against medical advice—something families are often tempted to do when their loved ones complain that they are being "mistreated" in the hospital. Everyone must be strong about not taking patients back before they complete treatment.

Although some patients do leave treatment against medical advice, others stay and rise to the challenge of recovery. At this stage of treatment, it is not unusual for patients who are not "rescued" by their loved ones and are forced to stay in the hospital to act out their anger or despondency about being "abandoned." This acting out can involve seductive behaviors with others on the unit, including invading boundaries of other patients in many ways, and can create turmoil that has destructive consequences for all involved. For example, many patients in treatment begin love affairs, due to the depth of emotions people experience during this stage of their recovery, but the affairs are destined to failure. Violent anger outbursts can be particularly frightening to both patients, who recognize the tremendous anger they are carrying, and to other patients, who may be reminded of their violent parents or spouse. The most difficult patients may create such turmoil in the addiction treatment unit that it even affects staff morale. Good psychiatrists will point this out to colleagues and encourage self-understanding by staff members, which can lead to a healthier environment for patients undergoing recovery.

HEALING: WHEN TREATMENT REQUIRES PROFESSIONAL SUPERVISION

We recommend that patients do not attempt to stop the use of addictive drugs or of problematic, out-of-control behavioral addictions, such as gambling or eating disorders, without psychiatric guidance. Stopping the use of some drugs, including heroin and marijuana, is simply uncomfortable and nerve-racking, but, absent a complicating physical or psychiatric disorder, is not really dangerous. However, withdrawal from other addictive drugs, especially central nervous system (CNS) depressants, including barbiturates, benzodiazepines (Ativan or Valium), and alcohol can have serious health consequences; in fact, if they are not properly supervised and cared for, patients undergoing withdrawal from these drugs can even die.

The most severe and dangerous withdrawal process occurs with withdrawal from high doses of CNS depressants. Barbiturates pose the greatest risk for severe withdrawal, followed by alcohol and benzodiazepines. Withdrawal from short acting depressants, which are most quickly eliminated from the body, often causes seizures and delirium. As recently as the 1960s, mortality rates for the worst cases of alcohol withdrawal were as high as 17 percent. Withdrawal from stimulants and marijuana is distressing, but it is unlikely to be dangerous, unless the patient becomes suicidal as withdrawal progresses. Withdrawal from heroin and other opioids is very uncomfortable, mimicking, in many of its symptoms, a severe flu. But, ultimately, it will not create any problems that significantly threaten patients' health, unless they also have a severe medical illness, such as heart disease.

As we explained in the last section, in order to decide on the best treatment protocol, the doctor takes a medical history, performs a physical examination, and uses urine and blood tests to determine which drug or drugs patients had been using and what else may be contributing to the problem. When more than one addictive drug is involved, the doctor will focus on the ones that pose a potentially dangerous withdrawal hazard. Once dangers to health have been overcome, the doctor tries to relieve the discomfort that patients will be feeling. However, as noted, this relief may not be to the degree that some patients would like. The reality is that some discomfort is inevitable when patients discontinue addictive drug use or other addictive behavior.

Even addicts who are highly motivated to withdraw from using drugs often experience painful and frightening symptoms. Dramatic episodes of withdrawal delirium are common in film and in fiction, so patients may dread undergoing withdrawal unless educated by the medical and nursing staff about what to expect. It is important for addicts entering treatment to recognize that, with modern medical care provided by a psychiatrist or other physician familiar with addictive disorders, they will not die or be severely affected by the withdrawal process. In fact, with proper treatment, only four to six days after their last use of the addictive drug, most patients will be relatively symptom-free from their acute withdrawal. It is extremely helpful to know there is light at the end of the tunnel, and patients and their loved ones should be continually reminded of this fact during the earliest stages of recovery.

After the patient has endured the course of acute withdrawal symptoms—that is, the first stage of treatment—the next stage of treatment—of protracted withdrawal symptoms—begins. At this point, patients who had been self-medicating an emotional or psychological disorder can no longer use their drug of choice to manage their psychiatric disturbances. It is therefore critical that patients undergo a careful psychiatric assessment at this point. The good news is that there are now many safe medications that can relieve these psychiatric problems. In fact, such treatment may actually alleviate the main reason that patients resorted to drug abuse in the first place.

However, the emotional disruptions that arise as a result of protracted withdrawal, including anxiety, depression, mood swings, and insomnia, are often difficult to distinguish from an underlying psychiatric problem that exists apart from and may have been the cause of the addiction itself. Complicating the situation further is the fact that cravings for the drug or preoccupation with the behavior that patients are trying to quit may persist for months after beginning treatment.

For these reasons, it is vital that the psychiatrist supervising addicts' treatment be trained in differentiating the effects of protracted withdrawal from the effects of comorbid, or simultaneously occurring, psychiatric problems. Psychiatrists who are not expert in addictive disorders often simply assume that patients' depression or mood swings indicate the existence of a psychiatric problem entirely separate from the problems arising from the addiction.

The treatments that would be effective in treating an independent psychiatric problem—for example, depression—may not be effective in treating similar symptoms in recovering addicts and in fact may be dangerous. For example, antidepressants like Prozac may not be as effective for treating depressed, recovering alcoholics as simply stopping drinking. Thus, the prescription of Prozac in the early stages of recovery is contraindicated in recovering alcoholics, in whom major depression cannot be diagnosed with confidence. Some medications are almost certain to do harm in these situations; others would just do no good. For example, doctors not experienced in addiction treatment may treat recovering addicts suffering from "panic attacks" with Xanax (alprazolam) or Klonipin (clonazepam), which is not good medical practice, because these two drugs are highly addictive in themselves. Addicted patients often tell psychiatrists who are planning to detoxify them from Xanax, "I was only taking the Xanax as prescribed by my doctor!" An effective response to such a comment is "Xanax is like alcohol in pill form, and I hope you understand that alcohol is very bad for you."

The golden rule is that pharmacotherapy—the use of medications to treat emotional problems—must not be instituted to treat disorders that are actually *consequences* of addiction. This rule is especially important when the medications prescribed are addictive and pose a high abuse potential in themselves.

A psychiatric assessment that is performed very close in time after patients last used drugs or when they are in turmoil from stopping a behavior addiction is not a reliable basis for making an accurate diagnosis of co-occurring psychiatric disorders. The only way to identify the proper focus for treatment is to document persistence or worsening of such symptoms during extended periods when patients were not using addictive drugs or engaging in other addictive behaviors.

Thus, in order to diagnose a recovering addict's psychiatric problems properly, psychiatrists must pay detailed attention to the patient's history of emotional problems, information obtained from family members and concerned friends who have had the chance to observe the patient over time, and, when available, the reports of therapists or physicians who have watched the patient's symptoms wax and wane in response to addictive use of drugs or addictive behaviors and treatments received in the past. Since the apple does not fall far from the tree, a family history of other psychiatric illness in biological relatives suggests a genetic predisposition to these disorders in the patient and may help the psychiatrist arrive at the correct diagnosis.

CHAPTER 8

Treatment Programs

AFTER ADDICTED PATIENTS have completed detoxification and withdrawal from the drug or drugs they had been using or have stopped engaging in addictive behaviors, their continuing rehabilitation, whether inpatient or outpatient, should consist of a combination of psychosocial and pharmacological treatments.

INPATIENT OR OUTPATIENT TREATMENT: WHICH IS MORE EFFECTIVE OR GIVES THE BETTER VALUE FOR THE MONEY?

After completing the acute stage of treatment, during which patients undergo withdrawal and detoxification from the drug to which they are addicted, patients and their families must decide on a course of more extended treatment that will enable them to learn how to begin a normal life.

Financial costs, including the expense of the treatment program, availability of insurance coverage for a particular treatment program, and the cost of taking time off from work, often assume primacy. Families now also must answer emotional questions, including about the possibility of the patient being separated from the family and how involved the family should be in the treatment. Fortunately, most good hospital addiction centers have capable staff members who can meet with patients and their families to help them make pragmatic choices.

The social services personnel can help answer many questions. For example, should patients seek treatment at a spa-like facility, halfway across the country, at exorbitant cost? Should patients be in a boot camp environment, where they will be immersed in a highly structured environment in which the rules of the community are enforced through firm discipline? Should patients live independently or in a supervised facility while attending outpatient treatment? How much financial assistance will be provided by insurance to cover the expenses involved, and how much is it reasonable for the family to provide? Have addicts already depleted the family coffers? To what extent should patients be encouraged to fend for themselves?

At this juncture, it is important for doctors to understand patients' histories and the psychiatric and medical factors that affect their condition, because not all facilities are well equipped to manage all of the problems associated with the various faces of addiction. For example, if a patient had been an addict for a relatively short time before undergoing withdrawal, outpatient treatment—the least expensive alternative—may be extremely effective. For patients who have returned to their addiction despite having received less intensive treatments, costly inpatient care may be the only alternative. Finally, because the patient's family usually must foot at least part of the bill, ambivalent feelings over the great amount of money and the emotional investment demanded to repeatedly bail out a loved one cannot be ignored.

What is most important is not to allow treatment to end simply with withdrawal and detoxification. Recovery treatment has a chance to achieve some permanence only when patients' brains have been cleared of the addictive substance.

In our judgment, treatment, whether inpatient or outpatient, should always be as close to home as possible, without sacrificing quality. The reason for staying close to patients' native environment is that recovery requires that people face the challenges of their lives without resorting to addictive drugs or addictive behaviors. Patients may find it difficult to apply coping strategies learned in a treatment program in a distant place, little related to their home ground, once they return to the realities of their life circumstances. In addition, sending someone "away" for treatment (a kind of "leper colony" model) tends to reinforce secretiveness and isolation. The world of the patient's family continues as if nothing happened, and the time and cost of travel greatly reduces the family's capacity to participate in the patient's recovery. Finally, most experienced clinicians recognize that the family should regard the patient's addiction as an illness rather than a moral flaw. And medical illnesses, such as heart disease, rarely require that patients be sent elsewhere for treatment.

WHO REALLY DECIDES
WHAT TREATMENT IS BEST?

Unfortunately, in the United States today, decisions about treatment are rarely made on purely clinical grounds. Most treatment professionals are handcuffed by the insurance industry, limited to sending patients to a level of care that is "covered" by their insurance policies. Addiction is a bona fide health problem, but there is a tremendous gap between the amounts of "standard" coverage provided for medical as opposed to mental health illnesses. To make matters worse, addiction treatment is considered the stepchild of mental health treatment. Despite the fact that addiction is as much of a psychiatric illness as mania or depression, addicts usually receive even less financial support from insurance payers than patients suffering from other mental health problems. Insurance companies are still allowed to reimburse less of the treatment cost for an addicted patient with multiple mental health and medical problems, including, for example, the risk of suicide, than they are required to provide for someone with a "pure" mental health problem, such as depression, who is suicidal. Often psychiatrists and other therapists combat this injustice by labeling patients as simply suicidal and depressed, to avoid acknowledging their addiction. This practice helps patients with their hospital bills, but it also supports their denial that addiction is the underlying cause of their problems. It is not unusual for patients to be hospitalized several times as "depressed" or even "psychotic," until the severity of drug or alcohol use becomes so obvious that it cannot be ignored. Clearly, the answer is hospitalization in a dual-diagnosis unit and parity for treatment of mental health and medical illnesses. Fortunately, Congress has initiated legislation to address this need.

Significant proportions of visits to primary care doctors have a mental health basis. In addition, the treatment of many medical disorders can be greatly improved by dealing with underlying mental health causes. Therefore, the fact that most insurance plans cover medical illnesses fully but greatly limit treatment for mental health care is especially unwarranted. Insurance companies get away with this by contracting out the mental health component of health care to other organizations (so-called behavioral health organizations, or BHOs), "carving out," as it were, expenditures on behavioral health care from other health insurance costs. As a result, only a small proportion of the total payout of general medical insurance policies goes to support mental health care, and mental health care organizations are rewarded for reducing utilization. Perhaps the worst consequence of this fragmentation is that it encourages physicians and hospitals to manage patients' difficulties piecemeal, instead of integrating the treatment of physical and mental problems.

In part, this inequity with respect to mental illnesses persists because the people who suffer from these illnesses, including the addictive disorders, are among the poorest and least represented members of our society. Few people in power appreciate the prevalence, impact, and potential for successful treatment of many mental illnesses. Further, because of the stigma associated with mental health problems, powerful members of our society who recover from mental illness, or who have family members who suffer from these disorders, are reluctant to identify themselves. Therefore, they rarely spearhead fundraising to support research into better mental health treatments. Contrast this with how many people have led initiatives on other, more "acceptable" illnesses, such as cancer and Alzheimer's disease. Probably one of the most important things people with addictive disorders and their loved ones can do to advance the cause of addiction treatment is to move out of the shadows and stop acting as if they are inferior.

Placement of many patients in treatment programs ultimately depends on what their insurance policies will permit. In a climate of cost containment, this makes some sense. Why expend 5 to 10 times as much money treating a patient's addiction if the same result can be obtained for less? The problem is that we are very good at calculating costs but extremely poor at determining "results." Answering the question of whether inpatient treatment is better than outpatient treatment becomes a judgment call; at this point, it cannot be answered in strictly scientific terms. The answer given to the question of how much money to spend is therefore the result of debate between addiction professionals and representatives of insurance companies, and debates can go both ways based on the talent of the debaters.

To keep the costs of addiction treatment low, insurance companies have developed an infrastructure of paid "advocates," who work with doctors trying to secure the best care for their patients. These include "hired-gun" physicians, who are not necessarily trained in an appropriate specialty and are much better reimbursed for time spent obstructing health care than providing it. Advocates may also include nurses and others with even less training. The primary job of these advocates is to win arguments with doctors who, although inclined to prescribe effective treatments and even to intercede on behalf of their patients, are not compensated for the time they devote to endless telephone debates.

Even concerned doctors have to move on to their next patient to earn their salaries and feed their families. The results are predictable: The insurance companies get their way most of the time, and recovering addicts are denied proper treatment.

In fairness to the insurance industry, their duty is to make money for shareholders. Obviously, unless it can be demonstrated that the more costly approach is substantially better than less costly alternatives, there is no reason not to save money by going the cheaper route. Even though it is difficult to predict how effective a given treatment will be for a given patient, the selection of the appropriate treatment is better left to physicians who know the patients and are expert in treatment of the disorders in question than to insurance company advocates. The best insurance companies do the process of "quality control" rather well. They actually assist physicians by helping to identify good treatment options that are covered by patients' insurance, treatment programs that have obtained good results with patients having similar problems, which physicians may not know about. To do this, these companies refer to their documentation on the quality of treatment programs to which they have sent previous referrals. However, whether a company does this is based on its business ethics rather than mandated rules. Unfortunately for Wall Street (and Main Street), business ethics are not necessarily the driving engine of our economy.

PSYCHOSOCIAL TREATMENT PROGRAMS

Psychosocial interventions organized within a treatment program include individual and group psychotherapy, family therapy, and self-help groups. These are the major elements of the care typically delivered in both inpatient and outpatient treatment settings. Orientation to self-help groups, namely the 12-step support groups such as Alcoholics Anonymous and Narcotics Anonymous, within the treatment program provides an empowering complement to professionally conducted psychotherapeutic modalities. For behavioral addictions, the 12-step model is also used.

Psychosocial treatments, which have evolved empirically (by trial and error) over the course of decades of medical practice, are unquestionably an effective, essential component of any successful treatment for addicted patients. This is true, despite the fact that psychotherapy is not an exact science and that it even has elements of an art form. In the course of psychotherapy, patients are taught to comprehend and get in touch with their feelings and to understand how their feelings can become triggers for drug use or irresistible, self-destructive behaviors. Patients are trained to recognize these triggers. Previously, they had no clue how their drug use or compulsive behavior was caused by life events or how to stop these feelings from pushing them back into the use of addictive drugs. In these programs, they are counseled on how to find outside supports to strengthen their resolve to remain sober, not to engage in their behavioral addictions, and to overcome craving and situations that otherwise would have precipitated a relapse.

Therapists experienced in treating addicted patients recognize the value of self-help groups. The urge to return to using drugs, despite "knowing" how devastating a relapse could be, is a primary characteristic of long-term abstinence. Recovering addicts remain vulnerable to relapsing, because they have become accustomed to relying on addictive drugs to cope with the stresses of daily living. In addition, some addicts who have maintained abstinence for years may inexplicably and irresistibly develop the desire to demonstrate to themselves and others that they can drink or use their drug of choice or gamble "just once." The consequence of this rationalization is predictable to everyone but the addicts themselves. In self-help groups, addicts meet others who have been through the same struggles that they are currently undergoing. A network of peers—people who are also trying to stay sober—can be mobilized 24 hours a day, seven days a week. This availability is important, because a nearly overwhelming impulse to use addictive drugs or engage in addictive behaviors can arise at any time. Obviously, no clinician can provide such total coverage. Any argument over which is more helpful—psychiatric care or self-help groups—misses the point that these two resources are highly compatible and should be used together.

The psychosocial therapeutic strategies that should be used in the care of individuals who suffer from the disease of addiction are self-examination, psychotherapeutic sessions that explore the emotional problems that led to the addiction, and the development of a support network to help protect a person from ever-recurring urges to use.

There are two major reasons why psychosocial treatment fails to enable a patient to begin leading a fulfilling and balanced life:

1. The therapist or addiction counselor may fail to recognize the presence of other psychiatric problems, in addition to the ones that are being treated.
2. Even if the therapist does recognize the problems, he or she may lack the experience necessary to provide successful treatment.

The long-term care needed by recovering addicts is similar, regardless of which specific drug they had been abusing or which irresistible behavioral urges they have been struggling to avoid. They may need help with housing, finding job opportunities, and, in general, feeding and clothing themselves, if they are living on their own. Many people must be involved in the management of long-term care. Family doctors, clergy, psychologists, social workers, nutritionists, and occupational, recreational, and art therapists, among others, are some of those who can provide this help.

MEDICAL MODEL

Pharmacological interventions, the vital, new component of the pharmacopsychosocial treatment model advocated in this book, are the result of an evolving body of research that proves medications are a viable, effective adjunct to the more traditional psychosocial approach to the treatment of addiction. The use of the right medications can increase the odds that psychosocial treatments will succeed and reduce the likelihood that a patient will return to using addictive drugs or engaging in addictive behaviors. Use of medications to minimize the discomforts of withdrawing from addictive drugs during the acute withdrawal stage has been part of the early stage of addiction treatment for a long time. New pharmacological agents specifically help patients reduce the craving for addictive drugs and thereby alleviate the distress of protracted withdrawal that would otherwise disturb people for months after discontinuing active addiction. In addition, other pharmacological agents are used to treat forms of mental illness that commonly afflict addicted patients and that frequently were the reason patients became addicted in the first place or did not fully recover with conventional psychosocial treatments.

The tension between the medical model and the psychosocial model is greatest at the time that long-term care is initiated. Part of the reason for this discord is that, until recently, psychiatrists lacked experience in treating drug addiction. The standard approach offered to young medical students by the community of psychiatrists was to tell patients "Until you stop drinking, I cannot work with you!" However, this attitude is outmoded, because today much more is known about the physiology and brain chemistry underlying the addictions. Also, this attitude is based on the misguided notion that patients choose to drink. In fact, their drinking *is* the problem for which they are seeking help.

The self-help movement to support recovering addicts arose initially due to psychiatrists' neglect of the field. Alcoholics Anonymous (AA) was founded in 1935 by Bill Wilson, a New York City stockbroker, and Robert Holbrook Smith, an Akron surgeon, both of whom had serious drinking problems. After years of bingeing followed by periods of abstinence, Wilson recognized that alcoholism was a disease, a disease that Smith had not learned to treat in medical school and for which neither man had been able to find help from their physicians. Wilson was convinced that "will power" could not keep a person from drinking once the person had become addicted to alcohol.

They began working with other alcoholics at Akron's City Hospital, calling themselves "Bill W." and "Dr. Bob," initiating the AA tradition of anonymity. They taught that alcoholics must recognize drinking as a sickness that required help from others to overcome. Indeed, Bill W. and Dr. Bob helped dozens of Akron alcoholics to quit drinking. Their approach has since been expanded to help those addicted to other drugs and harmful behaviors as well.

Unfortunately, the success of the self-help movement has discouraged generations of eager young physicians from getting involved in the care of recovering addicts. After doctors identify addiction as the problem, the standard—it has been argued, the only and best response—has been "Go to meetings." The irony is that the separation of addiction treatment from mainstream medical practice continues to some extent to this day, despite the fact that scientific research concerning the effects of addiction on the brain has confirmed the idea of Bill W. and Dr. Bob that addiction is, in fact, a disease.

Happily, over the last two decades, a rapprochement has begun between the medical community and the self-help movement. Psychiatrists and other physicians have begun to recognize that the principles advocated by the 12-step community offer tremendous insights to the medical treatment community. Physicians' acceptance of the self-help movement for recovering addicts has even led to the establishment of many other self-help organizations to support those suffering from other mental and medical illnesses, as diverse as obsessive compulsive disorder, diabetes, and Alzheimer's disease. One of the great contributions of the addiction field to the rest of medicine has been its emphasis on empowering patients to take significant responsibility for their own care through fellowship with others who are experiencing similar difficulties.

An important breakthrough in recent years has been the growing realization of the similarities among all the drug addictions and among behavioral addictions, including gambling and eating disorders. Some patients, even though they are recovering from the use of heroin or cocaine, feel more comfortable with the people in AA. And recovering alcoholics sometimes say that they see AA as "stodgy" and prefer NA (Narcotics Anonymous) or CA (Cocaine Anonymous), whose members are "younger and more like me." People suffering from the addictions of gambling, eating, and problematic hypersexuality have established 12-step self-help groups, modeled on AA, with considerable success. The structural elements, treatment strategies, and social focus of these support groups are remarkably similar.

SAFETY OF MEDICATIONS IN THE TREATMENT OF PRIMARY ADDICTION: WHY BECOME ADDICTED TO A DOCTOR-PRESCRIBED MEDICINE?

As we have noted, pharmacological agents now available for the long-term rehabilitation of addicts help them benefit from the spiritual growth fostered by self-help groups. The successful use of these medicines also help physicians to recognize that treating recovering addicts is as much their responsibility as treating patients who suffer from various other illnesses, such as hypertension or diabetes.

These new medicines, which directly treat drug addiction by reducing the intensity of craving for alcohol and drugs and the likelihood that a relapse will occur, reinforce the understanding that self-help groups have had since their inception: Addiction is a disease, not just a bad habit.

The medicines developed for treating addiction must be carefully distinguished from drugs used by addicts to self-medicate. It is simply not true that *all* addicts have an underlying psychiatric illness that they are self-medicating with addictive drugs, although most addicts do suffer from some psychiatric disorder in addition to addiction. However, some addicts are mentally healthy except for a problem in the "wiring" of brain reward mechanisms. Although we still do not fully understand these mechanisms, we can say with confidence that reward mechanisms are fundamentally important in the manifestations of emotional disorders other than addictions. Thus it is not surprising that a dysfunctional reward system can affect the course of or even cause the emotional illnesses that predispose people to developing an addiction. Stated in another way, mental illness and addiction often are like the proverbial chicken and the egg.

If addiction itself is considered the primary problem, and it is managed effectively so that patients stop using drugs, it might seem that no additional psychiatric intervention is necessary. But should the protracted withdrawal syndrome be considered a primary psychiatric disorder itself and warrant treatment in its own right?

A hypothetical question encapsulates this: If an alcoholic or a drug addict were placed on a deserted island with no access to alcohol or drugs, would he be psychiatrically "normal"? In a way, this scenario occurs frequently in the penal system, because, during incarceration, addicts are (mostly) prevented from using drugs. When they are discharged from prison, they frequently relapse into their former addiction. These relapses lead us to think that the emotional problems attending drug abuse are not simply a consequence of the availability and use of drugs themselves. It would seem that drug users' mental problems were present before drug use began and were in fact a factor that predisposed them to become addicted. Of course, this does not mean that the emotional problems a patient might have had before becoming an addict are not substantially worsened by drug use and are not greatly improved with sobriety.

Until recently, pharmaceutical companies, as well as physicians, have neglected patients who suffer from addictive disorders. As stated previously, whenever a new medication—for example, for the treatment of depression—is in development, patients suffering from alcoholism or drug addiction are typically excluded from all drug trials. Companies justify this exclusion by saying that, in order to exclude confounding factors, clinical trials of antidepressants should be confined to patients who have "pure" depression. But it must be acknowledged that addicted patients are also excluded for some of the same reasons psychiatrists tended to avoid treating them in the past. Alcoholics and drug addicts are a notoriously difficult population with which to work. In addition, no drug company wants to risk that the Food and Drug Administration will regard the new medicine as unsafe. Addicts typically have complicating illnesses, which, during clinical trials of the medicine, may mistakenly be attributed to the medicine being studied. However, the notion of "pure" psychiatric illnesses does not reflect the pervasiveness of addictive tendencies or disorders in the mental health population. In fact, after FDA approval, the drug will not actually be used to treat so-called pure depression in the "real world."

For all of these reasons, the treatment of addictive disorders should focus on the similarities, rather than the differences, between addiction to various drugs and behavioral addictions, such as gambling. The effectiveness of new medicines for treating addiction reflects the shared neurochemical underpinnings of drug-seeking behavior and different psychopathologies that may cause either the co-occurring mental disorders or addiction in a susceptible individual. The future of successful addiction treatment lies in better understanding the role of co-occurring psychiatric conditions, the development of new pharmacological treatments, and combining psychotherapy with pharmacotherapy in the management of these disorders.

PART III

Gaining Understanding: Treating Drug Addictions

CHAPTER 9

Alcohol

STATISTICS ABOUT ALCOHOL consumption vary from study to study and from year to year, but approximately 10 percent of men and 5 percent of women in the United States are alcoholics. About 95 percent of alcoholics eventually die from complications resulting from the disease, and their life expectancy is more than 25 years less than that of nonalcoholics. The harm caused by alcohol addiction is pervasive, and extends well beyond the deleterious effects this addiction has on the alcoholic. In addition to the personal and financial problems created for the alcoholic's family, friends, and coworkers, about 50 percent of homicides and 40 percent of assaults each year are related to the excessive use of alcohol. Fetal alcohol syndrome and fetal alcohol effects, which occur when pregnant women drink alcohol, is the leading cause of mental retardation in the country.

The terrible damage wrought by alcoholics on other people can create conflicting feelings in the doctors who treat them. When Dr. Martin was a young intern in the emergency room of a suburban Toronto hospital, three nurses with whom he had been working and who had just gone off duty were brought back to the emergency room, bleeding and unconscious, with severe internal injuries sustained as a result of an automobile accident. A very drunk man, who was crying "Oh my God, I didn't want to kill them," was led into the emergency room. He had a few superficial lacerations, which Dr. Martin was instructed to sew up. Of course, Dr. Martin treated the man; it was his duty to do so. But you can imagine the anger he felt over the terrible injustice of the serious injuries that the man had inflicted on his coworkers.

Alcoholic beverages are readily available at low cost and with minimal legal obstacles to their use. Accordingly, there is widespread use of alcohol in diverse recreational and work-related circumstances. Traumatic injuries sustained while under the influence of drunkenness—that is, elevated blood alcohol concentrations—are one of the most common public health problems today. On any given night, the emergency departments of most busy hospitals are beset with accident victims whose blood levels demonstrate severe alcohol intoxication. The care of these patients is enormously expensive. Heavy drinkers rarely recognize how severely their judgment and motor skills are impaired, and, because of their tolerance to some of alcohol's effects, they can appear to others "as sober as judges." The combination of alcohol that we drink (ethanol) with other central nervous system depressants, such as medications prescribed by physicians who are unaware that their patients are alcoholics, is the most common cause of severe drug overdoses.

As with other addictions, biopsychosocial risk factors increase the likelihood of a person developing the disease of alcoholism. The primary biological risk factor is a genetic predisposition to becoming a heavy drinker. It has been demonstrated that people who carry certain genetic risk factors are far more likely to become alcoholics once they begin drinking alcohol. Statistically, approximately 40 percent of the risk factor is traceable to genetics. Psychological risk factors include co-occurring psychiatric disorders. For example, people suffering from clinical depression, especially depression that disguises sublimated anger and dissatisfaction, often resort to drinking alcohol as a way of self-medicating, and thus escaping from the discomforts of depression. Social risk factors include the fact that alcohol is readily and legally available and inexpensive, and drinking is encouraged in some occupations or social circles.

Most alcoholics begin drinking at age 14 or younger. Of the children who begin drinking alcohol at that age, nearly half will become alcoholics. The disease usually takes about 15 years to develop. Like involvement with gambling or the Internet, drinking often starts out in an apparently innocent and nondestructive way. A young person may be taken to a bar by a parent or other family member or a friend, finds that he enjoys the effects of alcohol, and learns to use it as a way of managing stress. Drinking on this level often is regarded as healthy recreation. But some people increase the frequency and level of alcohol intoxication, and neurochemical changes in the brain begin to occur.

These neurochemical changes seem to accelerate the progression to the disease of addiction.

Alcoholism is frequently best understood as a primary addiction. For example, when strong genetic factors create the primary vulnerability to developing an addiction to alcohol, treatment should properly focus on controlling or combating this underlying biological problem. However, like other addictions, alcoholism can also be associated with another co-occurring psychiatric condition. That is, as we have said earlier, a person who is suffering from depression or anxiety or another psychiatric problem may turn to alcohol as a means of managing these problems. In such cases, treatment for the alcohol addiction must include treatment for the underlying condition.

THE CASE OF JOE A.

Joe was a short, feisty man, an entertaining conversationalist, with a ready sardonic smile, and a sharp, often hostile sense of humor. He regarded himself as flawed by lack of discipline but endowed with gifts that more than made up for his shortcomings. He had grown up in a middle class, Jewish neighborhood in Boston, and attended public schools. His father was in sales and the entire family suffered from the ups and downs of his flamboyant career. After each successful "deal," he was all smiles, brought roses to Joe's mother, took the family for a splendid meal in a fine restaurant—nothing could be better. However, when a deal went "sour," Joe's dad would come home with a hair-trigger temper. Joe's mom quickly hushed the children off to bed so when the drinking and yelling started they would be safe in their rooms. Joe was only five or six before he could forecast what was about to occur by the sound of his father's steps as he entered the apartment. His father could be very hurtful and sarcastic when things had not gone well at work—so Joe learned that that was the time to avoid him. However, Joe also realized he could not protect his mother from the abuse and that troubled him terribly.

Joe soon understood that his mother was "defenseless" against his overpowering father. Later, he started to see her as passive and ineffectual, and he promised himself that he would only marry someone who was able to take care of herself (and *him*, as he began to resent that his mother did not stand up to the bullying of his father). When he was fourteen, his father left his mother for a younger woman, forcing his mother and his sibs to fend for themselves. He was forced to help out around the house, as his mom became more and more despondent and less functional. He had little time to enjoy an extracurricular life, although he continued to do well in school, in spite of the responsibility of having to be the "man of the house." The only thing he got from his dad was the promise of money for college so that, "You can turn out to be more successful and could take care of me in my old age."

He entered college, relieved to be free of the pressures of home. It soon became one party after another. His grades started to fall, but partying allowed him to ignore his needy mom. Partying was accompanied by multiple "one-night stands." His ability to find women who "did not cling" was a great relief. Wanting Joe to make something of himself, his dad continued to subsidize his ongoing party. However, Joe became impatient to make his mark in business and show his dad how capable he really was. Finding that he spent most of his time partying, he dropped out before taking his degree.

Joe was a gifted designer with a distinctive understanding of patterns, textiles, and the taste to create clothes that upscale consumers found attractive. He lived in a world of colors and shapes. After a few years working for a leading tie manufacturer, selling ties to major department stores in and around Boston and New York, he borrowed money and formed a partnership with another talented designer, founding his own clothing company. In under a year, relying on their designs and Joe's salesmanship, the company turned a profit and prospects for growth looked good.

Joe was afflicted by frequent mood swings, especially periods when he seemed to have endless energy, slept little, and was highly sexual. Moreover, he began to see how his patterns somewhat resembled the "roller coaster" he and the family had been through with his father when he was growing up. He, however, denied that he had a problem, because he was not affecting others as his dad had. He felt that avoiding repeating his dad's abusive conduct was a compelling reason not to get "hooked up" in a steady relationship. He was able to "sell" himself the idea that he was "in control" and "having fun," even though others began to see that he was actually spiraling out of control. He started to use alcohol, much as his dad had, when things were not going well. He also drank when his thoughts were racing out of control, and he was manic, irritable, "really creative," and couldn't sleep.

His life had two parts: working and partying. When he worked, he focused on the drawing boards on which he created his designs and telephoned and made sales calls on his accounts, always alert, amicable, and assertive in the right combination to clinch deals. But, when he partied, which he did virtually every day after work, he really came to life. He lived in a one bedroom apartment in a luxury building in downtown Boston, located, as it happened, around the corner from one of the hottest bars and dance clubs in the city. At cocktail hour, the dance club offered a free buffet, set out on the dance floor, to members and their guests, and it filled up with "up and coming" men and women who assembled there after work to enjoy the food, have cocktails, and mingle. Later in the evening, the club transformed. The music was loud and the dance floor was occupied by dancers. And the crowd changed. There were still many businessmen in sports jackets and ties or suits and a number of conservatively dressed women. But the majority of the nighttime crowd was younger people, many in their twenties, who showed up in flashy, casual attire, often coming in groups of three or four or more. The young women came to get out for the evening with their friends, show off their newest outfits, have a few drinks, which, they hoped, they could induce men to buy them, and hunt for the man of their dreams. The young men came to get out for the evening with their friends, often to get drunk, and to try to pick up a woman who would go home with them.

His aging father—retired, again divorced, but financially comfortable—became an on-again, off-again drinking buddy for Joe. There was a bond between the two, and Joe's father seemed to live vicariously through Joe's many conquests. Fortunately for him, Joe's mother was now not much of a problem to him, now that she moved to live with Joe's younger sister and her family in Portland. The business was going well and life was reasonably good. Then his dad died of a heart attack, and Joe felt quite alone. The meaningless relationships and increased drinking caused him to become quite depressed. Thinking that marriage would offer a way out of his sense of aimlessness, Joe found time to find a wife and start a family. Unfortunately, his wife also suffered from emotional instabilities that prevented her from helping to "turn him around," so he continued his life much as he had before. Now, however, he felt some responsibility for the family. He was drawn particularly to his young son, Manny, whom he had named after his deceased father. He also began to understand for the first time what his dad must have experienced in an unfulfilling marriage. He did not want to divorce his wife, for Manny's sake. But he clearly made a choice to go elsewhere for his recreation! Joe, now in his early forties and mostly bald, had become a club regular who was lionized by the management, who saw him as an unofficial contributor to the club's entertainment, who even treated him to a steady supply of free drinks.

Joe spent little of his social time with his business associates. Instead, Joe was the self-appointed king of the dance club he frequented. He had gathered a circle of men around him, whom he dubbed "The Knights of the Round Table." It was a motley group, mostly near his own age, including a tall, handsome truck driver with a genial smile; a dark haired, good looking, bisexual pharmacist, with a dour expression, who dealt psychoactive drugs to supplement his income; a quiet, conservatively dressed, wealthy owner of a small steel foundry, with a natty beard; a young, unemployed lawyer, whose interest in life was English literature, with enough family money to escape, for a time, the need to find a job; a small, skinny hair stylist; and Joe's best buddy, a high school teacher, with a full beard and deep, soulful eyes, full of quiet quips and intellectual banter. These men would gather around Joe, who would hold court, presiding over their drinking, watching the colorful crowd, joking, talking, about politics, money or, more often, women and sex.

Joe went to bed drunk every night. He had dabbled in psychoactive drugs since his short tenure at college. He especially enjoyed taking a few hits of cocaine, a drug that would imbue him with energy and, he thought, make his usually sparkling conversation shine and scintillate like the bulbs on a theatrical marquee. And, after he tried marijuana, he liked the way it relaxed him and loosened him up so much that he was careful never to allow his supply to become exhausted. But his real penchant was for the expansive, inspiring effects of alcohol. He regarded himself a "serious drinker." He had no taste for liqueurs, brandy or port, even whiskey, and he had no patience for sugary, mixed drinks. He explained to his admirers at the club that alcohol had the same primary effect on a person, no matter in what matrix it was consumed. But the hangovers from what he saw as "adulterated" drinks were worse. Consequently, his drink of choice was vodka, which he considered the purest form of alcohol, either straight, or more often, mixed with orange juice and ice. Later on, when his drinking seemed to invade his life outside the club, he found it useful that it was difficult to smell vodka on his breath, so work colleagues would not know that he was a "lush."

Joe's acerbic personality, flamboyant affect, and nearly constant state of inebriation, began to destabilize his business activities. Competition with other manufacturers forced his partners, acting over Joe's objections, to accept a buyout offer. He came away with a handsome sum of money. But he was no happier in his personal life. The partying and drinking increased, and eventually he decided to leave his wife who "was stultifying my creativity and fun." Needless to say, he was now nearly broke after the divorce settlement. Long unemployed, he continued frequenting his favorite club, staying on until closing time in the middle of the night. Though both settlements had been fair, he brooded over how his partner had "cheated" him out of his company and how his wife had "cheated" him out of his house and children. Depressed and angry, he began drinking more than ever before.

When Joe entered his fifties, he needed a stiff drink to get out of bed in the morning. If he tried to skip it, he would suffer from the "shakes." He still measured out his alcohol intake during the day, taking in enough to avert withdrawal symptoms, but never so much as to significantly impair his judgment. When evening came, he relaxed his self-monitoring, and began downing doubles at the bar, one after another, until closing time. His doctors warned him that his heart and liver were in bad shape. Their advice was that Joe should get professional help to stop drinking entirely.

Joe had met Elaine, a divorcee, at the club. She was a woman of modest independent means, who after escaping from the boredom and confinement of a dull, unpleasant marriage found Joe's sparkling conversation, outrageous humor, and zest for his design work fascinating and endearing. This woman, the first strong-minded person to dedicate her efforts to helping Joe, used her determined, steady personality to help convince Joe to enter a psychiatric treatment facility in order to "dry out." While there, he was given Valium to help him through the worst stages of physical withdrawal from alcohol. After about two weeks in the hospital he started to notice that his head was beginning to clear. Even before he felt he was strong enough to do so, he was encouraged by his counselor and psychiatrist to attend Alcoholics Anonymous meetings on the hospital grounds. Initially, he was surprised how many other people were struggling with the same problems as he was. But, as his health returned, so did his brashness, and he soon felt he could do better "than these morons who are claiming to be treating me." For the first time, his doctor helped him see that he had profound mood swings that fueled his drinking and started prescribing a mood stabilizer.

With Elaine's support, Joe stayed sober for several months. He began eating more balanced and more regular meals than he had before undergoing treatment. And, a little subdued and slightly less outrageous, he seemed calmer and more at ease. Then, unfortunately, Joe and Elaine began to again frequent the club where Joe had been a regular, but now Joe would drink only ginger ale and club soda. Not surprisingly, Joe's resolve to remain sober didn't last long. And, since Elaine drank "moderately," one night Joe decided to join her "for old time's sake." It was only a matter of a few months that he stopped taking his mood stabilizer, and his drinking accelerated to previous levels.

PHARMACOLOGY

Sir William Osler, the legendary Canadian physician and one of the founding faculty members of the Johns Hopkins School of Medicine, was reputed to have remarked, "Alcohol does not make people do things better, it makes them less ashamed of doing them badly." This quotation superbly summarizes alcohol's pharmacological effects. The stimulation that apparently occurs in the early stages of drunkenness actually results from the suppression of so-called inhibitory control centers of the brain, the areas that allow us to make judgments and decisions.

Even low concentrations of alcohol in the blood affect the parts of the brain most sensitive to the drug, and the depression of these regions causes euphoria and impaired performance on tasks that depend on training, previous experience, and expectations. Higher alcohol concentrations in the blood cause a loss of motor coordination. It is this loss of coordination that is being tested by a police officer who asks a driver to walk a straight line or repeatedly touch his nose and the policeman's upheld finger. Still higher concentrations depress other brain functions and interfere with spinal reflexes and temperature regulation. The failure of temperature regulation explains why alcoholics sometimes have an abnormally low body temperature, if they have been drinking and, for example, sleep it off in a snowbank. The highest blood concentrations of alcohol depress the brain centers that control the heart and breathing, resulting in coma and respiratory failure.

Responses to different levels of alcohol in the blood have been carefully studied, and people's sensitivity to alcohol has been found to vary widely. For example, at blood alcohol concentrations of 50, 100 to 150, and 200 milligrams per 100 milliliter (mg/100 ml), it is estimated that approximately 10 percent, 66 percent, or almost all of the general population, respectively, would appear obviously intoxicated. Yet at blood levels as high as 300 mg/100 ml, some alcoholics may appear only mildly intoxicated, even though their coordination and judgment are, in fact, significantly impaired. According to the Council of Scientific Affairs of the American Medical Association, blood alcohol concentrations of 60 mg/100 ml double the odds of the drinker causing an automobile accident. Blood alcohol concentrations of 100 mg/100 ml multiply the chances of causing an accident by sixfold. And blood alcohol concentrations of 150 mg/ml increase these chances 25-fold. The legal limits of blood alcohol concentration for automobile drivers is 0.1 (i.e., 100 mg/100 ml) throughout most of the United States. It is slightly lower in most of western Europe and much lower in the Scandinavian and eastern European countries.

CHEMICAL CONSIDERATIONS

Therapeutic situations require a careful understanding of the amount of alcohol consumed by the patient.

Alcoholic drinks contain between 3 to 50 percent alcohol, and the typical "drink" has approximately 15 grams of ethanol. For example, the alcohol content of beer, wine, "fortified" wines (port, sherry), and whiskey are 3 to 5 percent, 10 to 12 percent, 18 to 20 percent, and 40 to 50 percent, respectively. The "proof" of alcohol is twice the percent by volume (i.e., 45 percent = 90 proof, etc.). Alcohol, U.S.P., is 95 percent ethanol. Absolute alcohol is 100 percent alcohol, but, because it takes up water rapidly when exposed to air, it quickly dilutes to 95 percent alcohol. The rule of thumb is that each drink contains about 15 grams of alcohol. Consuming 100 grams of alcohol per day for men (six or seven drinks) and 80 grams of alcohol per day for women (four or five drinks) is considered to be dangerous to long-term health.

So-called rubbing alcohol is 70 percent denatured ethanol, a percentage that kills bacteria better than higher concentrations. Denatured alcohol is the form of ethanol used in many household and industrial products. It contains small amounts of agents intended to discourage its consumption (e.g., pyridine, castor oil, acetone, sucrose octaacetate, amyl alcohol, gasoline, and benzene).

ABSORPTION, DISTRIBUTION, AND ELIMINATION

Absorption of alcohol is based on gastric emptying into the small intestine, because the absorption is much faster and more extensive from the small intestine than from the stomach.

When alcohol is consumed on an empty stomach, the increase in blood alcohol concentration is more rapid and the peak is higher. The alcohol is also absorbed faster from carbonated beverages, and the resulting blood concentration is greater than from noncarbonated ones. These facts explain the common wisdom that drinking on an empty stomach or drinking champagne gets you drunk faster.

In general, the average rate at which alcohol is metabolized, or eliminated from the bloodstream, is about 15 mg/100 ml per hour. Therefore, it takes about 1.5 hours to metabolize the alcohol in 1 ounce of 100-proof whiskey or in 12 ounces of beer.

Alcohol is mainly metabolized in the liver. Recent studies have demonstrated that alcohol has greater "oral bioavailability" in women than in men. This means that a greater proportion of the alcohol that is consumed reaches the bloodstream in women (about 90 percent) than in men (about 75 percent). This fact, combined with women's lower body weights and lower levels of body water, means that women receive more alcohol in their bloodstream for every drink they consume. This fact is compounded by the greater sensitivity of women to tissue damage by alcohol.

DRUG INTERACTIONS

For several decades, Antabuse (disulfiram) has been administered to block the use of alcohol. When patients taking Antabuse do not consume alcohol, they have no symptomatic effects. However, when patients taking Antabuse do drink alcohol, intense flushing of the face and neck, rapid heartbeat, low blood pressure, nausea, and vomiting ensue. Drinking while taking Antabuse can even cause death. Antabuse use in treating alcoholics must be combined with psychological counseling and social support. Calcium carbamide, a medicine available in Canada and other countries, but not in the United States, has a similar action to Antabuse but is thought to be less toxic.

There are a wide range of drug interactions between alcohol and prescribed medications, which can result in either increasing or decreasing the effects of these medicines or of the alcohol itself. Alcohol can change the rate at which certain medicines are absorbed; for example, it increases the absorption of Valium. When alcohol is taken in combination with such medicines, the medicine's effects may be increased or the effects of the alcohol may be prolonged. Two common mechanisms govern the interaction of alcohol with medicines: Because of the additive central nervous system (CNS) depression alcohol produces, it either increases the medicine's effects, or because of a "cross-tolerance" of alcohol with other drugs that depress the nervous system, it reduces the effects of the medicine. Because of these interactions, it is vital that patients inform their doctors about their drinking, so the doctors can warn them about any routine dangers of the medications being prescribed.

MEDICAL COMPLICATIONS

The primary medical complications of chronic alcoholism result from the direct effects of alcohol and the toxic effects of its by-products. The secondary effects created by chronic alcohol consumption include poor nutrition, accidental injuries, and general neglect of health.

CONSEQUENCES OF ALCOHOL METABOLISM

The metabolites of alcohol, or the substances into which alcohol is transformed by the body, make gout worse. This effect of alcohol consumption is illustrated by King Henry VIII, whose bacchanalian excesses are legend and likely a contributor to his painful experiences with gout, a disturbance occurring predominantly in males, characterized by painful inflammation of the joints, especially of the feet and hands, which can become chronic and result in deformity.

Heavy drinking after a period of not eating can cause severe, even fatal, hypoglycemia, or low blood sugar.

Even a single alcoholic drink can cause the buildup of some fat in the liver. An enlarged liver, caused by chronic alcohol consumption and greater accumulation of fat in the organ, usually abetted by poor nutrition, often progresses to alcoholic hepatitis and finally cirrhosis of the liver, a potentially fatal disorder. Alcoholics should not take Tylenol (acetaminophen), because the by-products of alcohol convert it to a compound that is toxic to the liver. Alcoholic cirrhosis of the liver is the second most common cause of death in the 24- to 44-year age group in large urban areas and the third most common cause of death in the 45- to 64-year group. Recently alcoholic cirrhosis has been complicated by viral infections contracted through exposure to the blood of people who have injected drugs from infected syringes or through sexual contact. These viral infections can create a more deadly form of hepatitis known as hepatitis C.

Methanol and isopropyl alcohol, compounds related to ethanol, are much more toxic than ethanol and can cause retinal damage and permanent blindness. Death can be caused by drinking as little as an ounce (60 ml) of methanol and blindness by drinking as little as 4 ml. Emergency room doctors should be aware of these metabolic dangers related to ingesting types of alcohol other than ethanol, as patients are often admitted to the hospital in coma, with little indication of the cause.

ENDOCRINE OR HORMONE EFFECTS

By acting on various hormones, ethanol causes diuresis, an increased urine flow. Alcohol inhibits the production of oxytocin, a hormone with many effects, including helping the bonding of a mother and child when it is released during breast-feeding.

Alcohol also increases the release of hormones that control the body's response to stress. In addition, it decreases the production of testosterone, the male hormone, and increases the speed at which it is metabolized (removed from the body). Alcoholic men often have shrunken gonads and feminization of their bodies. An important result of these effects is a diminished sexual drive, recognized in the famous quote from Shakespeare that alcohol increases the inclination to have sex but reduces the ability to perform sexually.

Gastrointestinal Effects

Alcohol stimulates the secretion of gastric and pancreatic juices, which, combined with the direct irritation to the stomach alcohol causes, explains why one in three heavy drinkers suffers from chronic gastritis. In the worst situation, alcoholics can develop bleeding ulcers. In the past, surgeons often removed the stomach to prevent deadly hemorrhaging. Nowadays there are many medications that reduce stomach acidity and prevent this dangerous outcome. Alcohol abuse also causes both acute and chronic pancreatitis and esophagitis. Heavy drinkers have an increased incidence of cancer of the pharynx, larynx, and esophagus. Emergency room physicians not uncommonly encounter alcoholic patients who are bleeding from both ends of the gastrointestinal tract because of chronic alcoholism. This can be a life-threatening emergency.

Malnutrition

Malnutrition is common among alcoholic patients, resulting in weight loss or obesity, an impaired immune system, and vitamin deficiencies. When their immune system is compromised, alcoholics become vulnerable to contracting infections of all sorts. Abnormally low vitamin levels can cause the failure of many bodily systems, especially the central nervous system and blood clotting.

Effects on Central Nervous System

Studies of alcoholic brain damage have revealed that brain dysfunction, or impairment of the various executive functions, is one of the earliest effects of regular alcohol abuse. For example, in a study of alcoholic men under 35 years old who had consumed large amounts of alcohol during the year prior to the study and in whom non–alcohol-related brain damage was not present, 60 percent were impaired and 50 percent showed shrinking brain mass (cerebral atrophy) on CT (computed tomography) scan. However, only 20 percent of these men had developed liver damage by this time. What these studies do not tell us is whether the functional deficits in alcoholics precede alcohol abuse and contribute to why they abuse alcohol, or whether these deficits are a consequence of alcohol consumption. Some cognitive deficits observed in alcoholics recover with abstinence from alcohol, whereas others do not.

Alcohol neurotoxicity, the poisoning of the nervous system, and lifestyle effects, including malnutrition, head trauma, liver disease, and the abuse of other drugs, combine to cause the brain damage seen in alcoholics. The most common manifestations of this brain damage are shrinkage of the cerebellum and reduced brain weight and volume.

Severe brain damage in alcoholics takes two different forms: alcoholic amnesia and alcoholic dementia. Of those alcoholics who suffer from acute ataxia (loss of the ability to coordinate muscular movement), confusion, and abnormalities of eye movement (so-called Wernicke's encephalopathy caused by deficiency of the B vitamin thiamine, associated with alcohol consumption), 80 percent to 90 percent develop Korsakoff's psychosis, a mental disorder characterized by subtle behavioral abnormalities and a significant impairment of memory. After a year of abstinence from alcohol, along with good nutrition, about 20 percent of patients with this memory problem and more subtle confusions completely recover and 20 percent recover partially. However, 60 percent have long-lasting brain damage, lose the ability to live independently, and must be institutionalized.

Treating brain damage caused by alcohol dependence requires alcoholics to abstain from alcohol and improve their nutrition. It is not known whether any medications can substantially augment the improvement that comes from abstinence and a good diet. This is a topic of continuing research.

FETAL ALCOHOL EFFECTS

Exposure of a developing fetus to alcohol during pregnancy has many serious consequences. The most severe cases involve malformations of the newborn child, retarded mental development or decreased IQ, fetal alcohol syndrome, and an increased likelihood of dying during or shortly after delivery.

The consequences of a woman drinking during pregnancy vary with the stage of pregnancy during which the drinking occurs. Exposure to alcohol during the first trimester can result in major abnormalities in the fetus. Exposure during the second trimester increases the risk of spontaneous abortion. And exposure to alcohol during the third trimester decreases the size and weight of the newborn.

The worst effects of alcohol on pregnancy are called fetal alcohol syndrome. Fetal alcohol syndrome is marked by a reduction in weight, height, and size of the head, structural abnormalities in the body, especially a distortion of facial features, and CNS damage, especially mental retardation. Manifestations of this CNS damage include a smaller-than-normal brain, irritability in infancy, weakened muscle tone, poor coordination, hyperactivity in childhood, and mental retardation.

Unfortunately, most women who drink regularly may be one or more months pregnant before they realize that they are pregnant, and the severe structural abnormalities caused by fetal alcohol exposure occur during the first trimester. Most physicians advise that women refrain from any alcohol use while pregnant. Even lower levels of alcohol exposure, insufficient to cause fetal alcohol syndrome, can cause behavioral problems in the developing child. These behavioral problems include hyperactivity and the tendency to begin drinking alcohol during adolescence.

Most women who have drug abuse problems also smoke cigarettes and use alcohol in addition to other drugs, and it is uncertain which substances are contributing the greatest toxicity. However, prenatal exposure to alcohol and reduction in oxygenation of the fetal brain due to maternal cigarette smoking probably have more serious effects than some of the other drugs discussed in this book.

LIVER DISEASE

The abnormal conditions caused by chronic alcohol dependence that injure the liver are fatty liver, alcoholic hepatitis, and alcoholic cirrhosis. Alcoholic fatty liver is completely reversible with abstinence and proper nutrition. Alcohol dependence is a major cause of cirrhosis of the liver in the United States and other developed nations. People who have been abusing alcohol for 10 years or more have a high probability of developing this disease.

Alcoholic hepatitis kills 20 percent of its victims and results in a chronic disease in about 40 percent. The remaining 40 percent of people afflicted with alcoholic hepatitis recover, displaying no residual symptoms of the condition. No one knows why some people with alcoholic hepatitis develop cirrhosis while the liver recovers entirely in others. Factors such as the amount and duration of drinking, the genetics of the drinker, the health of the immune system, and the quality of the diet probably all play a part in explaining why some people get better and others do not. However, the ability of patients to stop drinking is the major factor that determines the prognosis for alcoholic hepatitis patients. Some 80 percent of those who stop drinking recover or improve from alcoholic hepatitis and 20 percent develop cirrhosis. Of those who continue drinking, 30 percent to 50 percent continue to suffer from alcoholic hepatitis and 50 percent to 80 percent develop cirrhosis. The chances of surviving over five years following a diagnosis of alcoholic cirrhosis is nearly 65 percent in those patients who have stopped drinking, but it is only 40 percent in those who continue to drink. The rate of recovery from alcoholism-associated liver diseases is lower if an alcoholic has viral hepatitis, especially hepatitis C.

Having cirrhosis affects the choice of medicines that should be prescribed for other illnesses in alcoholics, because cirrhosis changes the way medicines are metabolized by the liver. In this circumstance, doctors either choose medicines that are not metabolized by the liver or lower the dose of liver-metabolized drugs.

CARDIOVASCULAR DISEASE

Heavy alcohol consumption worsens the prognosis for patients with cardiovascular and coronary heart disease. In contrast, light to moderate alcohol use may actually offer some protection against coronary heart disease. There is some evidence that this beneficial effect is particularly marked for those who drink red wine, which is rich in antioxidants.

OTHER ISSUES RELATED TO TREATING ALCOHOLISM

The initial treatment of an alcoholic requires diagnosis and, if necessary, treatment for the symptoms of alcohol withdrawal. The main treatment objectives at this stage include the relief of discomfort and the prevention or treatment of complications, such as seizures, irregular heartbeat, and delirium. A careful evaluation must be performed, with special attention to the severity and progression of the alcohol withdrawal syndrome and the presence of complications, including trauma, malnutrition, impaired CNS function, infections, gastritis, pancreatitis, and liver, heart, and lung disease. The doctor should also ask alcoholics if they have ever had seizures or delirium and if they use other addictive drugs.

It is estimated that only about 1 percent of recovering alcoholics can return to stable, moderate drinking habits. Because the ability to drink moderately is a rare outcome, the goal of long-term treatment for all alcoholics should be total abstinence rather than controlled drinking. Physicians should emphasize this point because self-knowledge is not a strong point of alcoholics, and many problematic drinkers see themselves as only "social drinkers."

Traditionally, psychotherapy and social support groups like Alcoholics Anonymous (AA) were the cornerstones of treatment for alcoholism. As we have stated, however, medicines now offer exciting new hope. The most common medicines employed in the past to reduce alcohol use were so-called aversive drugs, including alcohol-sensitizing drugs, such as Antabuse (disulfiram) and calcium carbamide, and emetics, such as apomorphine and emetine. The value of disulfiram in treatment has been called into question. Abstinence rates, time to first drink, employment, and social stability are not significantly improved among patients who are treated with this drug. However, drinking by nonabstinent people was reduced among those treated with disulfiram, suggesting some benefit. Because there are significant risks to taking disulfiram, its utility, despite some small benefits, must be considered marginal. Recently there has been a resurgence of interest in disulfiram for the treatment of cocaine dependence.

Better understanding of the neurological and biological mechanisms that control alcohol use may lead to developing medicines that can safely reduce the urge to drink.

Medicines that have been used in the past in the treatment of primary alcoholism include antidepressants, lithium (used to treat bipolar disorder), drugs that affect the dopamine neurotransmitter, vitamins, LSD, beta-blockers, carbamazepine, and hydroxyzine. More recent additions include naltrexone, topiramate, and acamprosate, each of which has clinically demonstrable benefits. Something that is not known yet is which of these three drugs produces the best outcome in an individual patient.

Drugs that have been used in the treatment of secondary alcoholism—that is, alcoholism that has been caused by the attempt to self-medicate a psychiatric disorder—must address the underlying mental problems. These drugs include minor tranquilizers, antidepressants, lithium, and neuroleptics (tranquilizing drugs).

Medicines used to treat alcoholism should reduce alcohol use without themselves having a potential for being abused. Furthermore, such medicines should have no harmful interactions with alcohol, should be taken orally, and should be long-acting and well tolerated, in order to encourage patients to continue taking them as prescribed.

An extended release formulation of naltrexone, which must be administered by intramuscular injection once a month, has recently been approved by the Food and Drug Administration. Its benefits are quite promising. One advantage of this formulation is that, because it is administered by a physician or nurse, there can be no question about compliance with the prescribed regimen for its use, which is a serious problem in the case of most medicines used in treating addictive disorders.

Finally, the medicines used in treating addictions should have little risk of an overdose and no serious drug-related toxicity, especially to organs that may have been already been damaged by alcohol abuse, such as the liver or brain.

ALCOHOLISM AS A PARADIGM FOR
UNDERSTANDING DRUG ADDICTION

Alcoholism is the best studied of all drug use disorders and can serve as a general paradigm for understanding the abuse of other drugs. (See chapters about each drug.) The next sections discuss elements of this paradigm, which are highly interrelated and can influence each other.

INHERITANCE OF ALCOHOL DEPENDENCE

Alcohol abuse in a family member disrupts family life and affects development of children within the family. It is not surprising that children of alcoholics have a greater chance of developing alcoholism or other mental disorders than do children from nonalcoholic families.

Studies of twins and adopted children have enabled scientists to separate the genetic and environmental factors in the development of alcoholism. When one identical twin has a severe alcohol problem—that is, when one twin is addicted to alcohol—the chances are 70 percent that the other twin will be similarly afflicted. Among nonidentical twins, the chances are only 33 percent. In contrast, identical and nonidentical twins each have an 80 percent likelihood of developing a less severe alcohol problem, so-called alcohol abuse, which falls short of alcohol addiction, when the other twin is so afflicted. Adoptee studies show that adopted men with alcoholic biological parents have an increased likelihood of developing alcoholism, whether they are raised in an alcoholic environment or not. When the biological parents are severely alcoholic, the odds are good that the children, even if brought up by nonalcoholics, will develop the disease of alcoholism. The conclusion is that genetic factors play an important part in determining who will become an alcoholic and that the influence of environmental factors varies with the severity of the parents' alcoholism.

HETEROGENEITY OF ALCOHOLISM

Large differences exist among the members of any group of alcoholic patients. The challenge has been to identify characteristics of these patients that would allow researchers to divide them into more homogenous subgroups, which are useful predictors of the causes of the disease, its prognosis, and its response to various treatments. One classification system is based mainly on the age when alcoholism began: Type 1 (after age 25) and Type 2 (before age 25). Alcohol-related problems and personality traits are different in the members of these two groups. In general, Type 2 patients tend to be more resistant to treatment, and environment plays a less important part in the development of their alcoholism.

WOMEN AND ADDICTION

Men and women follow different courses when they become alcoholics. It is particularly important to understand alcoholism in women, because of the damaging effects of drinking on the developing fetus and the ways alcoholism disrupts the relationship between mother and child. Both factors can perpetuate the transmission of alcoholism from one generation to the next. Women have lower rates of alcoholism than men, and genetic factors contribute less to their chances of becoming alcoholics. Although, on average, women start drinking later than males, they tend to develop more serious complications relating to alcohol abuse at about the same age as men.

GENETIC FACTORS IN DEVELOPMENT OF ALCOHOLISM

An exciting area of research has been to determine how genetic factors play out to cause addiction. As yet no viable explanations have clinical applicability. Promising examples include differences in subjective intoxication, ethanol metabolism, and electroencephalogram (EEG) evoked potentials between children who have a biological parent with alcoholism and those who do not.

INHERITANCE OF DRUG ADDICTION

It is not yet known if genetic factors that influence the development of alcohol dependence are the same as or different from those that influence the development of other drug addictions. This question is difficult to study, because younger people tend to mix alcohol with other psychoactive drugs. However, it is clear that interactions of genetic and environmental factors are important in the development of drug addictions, just as they are in alcoholism. Furthermore, because the inheritance of addictions to drugs and alcohol is multifactorial, it is likely that some of the same factors (perhaps those that determine temperament and brain functioning) contribute to all addictions. In contrast are the drug-specific factors, such as those that are unique to the metabolism of any given drug or those that create specific actions of the drug on the brain.

CHAPTER 10

Heroin and Other Morphine-Related Drugs

INTOXICATION

THE PRIMARY WAY in which psychoactive drugs affect our feelings is by changing the amounts of neurotransmitters that mediate the flow of information between cells in specific regions of the brain. Neurotransmitters transmit signals that alter the inner workings of the brain cells, carrying precise instructions from one brain cell to another via receptors. There are three main types of opiate receptors, only one of which is primarily involved in addiction. Heroin, morphine, and other opiates, such as meperidine (Demerol), activate these receptors and, as a result, cause many changes in the way the brain functions. These brain effects are the reason people get high when they take heroin, become dependent on and crave more heroin, and experience withdrawal when they stop using it.

The characteristic pharmacologic action of opioids is analgesia (the relief of pain). Opioids are energizing at low dosages and sedating at higher dosages. Depending on the dose used, heroin and other opioids can have these effects on users' mental states:

- A "rush," or sudden intoxication, experienced shortly after taking the drug

- A "nod," or feelings of apathy, sedation, and dreaming, experienced immediately with high doses or after a period of drowsiness with lower doses
- Euphoria (feelings of well-being) or dysphoria (feelings of discomfort)
- Impaired judgment, attention, and/or memory

Heroin and other opioids have these physical effects on users:

- Feelings of warmth, facial flushing, or itching
- Analgesia (If the user was feeling pain, the pain is reduced or eliminated.)
- Constipation
- Constricted ("pinpoint") pupils of the eye
- Shallow breathing, lowered blood pressure, increased heartbeat, and, as the dose reaches toxic levels, cyanosis ("turning blue" due to lack of oxygen in the bloodstream); coma and death by overdose can occur at this stage

These effects are particularly powerful and short-lived when heroin is administered in an intravenous injection directly into the bloodstream. In fact, the "rush" associated with intravenous use can cause lower abdominal sensations that have been described as resembling an orgasm. The effects are less intense and more drawn out when addicts snort heroin or take long-acting opioid pills or liquid opioid formulations. Because the stomach destroys much of any opioid that is ingested by mouth, oral administration is not particularly effective. For this reason, when a patient is experiencing severe pain—for example, after a trauma or a heart attack—the physician will administer morphine intravenously to control pain.

Most doctors avoid prescribing the most powerful opioids to patients suffering from long-term, or chronic, pain because of the risks of narcotic addiction and also because of the inconvenience and hazards of repeated intravenous injections. Recently, formulations of long-acting morphine that can be given by mouth have been developed for controlling chronic pain. The unintended consequence these drugs has been a significant increase in opioid dependence in the middle class, among people who would never have snorted or injected the illegal drug. These new opioid formulations have thus created a new class of narcotic addicts. This is a striking example of the way that therapeutic advances have the potential for both benefit and harm, and it seems to be a characteristic of human beings that they seek out both the beneficial and harmful aspects. Moreover, some people, because of their physical and psychological makeup, are particularly prone to seeking out the harmful aspects. Thus, a person who could not imagine himself lying in a filthy room injecting himself with heroin may find opioids attractive—even irresistible—when they are offered in a more palatable pharmaceutical formulation. The appearance of this new group of middle-class narcotics addicts has prompted Congress to support the newer forms of office-based therapy for opiate dependence that are discussed in this chapter.

THE CASE OF BOB R.

Bob R. grew up in an upper-middle-class family in the suburbs of Chicago. During his grade school years, he was well behaved, slightly introverted, and an above-average student. In his junior year in high school, Hugh, his best friend, a talented lead guitarist in a five-member rock-and-roll band, badgered him into trying marijuana. Although Bob didn't recognize it at the time, this apparently small step was the start on a journey that would take him far from the world he knew, through a place filled with pleasure and pain, and, finally, leave him alone, despairing, and near death.

After smoking marijuana a few times and experiencing no effects but a cough and a dry mouth, Bob began to like the way the drug made him feel. He had always enjoyed rock music and attending Hugh's jam sessions, but after smoking a joint, the music seemed to come alive with excitement. Most of the students in his high school did not use illegal drugs. The clandestine rolling and passing of joints with the band members deepened Bob's camaraderie with them. They became, and fancied becoming, outlaws of a sort, banding together in secret to enjoy a forbidden pleasure. Two members of the group began using other drugs, white, powdered cocaine and stimulant tablets, and depressants, such as barbiturates, that came in capsules or tablets. However, cocaine cost too much. And barbiturates seemed to impair their musical performance. So the young men stopped buying cocaine and barbiturates, but they increased their use of marijuana and amphetamines, both of which, especially when taken together, seemed to give their music a boost.

Bob stuck to marijuana. His school had provided cautionary lectures about the dangers of drug use. Despite his affectation of disdain for "official" warnings, they did scare him and keep him from using other illegal substances. The stern words of his father had even more effect; his father often emphasized the disaster that would overtake Bob, were he stupid enough to fool around with these dangerous substances.

At the age of 18, Bob entered Columbia College in New York City. He found the college and the city environment replete with novelties and challenges, both academically and socially, and he met both with energy and excitement. One of the first things he determined to do, however, was to find someone who could sell him marijuana. This turned out to be as easy as asking a couple of fellows living on his floor in the dormitory.

Always shy in the company of girls, Bob nevertheless made an effort to date, and during the second semester of his freshman year, he found Maryellen, a Barnard freshman. They saw each other for two months. However, Maryellen met and became smitten with a Columbia junior, and she and Bob parted company. After losing Maryellen, Bob became lonely and depressed. Never confident in affairs of the heart, his self-esteem hit a new low. He began smoking marijuana every day, passing his days in a cloud of pot smoke. Every morning he would get out of bed and roll and smoke a joint. Whenever he found the opportunity, he would continue smoking throughout the day, until he dropped off to sleep. Dark rings began to form under his eyes; his skin became pasty and pale. His new friends at college, a ready-made circle of acquaintances who all smoked pot (and many of whom used other drugs as well), established a new standard of conduct: Nearly constant indulgence in intoxicating drugs was the rule and, indeed, the central unifying fact of their association. As they gathered in their dorm rooms in the afternoons and evenings, whether they were listening to music, playing poker, or just talking, they would invariably get high. These students attended fewer and fewer classes and did less and less of their assigned academic work.

Chris was the star rock-and-roll guitarist on campus, who was known and looked up to by nearly half the students. Bob and Chris, who had met while passing a joint around a circle of friends after one of Chris's campus concerts, hit it off immediately. Bob bought a guitar, and Chris began teaching him to play. They would meet for a lesson almost every night in Chris's off-campus apartment, where they would listen to music and smoke pot. Chris, the son of a diplomat from Washington, D.C., was a heroin addict. He had been turned on to heroin by Suzanne, his girlfriend, the daughter of a heart surgeon from the posh Westchester suburbs of New York. Suzanne was a brilliant, unstable Barnard freshman who had had the money to begin indulging in the drug while still in high school. Chris loved heroin from the first and now injected it once or, more often, twice a day. Bob was somewhat shocked when he discovered that Chris used heroin. But because he regarded Chris as the "coolest" guy he knew—funny, savvy, popular, and endowed with genuine musical talent—Bob tried hard to suspend his judgment. Chris, who genuinely liked Bob, was in no hurry to get him involved in heroin. Despite his use of the heroin—or perhaps because of his experience—he recognized the dangers it posed. Nevertheless, late one winter night in Chris's apartment, Bob and Chris decided that Bob should sniff a couple of match heads of the white powder.

Bob became a heroin addict. This didn't happen overnight. For months he used the drug only rarely. Then one day Chris bought an ounce, a large score, of especially pure heroin, which he began dealing to help pay for his own habit. Bob had access to this heroin at a bargain price, and he began sniffing it every day. In less than two weeks, he woke up one morning and felt a little queasy. When he looked in the bathroom mirror, he saw his pupils were black saucers. He was, he knew, for the first time experiencing the symptoms of heroin withdrawal. He felt a stab of fear, but then quickly calmed down. It was, he thought, no big deal. He had a choice: He could let the withdrawal run its course; in a few days he would again become metabolically free from the drug. Or he could take some more heroin, feel better, get high, and put off the time when he would break the chain of using. Wavering between these alternatives, he decided to take some more heroin. Minutes after sniffing it, he felt good and confident that he had made the right choice. Although he felt a pang of remorse when he remembered his father's harsh admonitions, the drug made him relaxed and warm and optimistic, with energy to spare. Shrugging off his guilt, he decided to celebrate by cutting class and practicing his guitar.

Bob finally went through heroin withdrawal when the spring semester ended, and he was forced to return home for the summer. He brought a little heroin with him, to help him taper off his regular use of the drug, and some minor tranquilizers to help him sleep despite the discomfort he knew he would feel. To his parents' consternation, for his first two weeks at home, he spent most of his time in his room. They did not understand why he had become so sickly and attributed his withdrawal from them as readjustment from his independent existence as a "college man." They tolerantly waited while he began to be more sociable. His withdrawal was an unpleasant experience, but, in the comfort and security of his home, and without any way to acquire more heroin, Bob endured the aches and pains, the sweating, the physical and mental craving, and soon he thought he was back to his old self again. However, when he returned to Columbia in the fall, the first thing he did was seek out Chris—ostensibly to get together with a friend, but, in fact, his uppermost purpose was to buy heroin and get high. He had been anticipating doing this for weeks. He sniffed his first hits of heroin with a feeling of expectation and confidence: He had proven that he could beat the drug. As long as he didn't go crazy and greatly increase his dose, he told himself, he could enjoy himself with little fear.

The details don't concern us here, but as his sophomore year went by, Bob became a daily heroin user. He still imagined that he could stop using, but he was no longer either inclined to or capable of doing without the drug. Because it is illegal, heroin is expensive. Even as Chris's preferred customer, Bob needed every dollar he could get to feed his habit. He turned all his money from home, intended for food, books, clothes, and recreation, into white powder. Along the way, he stopped sniffing heroin and, like Chris, began injecting the drug in his veins. This method of administration not only provided more efficient delivery of the drug to his system but also supplied a "rush," the feeling of the acute, sudden onset of intoxication, an experience Bob began to desire repeating with a growing intensity. Although he continued to live in the dorm, he basically stopped attending classes, becoming, in effect, a dropout in residence. After a few months of this marginal existence, he became afraid that he was losing control of his life. He repeatedly resolved to taper off heroin and stay clean, at least for a while. However, despite promises to himself and his self-imposed deadlines, his heroin use slowly but steadily increased. When he received his next tuition check from home, he "borrowed" the money to make a heroin deal with Chris, planning to recover the money by selling some of the drug at a profit. But the deal went bad, and he lost most of his money. He was now out of school, strung out on narcotics, and afraid to confess his problems and seek help from his family.

DRUG-SEEKING BEHAVIOR: SOUGHT-AFTER EFFECTS

The actions of heroin and other opiates on the nucleus accumbens, the ventral tegmentum, the hippocampus, and hypothalamus of the brain are responsible for the fact that people using these drugs feel "rewarded" and therefore want to take the drugs over and over again.

Opiates, like other addictive drugs, increase the release of the neurotransmitter dopamine in the nucleus accumbens, demonstrating the overlap in the ways opiates and other addictive drugs "reward" the user and reinforce repeated use of the drugs. However, the addictive power of opiates depends on their effects on other neurotransmitters, independent of their effects on the dopamine system.

Opioids are produced naturally by the brain. These so-called endogenous opioids play a part in maintaining normal moods and normal drives, such as for food and sex. Part of the reason why some people are vulnerable to becoming addicted to heroin and other opiates may be related to how their brains utilize these naturally occurring opioids.

NEUROADAPTATION

Heroin and other opiates increase the activity of cells in the reward circuits of the brain that have what are called mu-opioid receptors on their surface. These mu-opioid receptors are considered to be the primary sites responsible for the acquisition, maintenance, and relapse of opiate addiction.

TOLERANCE

Tolerance, or decreased response to the effects of a drug as a result of repeated use, develops to some specific effects of heroin and other opiates, such their ability to alleviate pain and to their general depressant properties. However, responses to the stimulating effects of heroin actually increase when the drug is used regularly. As a result, when people abuse heroin, its unpleasant side effects quickly decline while its pleasant, or reinforcing, effects increase. This same pattern of adaptation—tolerance to their depressing effects on the central nervous system and increased response to their stimulating effects—occurs with some of the other drugs of abuse discussed in this book.

DEPENDENCE

People who use other addictive drugs in addition to heroin have a powerful pharmacological incentive for continuing their heroin addiction. This phenomenon teaches us that an enduring *learned response* forms the underpinnings of addiction to all addictive drugs. Because of the overlapping causes of all drug addictions, psychiatrists advise that, in order to recover from heroin addiction, addicts must not only stop using heroin but must stop using other addictive drugs and become completely abstinent. The notion that "I'll stop heroin but keep drinking or smoking marijuana" just does not work. For this reason, buprenorphine, a medicine that has mixed (activating and blocking) actions at the mu-opioid receptor, is probably more effective in treating moderately dependent opioid addicts (who are using moderate amounts of opiates) than methadone, a specific substitute for heroin that activates the mu-opioid receptor. Buprenorphine may not be suitable for use with the most severely addicted opioid addicts (who are using large amounts of opiates); methadone treatment may be more successful with this group. Nevertheless, it should be stressed to these patients that they need to stop all other drugs of abuse. CNS depressants are particularly dangerous and can cause death by overdose.

Withdrawal

When addicts stop chronic use of heroin or other opiates, they experience withdrawal effects. The unpleasant symptoms of withdrawal include:

- Joint and muscle aches and general hypersensitivity to pain of all types
- Diarrhea and gastrointestinal cramping, nausea, and vomiting
- Depression, anxiety, and generally not feeling well (like having the worst flu ever)
- Craving for heroin or other opioids that they had been using
- "Goose flesh" and chills
- Teary eyes and a running nose
- Dilation of the pupils and consequent sensitivity to light
- Insomnia
- Rapid heartbeat and high blood pressure
- Yawning

Withdrawal results in no predictable release of the neurotransmitter dopamine that occurs with repeated drug use, which is essential to feelings of well-being. Interestingly, the degree of physical dependence does not predict the intensity of addicts' craving for the drug during withdrawal. After recovering from physical dependence, former addicts are vulnerable to returning to heroin use and to becoming readdicted. This continued vulnerability is the reason long-term recovery is so difficult to achieve. Recovering heroin addicts remain highly prone to relapsing when they encounter trigger events, or situations in which they previously used heroin, and also whenever they are disappointed about anything in life. Self-help groups encourage their members to avoid situations in which they might experience hunger, anger, loneliness, or tiredness (designated by the acronym HALT), because these unpleasant experiences can prompt recovering addicts to use drugs again and to relapse into addiction. As we have noted, the feelings surrounding withdrawal are independent of the intensity of its physical symptoms. During abstinence, less dopamine is released into the brain than when addicts were using the drug and less dopamine than is released in non-addicted people. Because using heroin or other opiates reverses the effects of withdrawal and again counteracts the unpleasant mood effects produced by the decreased amount of dopamine into the brain reward centers during abstinence, addicts may perceive the effects of the drugs as "beneficial." This mechanism of encouraging the continued use of heroin to counteract the aversive effects of withdrawal is called "negative reinforcement."

CHAPTER 11

CNS Depressants: Barbiturates, Benzodiazepines, and Other Hypnotics and Tranquilizers

BARBITURATES ARE MEMBERS of a class of drugs called "hypnotics," or "hypnosedatives." Hypnotics make people sleepy, and, consequently, one of their primary medical uses is to induce sleep. They are also calming to some people, and, prior to the advent of modern tranquilizers, doctors used hypnotics to soothe people in emotional crisis. The alert reader will see how very much these agents resemble alcohol, although they are in pill form.

Barbiturates, in the form of barbital, or barbituric acid, were first used clinically in 1903, and a case study of barbital abuse was published within a year. Approximately 50 barbituric acid derivatives were eventually marketed for therapeutic use. Common barbiturates include phenobarbital, Seconal, Tuinal, and Nembutal. Except for phenobarbital, which is used to help control epileptic seizures, barbiturates are rarely prescribed nowadays. Because of the demand for barbiturates as psychoactive drugs of abuse, they are sometimes still manufactured in underground or bootleg laboratories.

In the mid-1950s, a number of nonbarbiturate hypnosedatives, including ethinamate (Valmid), glutethimide (Doriden), meprobamate (Miltown), methaqualone (Quaalude), methyprylon (Noludar), and ethchlorvynol (Placidyl), became available. As with barbiturates, reports of the abuse of these drugs followed shortly thereafter. The 1960s and 1970s witnessed the introduction and unprecedented clinical popularity of the benzodiazepines, followed by a myriad of publications documenting their abuse.

The adverse side effects of barbiturates and other hypnotics, including hangovers and addiction, have caused them to fall out of favor in recent decades. Today physicians generally prefer to prescribe benzodiazepines, such as Ativan and Valium, or "nonbenzodiazepine" anxiolytic/hypnotics like Ambien (zolpidem), which are minor tranquilizers, as sleep aids or to calm anxiety, because they are less toxic and have fewer side effects than barbiturates.

Central nervous system (CNS) depressants are often prescribed to patients for management of anxiety, insomnia, or chronic pain. With continued use, tolerance develops and larger doses are needed in order to achieve symptomatic relief. If physicians do not educate patients and carefully monitor prescriptions, patients may eventually receive large doses of these medications, with attendant side effects, including mood disorders, cognitive dysfunction, social difficulties, impaired work performance, and traumatic injury due to falls or vehicular accidents. In order to maintain symptomatic relief in the face of tighter controls by the prescribing physician, patients may combine alcohol or other prescribed medications or illicit drugs (e.g., marijuana, opiates) with the prescribed dose of CNS depressant, "doctor shop" for other physicians to provide additional prescriptions, or even engage in illegal activities, such as forging prescriptions. Cessation of CNS depressants leads to undesirable and even potentially harmful withdrawal symptoms, and addicts continue their drug-seeking behavior and drug use in order to avoid the onset of these effects. Occasionally patients who are forced to discontinue use of CNS depressants because of illness or other unforeseen circumstances, such as hospitalization for a motor vehicle accident, suffer fulminant (sudden and severe) withdrawal, characterized by profuse diaphoresis (sweating), tremors, anxiety, and seizures, if their physician is not aware of the drug dependence.

Each new wave of CNS depressants, synthesized and developed for use by the pharmaceutical industry (barbiturates, nonbarbiturate hypnosedatives, benzodiazepines, and nonbenzodiazepine hypnosedatives), was initially marketed with claims of pharmacologic novelty—particularly, a lack of the dependence liability and hence minimal risk of abuse. However, as these medications become more widely available, strikingly similar problems with abuse and dependence (which they share with alcoholic beverages) have emerged. Indeed, pharmaceutical marketing efforts often lead to significant problems as physicians begin prescribing this ever-expanding class of drugs, believing that they are safe for most, if not all, patients. As a consequence, many distressed patients who may not have had problems with drug abuse become dependent on CNS depressant drugs, such as Valium, Xanax, or Klonopin, even when they take these medications "exactly as prescribed." Moreover, some alcoholics convince themselves and their physicians that they could stop drinking alcohol, if only someone would prescribe them these *safe* CNS depressant drugs. Unfortunately, the eventual outcome is that they start using alcohol and the prescription drugs together. Because most physicians view these drugs as relatively benign, it is not unusual to find patients who have been taking them for years before the drug use is recognized as problematic. As they require increasingly higher doses, family members point out that they are "not themselves anymore"; or they may want to stop taking the drugs and find they cannot do so without experiencing the serious symptoms mentioned earlier. This situation typically occurs after users realize that their family's comments are valid, or after they change doctors and the new physician will not continue to prescribe these drugs for "no apparent reason." The emergence of withdrawal symptoms or even a spontaneous seizure in patients who stop the chronic use of CNS depressants often precipitates addiction treatment.

To date, no CNS depressant has been developed that is free of abuse liability and the potential for withdrawal upon drug discontinuation. Benzodiazepines are currently among the most widely prescribed drugs in the world, ranking in the top 50 most commonly prescribed drugs since the late 1960s. Furthermore, this drug class is the most commonly misused and abused type of prescription drug. Recently attempts to find drug treatments for anxiety and insomnia that have no dependence liability have led to the development and use of the nonbenzodiazepine anxiolytic/hypnotics zolpidem (Ambien), eszopiclone (Lunesta), and zaleplon (Sonata). Unfortunately, we can predict the eventual consequences of using these new agents indiscriminately to treat insomnia and anxiety, to take the edge off pain, and to foster restful sleep.

An important lesson should be gleaned from this rather unequivocal historical perspective: The treatment of anxiety, insomnia, or pain is a minefield for the unwary physician *and* patient. Without understanding the medical or psychiatric condition that is causing these symptoms, physicians cannot hope to address the root cause. Treatment of the primary disorder—that is, depression—which is often associated with sleep problems, anxiety, and chronic pain, is the only effective and safe way to treat these symptoms. (A useful analogy is the futility of treating the fever of severe pneumonia with only aspirin without treating the underlying infection with an antibiotic.) When a person takes a barbiturate or other CNS depressant but does not go to sleep, he experiences a form of intoxication: "barbiturate high" or its nonbarbiturate analog. The desire to experience this effect is the reason that barbiturates and nonbarbiturate CNS depressants have become drugs of abuse.

The barbiturate high is roughly similar to the high experienced from consuming alcohol. The short-acting barbiturates (Seconal, Tuinal, and Nembutal) produce the strongest high and therefore are most sought after by those seeking their intoxicating effects. Fifteen to 20 minutes after taking a barbiturate capsule or tablet, users begin to experience euphoria, relaxation, diminished judgment, and loss of motor coordination. Users may take hypnosedatives to "come out of their shell" at a party by becoming less shy and self-conscious, and even disinhibited. Because these effects begin to wear off after about an hour or two, drug users may take an additional dose to extend the period of intoxication. Eventually, after taking a course of barbiturates, even regular users will be overcome with sleepiness and fall into an exhausted sleep.

PATTERNS OF USE

The use of barbiturates or other hypnosedatives to achieve intoxication is a dangerous and often fatal pursuit. These drugs can cause a tolerance, which means that, if they are taken regularly, it is necessary to keep increasing the dose in order to achieve the desired effects. Too large a dose of barbiturates suppresses breathing and results in death. Unfortunately, the fatal dosage level of barbiturates does not increase as the tolerance to the drug's intoxicating effects increase. Therefore, as people increase their dose, they approach the point where the amount they require to get high actually exceeds the amount their body can tolerate.

In addition, because of the similarity of barbiturate effects to the effects of alcohol, many people who take barbiturates to get high also drink alcohol. *Mixing barbiturates with alcohol is one of the most hazardous activities in the entire world of drug abuse.* The combination of even relatively modest doses of barbiturates and alcohol is extremely toxic and frequently results in death.

Barbiturates are generally available in pill form. Often addicts mix the crushed pills or contents of the capsules with water and inject them into their veins. When barbiturates are mixed with water, they yield a messy paste that can, with some difficulty, be drawn into a syringe through a piece of cotton, which filters out the viscous components of the mixture. Intravenous injection of barbiturates creates a rush—a sudden onset of intoxication that is greatly prized by drug abusers. It also delivers the entire chemical contents of the drug directly into the bloodstream, bypassing the losses that occur when the drug is consumed orally and must pass through the stomach and be metabolized by the liver. Thus, a shot of barbiturates produces a much faster-acting and stronger intoxication. Unfortunately, injecting barbiturates is far more risky than taking them orally, as the chances of an accidental overdose are much higher. In addition, addicts often fail to inject the entire contents of the syringe into the vein, but spill some of the drug into the tissue surrounding the injection site. Because barbiturates are not very water soluble, they do not disperse readily from the injection site. Deposits of barbiturates create irritated lumps under the skin that can be painful and often become infected.

As the case study that follows illustrates, people who regularly use barbiturates or other hypnosedatives to get high find that the drugs interfere with their capacity to function. The cognitive and motor disturbances induced by barbiturates are so disruptive that they virtually preclude working and having normal social interactions. The effects of benzodiazepines may at first be less noticeable to others, but, at high enough doses, benzodiazepines cause the same symptoms of intoxication. The prognosis for those who chronically abuse barbiturates or other hypnosedatives is not good. Hypnosedative users, like chronic alcohol drinkers, lose the capacity to moderate their conduct, take normal safety precautions, control their tempers, and care for themselves. In addition, they are subject to passing out, or experiencing periods of retrograde amnesia (inability to remember the episode) without passing out, sometimes called a "blackout." The lives of barbiturate or other hypnosedative addicts is marked by periods of extreme intoxication and exhausted intervals of rest followed by intense hangovers, characterized by anxiety or even panic attacks. Constructive or goal-directed activity therefore becomes virtually impossible.

THE CASE OF MIKE R.

Mike R. came from a happy large family where he had learned to work hard and appreciate everything life had to give him. Since there was no money for college, when he graduated from high school, he married his high school sweetheart, and enlisted in the army. Stationed in Fort Dix, New Jersey, he completed basic training and began what he expected would be a quiet, secure life that offered a decent regular paycheck, the possibility of advancement, and training in skills that could later be used to win him a good job in civilian life. Mike's family was very proud of him—his wife, all his sisters, and mother would dote on him in his sharp military uniform. Mike's dad had been in the army in Korea, and there was a quiet and strong bond formed between them. When the war with Iraq erupted, Mike was appalled to find himself stationed in the Middle East, many United States soldiers dispatched to Iraq to end the threat of Saddam Hussein. This was the "other side" of the military, which neither he nor his family were really prepared for. Arriving in Kuwait, he was among the troops assigned to enter Iraq to search for and dismantle secret facilities created to support biological warfare. For months, he endured the physical hardships of the desert climate and the psychological strain of being far from home in an alien, hostile environment. He was homesick and kept in touch with e-mails and the occasional phone call. Mike could hardly wait for his next furlough. During most of his stay, his only contact with actual fighting was hearing the sounds of distant artillery barrages. However, late one night, while heading down a desert highway, his company was ambushed by Iraqi troops. He watched, horrified, as several of his companions were cut down by enemy fire. Then, suddenly, a mortar blast blew him off his feet and rendered him unconscious. He awoke the next day in a field hospital to discover that his body was riddled with shrapnel and both his legs were broken. Fortunately, his injuries, though serious, were not fatal, and, in a few weeks, he recovered sufficiently to be put on a transport plane for home. He had a long scar on his face, and his left leg was seriously, perhaps permanently impaired, but, otherwise, his wounds healed and he was relieved to be back with Madeleine, his wife. He now looked forward to leaving the military and, after his discharge, finding civilian employment.

His injuries required that he embark on a long process of multiple surgical procedures to restore use of his leg, to be followed by physical therapy, painful procedures that were both tedious and debilitating. He was given narcotic painkillers and sleeping pills to help him endure the period of recuperation. With his wife's support, he persisted in the struggle to recover. His family members, especially his dad, were "there for him." Within a few months, he was walking without a cane and seemed ready to start looking for a job.

Unfortunately, since his return to the United States, he had begun suffering from nightmares. Almost every night, he awoke, drenched in perspiration, his mind filled with images of the ambush in which he had been injured. He kept seeing the faces of the two men, who had been standing right next to him, just before they were cut down by enemy fire. One had been shot in the chest. The other was hit in the temple, and his skull fragmented, blood and bone fragments erupting in all directions—he could almost feel the unctuous blood on his own skin. And he kept hearing the massive explosion of the mortar that knocked him off his feet and plunged him into agony and then unconsciousness. During the day, he sat in front of the television, drinking beer, silent for long periods of time. When he spoke, it was frequently to retell the trauma of the ambush. Madeleine became worried about his emotional disturbances. But she reasoned that, with the passage of time and her help, Mike would gradually put these horrifying memories behind him.

However, the nightmares continued and, on the advice of the counselor from the Veterans' Administration and his wife, he decided to get professional help in the form of a PTSD (Post-Traumatic Stress Disorder) Group that was ongoing at the local VA Medical Center. The groups offered some bonding and commiseration from others who had been through the same experiences. But for some reason he could not see himself getting close to his fellow soldiers again, as he had to his original platoon. His drinking steadily increased. At night, his most difficult time of the day, he more and more often combined the Valium, which he was still being prescribed to help him sleep, with a couple of beers, becoming strongly intoxicated and finally collapsing into unconsciousness.

His plan to find employment reached an impasse. His recurring nightmares and waking flashbacks to the mortar attack, cast a shadow over his days, putting him in a state of nearly unbroken depression. He avoided going out without his wife, expressing a variety of concerns that were not assuaged by reassurance. His leg still ached, but the doctors, fearing that he would develop an addiction, stopped giving him narcotic analgesics. To help him tolerate the pain and counteract his depression, he increased his alcohol consumption, starting each day with a stiff drink and continuing to drink until retiring. He stopped shaving and showering regularly and, after climbing out of bed toward noon, exhausted from a troubled night, sat in his bathrobe and underwear, watching television and drinking, until his wife returned from work. In the evenings, he would dress and go to the corner bar, where he would meet Ralph, a high school friend who worked on the loading docks, who had always been a hard drinker and who dabbled in a variety of psychoactive drugs. Their conversation focused on a discussion of the latest sports results. Mike stoically kept his troubles to himself, so neither Ralph, nor any of his other associates, knew what was bothering him. Seeking to help Mike cope with his depression, Ralph began selling Mike Percocet and Oxycontin (a long acting form of the Percocet), which "picked him up" and helped his pain. Meanwhile, he continued to receive Valiums from his VA doctor. Even though the immediate effect of alcohol and Lortabs (hyrdocodone) was brief, it gave Mike periods of energy, during which the pain of Mike's traumatic memories seemed to fade into the background. Overall, however, the more Mike drank and the more pills he took, the more intense his unhappiness became. Several times, he passed out at the bar, and Ralph had to take him home.

Madeleine felt she was living with a stranger. Mike hardly spoke to her. When she tried to approach him with the thought of starting to look for a job or of reentering therapy, he complained that he wasn't ready for work and that therapy hadn't helped him in the past. Mike's father also tried to get through to him, but to no avail, as Mike could not see disappointing his old man about what a "lousy soldier I was." He thought, "Why did I survive, while the others were cut down? It should have been me. . . ." And so Mike drifted off from everyone he loved and held dear into a hell of guilt and remorse.

Since Madeleine could not take the deepening tension at home, after work she began going out to a bar with friends from her job. When she finally arrived home, Mike would receive her with angry suspicions and accuse her of neglecting him or having an affair. Mike and Madeleine stopped making love, as Mike was usually too exhausted to do more than pass out in bed and Madeleine was repelled by his occasional drunken overtures. She was now repulsed by his poor hygiene and the smell of alcohol on his breath. But at times when he was quietly sleeping, a rare event these days, she still longed for the past when they were so passionately in love. One evening, after several days of morose quarreling, Madeleine gave in to the advances of Bill, one of her coworkers, and began a fitful affair that made her feel guilty and angry at Mike for having, as she saw it, driven her away.

DRUG-SEEKING BEHAVIOR:
SOUGHT-AFTER EFFECTS

The intoxicating effects of CNS depressants depend on the amount of the drug taken and the time that has passed after taking it. Low doses of CNS depressants create in users an excited state, which is characterized by increased activity, talking, and aggressive behavior. These same effects may also be seen minutes after administration of higher doses. Users often report euphoria—that is, happy feelings—and reduced inhibitions during the early stage of intoxication, and these feelings are typically why CNS depressants are used recreationally. An example is a shy boy who has a difficult time approaching girls but who becomes smooth-talking and uninhibited after he has taken one or two "downers," such as Seconals or Tuinals, at a dance. When combination of alcohol with other CNS depressants reaches very high concentrations, it has a synergistic effect that can induce a coma, cause breathing to stop, and even cause death.

Alcohol, barbiturates (e.g., Seconal, Tuinal, Nebutal) and benzodiazepines (e.g., Ativan and Valium) all produce an anxiolytic, or tranquilizing, effect by enhancing in users' brains the inhibitory effect on nerve cell firing by a neurotransmitter called gamma-amino butyric acid (GABA). The power of CNS depressants to reduce tension is a major reason why users of these drugs continue taking them and why their continued use results in addiction. This effect is an example of how *reinforcement* is distinct from *pleasure*. Paradoxically, stimulants that create pleasurable feelings can also create anxiety, which, during excessive or compulsive use, can develop into paranoia and fearfulness. Users often combine stimulants, such as cocaine or amphetamines, with CNS depressants to "take the edge off" a cocaine binge or help them to sleep after the binge. It is also why addicts may be spurred on to take higher doses of CNS depressants, resulting in accidental death by an overdose.

NEUROADAPTATION

The continued use of CNS depressants causes changes in the brain, so-called neuroadaptation, that include the development of both tolerance and dependence. The length of time required for tolerance and dependence to arise varies with different drugs. But the neuroadaptive changes that eventually are caused by benzodiazepines, barbiturates, and other hypnotics and sedatives (and alcohol) are much the same.

TOLERANCE AND DEPENDENCE

The development of tolerance to and dependence on all CNS depressants can occur after taking these drugs for only a few days. Tolerance and dependence arise in tandem. As with all psychoactive drugs, these effects are determined by the dose of the CNS depressant that is taken and the frequency with which it is used. The speed at which these neuroadaptive changes can develop can be seen in the hangover that college students who are weekend drinkers often experience after use of barbiturates and other CNS depressants. A hangover is actually a manifestation of the withdrawal syndrome. As mentioned, with continued use, users of CNS depressants develop a tolerance to the effects of the drugs, so that the dose that initially reduced anxiety or helped them to sleep will no longer achieve these effects. As a result, users need higher doses to achieve these "therapeutic" goals.

Tolerance to all of the effects of a CNS depressant does not develop at the same rate. For example, the power of Ativan and Valium to induce sedation usually diminishes after the first few days of treatment; their power to relieve tension may persist for months without the need to increase the dose. The power of CNS depressants to create euphoria in users also seems to decline quickly. Users who are prone to addiction and who are using CNS depressants primarily to improve their moods must increase their dose of the drugs quickly to compensate for this tolerance. Because tolerance to these mood effects occurs quickly in most people, benzodiazepines should not be prescribed for more than a few days.

In general, even after repeated use of all CNS depressants causes users to have a tolerance to their "beneficial" effects, the amount needed for a lethal dose does not increase significantly. Thus, the amount of a CNS depressant—particularly barbiturates and some other hypnosedatives—that users need to achieve the effects they desire will eventually become great enough to kill them. Benzodiazepines alone are rarely associated with death due to overdose unless they are combined in overdose with other drugs in this class, most commonly alcohol.

WITHDRAWAL

Stopping the use of CNS depressants after long-term use causes physiological changes in the brain that give rise to anxiety, apprehension, restlessness, irritability, and insomnia. Often, if cessation is abrupt, patients experience rapid heartbeat, increased blood pressure, profuse perspiration, and loss of appetite, nausea, and vomiting. Eventually the most severe cases may develop delirium, which includes severe agitation, disorientation, fluctuating level of awareness, and visual and auditory hallucinations. As noted, the effects of the withdrawal from CNS depressants can be fatal.

The most severe and potentially dangerous withdrawal syndrome caused by stopping the use of CNS depressants results from cutting the intake of short-acting barbiturates and nonbarbiturate sleeping pills. The effects of withdrawing from alcohol and benzodiazepines are less dangerous. The speed at which the drug and its by-products are eliminated, or "cleared," from the body determines the degree and duration of the withdrawal effects addicts experience after stopping the use of CNS depressants. Withdrawal usually begins within 12 hours after stopping the use of short-acting barbiturates, nonbarbiturate sleeping pills, and benzodiazepines. Withdrawal effects are most severe for rapidly eliminated compounds, such as amobarbital, methyprylon, triazolam, and alprazolam. For slowly metabolized compounds, such as phenobarbital, diazepam, and clonazepam, the onset of withdrawal may be delayed for several days after drug discontinuation. It is worth remembering that barbiturates and other depressant drugs are like "alcohol in tablets," and subject the user to many of the same hazards as alcohol use.

Cross-tolerance and cross-dependence among alcohol and other CNS depressants provides evidence that the same cellular and molecular mechanisms underlie the development of tolerance and dependence to these drugs. Cross-tolerance and cross-dependence also provide us with leads to formulate a pharmacological treatment for CNS depressant withdrawal. The general approach of treating withdrawal from CNS depressants is to give patients a CNS depressant that is eliminated from the body more slowly than the one from which they are being withdrawn. For example, a long-acting benzodiazepine, such as Valium, is the treatment of choice for alcohol withdrawal. The slowly eliminated barbiturate phenobarbital is the best choice for treating addiction to the other CNS depressants, such as Valium itself. In the treatment of alcohol withdrawal, hourly doses of Valium are administered until the withdrawal symptoms are suppressed. In the treatment of withdrawal from other CNS depressants, hourly doses of phenobarbital are administered until the patient displays signs of mild intoxication. The typical patient who manifests moderately severe signs of alcohol withdrawal requires 60 milligrams of Valium. Those withdrawing from barbiturates, nonbarbiturate sleeping pills, or benzodiazepines may need 900 to 1,500 mg of phenobarbital.

All drugs currently used for the treatment of CNS depressant with-drawal can themselves cause drug dependence. Accordingly, a major challenge for research pharmacologists is to develop drugs that can ease this withdrawal but that have little liability for abuse and dependence themselves. However, in our opinion, such research is unlikely to be successful any time soon. Therefore, psychiatrists must concentrate on balancing the risks and benefits of using the drugs currently available for withdrawing patients from CNS depressants and avoid their use, af-ter withdrawal has been completed.

CHAPTER 12

Stimulants: Cocaine and Amphetamines

COCAINE AND AMPHETAMINES are pharmacologically distinct drugs that are both classified as stimulants. Each produces strong euphoria and self-confidence, imbues users with physical energy and increases endurance, diminishes the appetite for food, and delays the onset of sleep. After taking a stimulant, users become hyperactive and talkative and often find extended concentration difficult. A dose of a stimulant can keep a person high from five minutes to several hours, depending on the drug used and the way it is ingested.

Since before recorded history, South American natives have chewed the leaves of the coca plant, the source for cocaine. Chewing the leaves resulted in the slow release of a relatively small amount of the drug, and natives used it to increase their stamina and stave off hunger. Cocaine itself is a white or off-white crystalline powder that was first isolated by Europeans from coca leaves in 1860. Initially it was used in compounding medicinal tonics and elixirs.

After 1884, cocaine became the first effective local anesthetic. Now this is its only bona fide medical use. Until 1914, when cocaine was placed under the same laws as morphine and heroin and was legally classified as a narcotic, it was used "therapeutically" in a variety of ways, including as food additives. (Back then cocaine was the "real thing" in Coca-Cola, before it was replaced by caffeine.)

The main clinically relevant pharmacological effect of cocaine is blocking the reuptake of the catecholamine neurotransmitters, dopamine and norepinephrine. The effects of dopamine reuptake blockade include: stimulation, anorexia, stereotyped movements, hyperactivity, and sexual excitement. The consequences of noradrenergic reuptake blockade include: tachycardia (rapid heartbeat), hypertension (high blood pressure), vasoconstriction (impeding blood flow), mydriasis (dilation of the pupils), diaphoresis (perspiring), and tremor.

Toward the end of the nineteenth century, cocaine became recognized as a mental stimulant that could kindle ideas, fire the imagination, and lift depressive thoughts. In literature, the detective Sherlock Holmes, who embodied the ideal of a man who used his powers of deductive reasoning to solve problems, used cocaine to sharpen his mind. It was also used by Sigmund Freud, for example, for these purposes. In fact, Dr. Freud initially thought that cocaine would be a useful cure for morphine dependence, until it became evident that, even when those opioid addicts to whom cocaine was administered stopped using morphine, they became hooked on cocaine instead. Unfortunately, this is a recurrent theme in the story of medications for treating addiction. That is why only those medications that do not themselves have abuse liability should be used in addiction therapy.

Today drug users sniff (insufflate), intravenously inject, or smoke crack cocaine (freebase). The route of ingestion dramatically alters the intensity of the drug's pharmacological effects. When cocaine is sniffed, it is absorbed into the bloodstream through the nasal mucosal blood vessels. Effects are achieved within about 10 minutes and wear off within an hour or so. When cocaine is injected into the bloodstream or when cocaine vapor is inhaled into the lungs, it is carried directly to the brain. An almost instantaneous intense, pleasurable euphoria occurs that subsides in a few minutes, leaving users with a desire to repeat the experience. Injecting and smoking cocaine allow rapid access of the drug to the brain, thereby increasing its reinforcing effect as well as its toxicity. The more quickly the drug is absorbed, the more intense is the high that is experienced and the shorter the duration of its action.

PHARMACOLOGY

Normally, when a neurotransmitter like dopamine is released by a presynaptic nerve cell, it crosses the dead space between the cells—the synapse—very rapidly and instructs the next, or postsynaptic, cell to carry on the neurochemical message by binding to the dopamine receptors on that cell's surface. The presynaptic cell contains a large number of vacuum cleaner–like molecules (transporters), which very quickly remove dopamine from the synapse before it can bind to the dopamine receptors. This is how the brain naturally blocks the action of dopamine to keep the dopamine message from overloading the postsynaptic cell. Dopamine is a chemical messenger that is released as a critical component of the brain's reward system.

Cocaine specifically interferes with the dopamine transporter in the presynaptic cell and prevents the "vacuum cleaner" from removing dopamine from the synapse. Excess dopamine builds up in the synapse and becomes available to bind to the postsynaptic cell. The characteristic euphoria associated with cocaine use is due to the fact that the drug increases the levels of dopamine circulating in the synapses of the cells in the brain reward pathway. The effects of increased levels of dopamine are so powerful that people will stop doing anything else if cocaine is available and continue self-administering it until their supply is exhausted. In fact, users will try to get some more as soon as they have recovered, or slept off the binge. With continued use, users become so enslaved by cocaine that they can no longer experience the pleasures of natural rewards, such as those that come from food or sex.

Cocaine use thus tends to displace the enjoyment of other pleasures, leaving users to rely increasingly on the drug as their exclusive source of pleasure. However, as with other drugs of abuse, with continued use, cocaine is no longer able to cause the pleasure it did initially. Addicts try but can never again recapture the original high. They can enhance and prolong euphoric effects by consuming cocaine and alcohol at the same time, but by doing so, they also increase their risk of sudden death from cardiac or respiratory arrest. Also, taking the drugs together causes the liver to produce cocaethylene. Cocaethylene has similar euphoric properties to cocaine, but is longer lasting in the body. Some studies suggest that it is more toxic than cocaine itself, particularly to the heart.

The most striking pharmacological characteristic of cocaine is its tremendous reinforcing power. Studies with laboratory animals have shown that animals will self-administer cocaine preferentially over food, leading to emaciation and death (in contradistinction to other highly reinforcing agents such as opiates). In fact, one of the most common clinical findings among chronic cocaine abusers is their striking anorexia and weight loss; moreover, after the initial preoccupation with sexuality, most cocaine addicts forgo sexual relations with persons of significance to them, in favor of cocaine, or use sexual favors as a way to obtain cocaine.

Although cocaine is clearly a powerful positive reinforcer, laboratory experiments with animals have shown that environmental manipulations, such as punishment, increasing the amount of effort required to obtain the drug, or offering alternative pleasurable substances, can decrease its self-administration. Dopamine seems to be the major neurotransmitter involved in the positive reinforcement of cocaine, but the neuropharmacological effects involve other brain chemicals as well. Cocaine's effects on other neurotransmitters, including serotonin and glutamate (on the NMDA receptor), are also significant. The NMDA effects of glutamate are especially important to the learning, or psychological, effects of cocaine, the process by which cocaine trains the brains of users to crave its use.

Prolonged use of cocaine triggers the onset of a progressive mental illness to some degree in most people. This illness begins with feeling of anxiety and restlessness, develops into ideas of reference—that is, the notion that people are thinking and talking about them—and finally culminates in a full-blown psychotic paranoia that frequently engenders violence. Unlike other psychoactive drugs of abuse, cocaine use does not create an increasing tolerance for most its effects. That is, a given dose will continue to produce the same effect, no matter how long the drug is taken. The one exception is that the pleasure derived from a hit of cocaine becomes progressively less as use continues, and, as mentioned, addicts can never recapture the euphoria from the first experience with the drug. Attempts to curtail or stop cocaine use are usually foiled by the fact that doing so gives rise to a severe, nearly unendurable depression.

AMPHETAMINES, INCLUDING METHAMPHETAMINE

Amphetamine and methamphetamine (meth), a more powerful derivative of amphetamine that is manufactured in underground laboratories, are pharmacologically distinct from cocaine, but the profile of their effects and the ways in which they lead to addiction are very similar to those of cocaine. Historically, amphetamines were used as nasal decongestants, for the treatment of narcolepsy, and for the management of obesity. More recently, amphetamines have been used, as have other stimulants, in the control of attention deficit/hyperactivity disorder. They have also been and continue to be used by military personnel, especially pilots or those in combat situations, to reduce reaction time, sharpen reflexes, and maintain wakeful attention despite sleep deprivation.

The clinical characteristics and consequences of amphetamines and methamphetamine are not dissimilar to cocaine. However, certain striking differences should be mentioned. Meth has a longer duration of action than cocaine. Most worrisome is the fact that, unlike cocaine, the direct neurotoxicity of which has not been established, meth appears to be specifically toxic to the dopamine system of the brain and kills dopamine neurons. This brain injury may not be fully reversible and can compromise brain functions such as memory, cognition, and decision making. The diminution of dopamine may result in a loss of motor control similar to the effects of early Parkinson's disease. Methamphetamine, like cocaine, also increases heart rate and blood pressure and may cause irreversible damage to the brain from strokes sustained from high blood pressure and constriction of blood vessels after its administration. In a recent press conference, Mike Levitt, the director of the Department of Health and Human Services, proclaimed: "Meth fries the brain." In all fairness, this lurid expression may not have been simply political superlative, since the consequences of meth addiction have reached gargantuan proportions. Much more research must be conducted to establish whether these detrimental effects on the brain can be effectively managed so that addicts can recover to lead a fulfilling life. Currently, there are examples of combining the medical and legal systems through drug courts to help meth addicts stay sober for prolonged periods and thereby allow their brains to heal. It remains to be determined whether certain medications may help this process of recovery.

Amphetamines can be taken orally, in pill form, or, like cocaine, they can be sniffed as a powder or dissolved in water and injected intravenously. What is particularly devastating about methamphetamine is that it is relatively easy to manufacture in home labs using an over-the-counter cold remedy, pseudoephedrine, cooked with toxic chemicals. The toxic wastes produced by this process and the severe chemical burns sustained by those who prepare this witches' brew, often while half intoxicated, are legend in the burn centers of major academic medical centers throughout the nation.

Like the chronic use of cocaine, the chronic use of methamphetamine leads to the development of a psychosis characterized by paranoia, visual and auditory hallucinations, and outbursts of uncontrollable, violent rage. Unlike cocaine's actions, which are relatively short-lived, meth has a longer duration of action, and, if it used continuously in a binge, blood levels may build. This cumulative dosage increases the chances of toxic side effects and even death.

THE CASE OF ROY T.

When he finally graduated medical school and passed the qualifying examination to become a doctor, Roy T. felt like he was leaving his past behind him and entering a new, independent, fulfilling life. He then entered residency training in anesthesiology, one of the less competitive areas of practice, but one that offered a stable life, with few disruptive surprises or emergencies. Roy's father had been an alcoholic, and, when Roy was still a child, had lost his business and, ultimately, his life, as a consequence of heavy drinking. Roy's mother had always been afflicted with depression, a condition worsened by her husband's unpredictable, abusive conduct. Roy escaped actual abuse from either of his parents. Roy was the only light in his mother's life, and his mother doted on the boy and impressed upon him that he should, at all costs, avoid the dissolution that had overtaken his father. Roy did not understand his mother's bouts with depression. He felt guilty when his mother was unhappy, feeling that, somehow, he was responsible. As he entered adolescence, these feelings of guilt translated into shyness with girls, whom he unconsciously felt he would disappoint.

Roy was never academically brilliant. But he was a hard worker and he devoted himself to his undergraduate and medical studies. He felt that, somehow, by succeeding in his studies he could compensate his mother for the absence of his father. While in school, he considered himself an outsider. He explained his reclusiveness to himself by his need to concentrate his time and energy on his work. His isolation was reinforced by the fact that he lived at home with his mother, and she, evidently wanting to keep Roy all to herself, had no patience with visitors. Envisioning himself becoming the center of attention at the hospital, attending parties, and dating, he told himself that, once he became a doctor, his social isolation would come to an end. His mother had become a heavy millstone around his neck. Yet, despite the fact that she was smothering him, he still felt he had to protect her.

Roy was pleased to be making a decent living as a hospital resident and to have finally moved into his own apartment. But he was not pleased with the other aspects of his work or his life. Unfortunately, his dream of a changed life due to becoming a doctor was little more than "magical thinking." Roy had none of the socialization skills that would have been required to fulfill his fantasies. Instead of dates, he just masturbated and fantasized about wonderful girls he would one day have. As a resident, he was low man on the totem pole of the medical hierarchy. Though he had moved out of his mother's house, her incessant emotional demands and his painful shyness made it difficult for him to relate to his colleagues and. supervisors. And as an anesthesiologist, he was regarded by many of the other students as saddled with a dull, unheroic specialty. The stars in the hospital were the surgical residents and they competed for status with medical residents such as cardiologists. The nursing staff treated him with courtesy, but offered him little flattering attention. After all, he began to realize, everyone was a doctor there. Nevertheless, even though he couldn't "stand out" in the crowd, he held on to his precious ambitions to achieve status and independence from his mother by becoming a doctor.

In the cafeteria, he met and struck up a friendship with George, a lab technician in the radiology department. George was a relaxed, attractive young man, and, after a few weeks, they began going out for drinks together. Then George invited Roy to a party. Roy had always been wary of alcohol, because of his father's example and his mother's continual warnings. After one drink, he usually decided to call it quits. He resented the fun that other people were able to have when they were drinking. Calling Roy to the bedroom, George laid out a few lines of cocaine on the dresser and invited Roy to sniff it.

Roy had never tried cocaine, but, of course, as a doctor, he knew what it was. He had fantasized about taking drugs, escaping from himself and going against his mother's orders. He also felt, unconsciously, that trying drugs would help liberate his natural sexual urges, which his mother's overbearing treatment of him seemed to have suppressed. He decided that a little cocaine wouldn't do him any harm and might be a great deal of fun.

After about 10 minutes, Roy began feeling an expansive pleasure. He had been tired when he had arrived at the party. He had been feeling depressed, as he frequently did. Now, suddenly, he was full of energy and felt cheerful, optimistic. Instead of being his usual, quiet, soft-spoken self, he found himself full of exciting things to say. In fact, he walked up to Melinda, a desirable young lady at the party, invited her home, and scored! The release he felt was not only sexual. He also felt liberated from the domination of his mother. Roy and Melinda carried on an intense conversation that ranged over sports, current events, travel plans, and hospital politics. They began sniffing more lines. Melinda seemed more likeable to Roy, more appealing, more affable than she ever had before. Roy began to realize how much he really liked Melinda, a feeling he somehow ached to express. In the course of their conversation, Melinda asked Roy if he could get coke, something he knew he could accomplish through his friendship with George.

Over the ensuing weeks, Roy began meeting with Melinda with the expectation that they would do cocaine together. Although at first it had seemed inconsequential, Roy became surprised how much money this recreation was costing him. George knew a man whom he considered "a good connection." But a gram of cocaine cost $100. And Roy and Melinda had started consuming over a gram every time they met, which quickly became three or four times a week. The expense was made worse by the fact that Melinda couldn't afford to pay for the cocaine she was using, and Roy, who wanted Melinda's companionship, had to pay the entire bill.

During their nighttime cocaine parties, Roy and Melinda continued to make love. But, whenever their sexual encounters were over, Roy felt confused and unsettled, perhaps even a little guilty. He also felt as if he had finally "grown up" into having an adult relationship. But, as always, he also felt that somehow, he was betraying his mother by entering a new relationship. Although he worried about his increasing involvement with cocaine, he recognized that it had opened up a new world of pleasure for him that he never was able to enjoy before. If he kept control over the cocaine and put his responsibilities to his mother out of his mind, life would be wonderful.

PATTERNS OF USE

There were two epidemics of cocaine use in the twentieth century, each preceded by a period of time when it was considered harmless fun, followed by a period when cocaine's tremendous addictive power was recognized and feared. The most recent epidemic started in the late 1970s. It is now possibly waning, as cocaine is being replaced by amphetamines, heroin, and "club drugs" as the substances of choice among drug addicts. Cocaine is almost always taken in combination with another psychoactive drug, most commonly alcohol, by people who have previously used marijuana as their first illicit drug. Therefore, in a sense, marijuana is a "gateway" drug for cocaine use. However, alcohol accentuates the cocaine high and alleviates some of cocaine's adverse effects, such as feeling edgy or "wired." There may well be common genetic and environmental factors that lead to developing addictions to both substances. Cocaine is also often combined with heroin or other narcotics to create a "speedball," a particularly dangerous intravenous cocktail, the use of which can easily result in a heart attack, respiratory arrest, and death.

DRUG-SEEKING BEHAVIOR: SOUGHT-AFTER EFFECTS

To become free of cocaine use in the long term, cocaine addicts must stay away from cocaine beyond the time needed for withdrawal to subside. Therefore, treatment for cocaine addiction must address the conditions that lead to relapse; that is, treatment must reduce the effects of conditioned cues that trigger craving, such as people, situations, or feelings that have prompted addicts to use cocaine in the past. (This is the meaning of avoiding the "playgrounds and playmates," an adage of the 12-step movement.)

NEUROADAPTATION

TOLERANCE

Tolerance develops to the euphoria created by cocaine, and this tolerance is one of the main reasons cocaine addicts continue to increase the dose they use. Addicted patients continue to "chase the high," which, as we have explained, may never be possible to achieve again. As cocaine addicts become resistant to the drug's euphoric feelings, they become more sensitive to its unpleasant effects, such as panic attacks, paranoia, seizures, and disturbances of perception, and they are more likely to die as a result of using cocaine. It should be noted, however, that sudden death from cocaine-induced heart attacks can occur in some people taking even low doses or the first time they use the drug. A so-called inverse tolerance results from continued use of cocaine: Lower doses can cause unpleasant and dangerous reactions that can be very frightening to addicts and the people they know. (At these doses, euphoria does not occur.)

DEPENDENCE

Because cocaine use does not cause the same kind of tolerance and withdrawal as alcohol and heroin, in the past it was not thought to cause drug dependence. However, now that dependence is understood in terms of drug-seeking behaviors and loss of control, it is evident that using cocaine quickly becomes strikingly compelling, to the extent that it easily becomes addicts' primary focus at the expense of all other aspects of a balanced life, even though they recognize that their cocaine abuse has significant harmful consequences.

WITHDRAWAL

Suddenly stopping cocaine use initiates a so-called crash, which is caused by severe depletion of several neurotransmitters in the brain. When these neurotransmitters—dopamine, noradrenaline, and serotonin—are depleted, a strong craving for cocaine results. In addition, the depletion of these neurotransmitters causes sleepiness, sadness, and loss of energy—all symptoms that can easily be confused with primary depression. The tremendous craving that addicts experience during the cocaine crash causes them to seek out and repeatedly use cocaine, as long as they can get the money to buy more. One of the most striking features of cocaine addiction is the extent to which addicts will violate their moral principles to get funds to obtain more of the drug. To satisfy their drug craving, cocaine addicts, although previously upright, law-abiding citizens, often resort to violent criminality, prostitution, stealing from friends and family, and the destruction of trusting relationships.

The typical cycle of cocaine use consists of periods of bingeing, followed by the crash, which lasts from nine hours to four days. Many users will go through a period of protracted withdrawal of 1 to 10 weeks, during which relapse to cocaine use is very common. Cocaine addicts seem to be most greatly disturbed by anhedonia, an inability to derive joy from the ordinary aspects of life that previously gave them pleasure or satisfaction, such as an encounter with a friend's smile, the sound of a favorite piece of music, the sight of a beautiful flower, or the warmth of relations with loved ones.

In recent years, the methamphetamine epidemic has come to the forefront of public concern. The characteristics and consequences of methamphetamine addiction are similar to cocaine and other stimulants. In regions of the country where methamphetamine addiction is widespread, the socioeconomic effects of the drug's use are enormous, including greatly increasing criminality, destroyed families, neglected and abandoned children, and poisoning in the users from impurities found in drugs manufactured in amateur meth labs.

One major difference between the effects of cocaine and methamphetamine is the extent to which the latter drug physically damages the brain terminals that produce the neurotransmitter dopamine. Some of this damage is reversible with abstinence from the drug. Brain damage caused by methamphetamine use also can lead to obvious and permanent neurological and emotional damage, including lack of motivation and anhedonia. This lasting damage is instrumental in inducing addicts to relapse and accelerates their downhill course.

MEDICAL AND OTHER COMPLICATIONS

Physical disturbances reported by addicts who snort cocaine include sleep problems, chronic fatigue, severe headaches, nasal sores and bleeding, chronic cough and sore throat, nausea, vomiting, and seizures or loss of consciousness. Emotional disturbances include depression, anxiety, irritability, apathy or decreased energy, paranoia, difficulty concentrating, memory problems, loss of interest in sex, and panic attacks. The damaging social effects of prolonged cocaine use include dealing cocaine to support one's increasing habit; stealing from work, family, or friends; arrest for dealing or possession of cocaine; automobile accidents; loss of a job; loss of a spouse; and severe financial debt.

The neurological and psychiatric complications of cocaine abuse include:

- Organic mental disorders (intoxication, withdrawal, delirium, delusional disorder)
- Organic mental syndromes, which may be difficult to unequivocally attribute to the cocaine and are long-term problems:
  - Psychosis that cannot be differentiated from schizophrenia
  - Affective disorders, including both depression and mania
  - Anxiety disorders
  - Loss of the ability to perform sexually

Affective disorders, a particularly important complicating factor in treating cocaine addiction, affect men and women differently. Women who are cocaine addicts have higher rates of major depression than men, suggesting that their use of the drug is prompted by the desire to "self-medicate" depression. Men who are cocaine addicts have higher rates of antisocial personality disorder than women.

Cocaine abuse can cause a whole laundry list of neurological problems, including:

- Seizures
- Stroke

- Excessive firing of muscle cell fibers, which leads to fevers and, ultimately, the breakdown of muscle fibers
- Abnormal body movements
- Headaches

One of the most common reasons cocaine addicts seek hospital treatment is for a variety of heart problems caused by acute or prolonged use of cocaine. Chest pain can be caused by insufficient blood flow to the heart muscle due to spasm of the blood vessels that supply oxygen to the heart, which can precede a heart attack. Pulmonary edema—the filling of the lungs with fluid—as a result of heart failure can ensue. Sudden death can result from a change in heart rhythm due to cocaine's effects on the electrical system of the heart muscle. Sudden loss of consciousness can occur due to lack of blood flow to the brain related to a disturbance of the heart. A rapid increase in blood pressure due to cocaine use can cause rupture of the aorta or other vessels in the body.

Methamphetamine and other amphetamines have many of these same medical complications. But, in addition, these drugs, particularly methamphetamine, directly destroy the neurons in the brain that produce dopamine and tend to lead users to neglect their health as severely out-of-control methamphetamine use continues. All of the conditions described for cocaine can result from methamphetamine use. However, they occur more quickly.

CHAPTER 13

Marijuana and Tobacco

MARIJUANA, OR *Cannabis sativa*, is a plant that grows wild as a weed or as a crop under cultivation in hot, dry climates around the world. To protect themselves from the scorching rays of the sun, marijuana flowers exude a brown, gummy resin. This resin contains the primary psychoactive constituent of marijuana, tetrahydrocannabinol (THC), called "delta^9-THC," and 60 other cannabinoids, only some of which contribute to the brain effects of smoking marijuana. When the dried, crushed flowers are smoked, these chemicals are released from the lungs of the smoker into the bloodstream and are carried to the brain. Marijuana (pot) is often thought of as a hallucinogen, because its primary effects include visual and cognitive distortions. However, unlike the powerful hallucinogens LSD and mescaline, marijuana does not ordinarily produce actual hallucinations.

One of the most confusing things about marijuana is that its effects are highly idiosyncratic. After smoking marijuana, users typically experience a relaxed euphoria, sometimes accompanied by an increased appetite for food and an intensified response to visual, auditory, gustatory, and tactile stimuli, which increases the response to and the enjoyment of music, art, motion pictures, and eating and sexual contact and often prompts animated conversation that seems sparkling but is often inane. Marijuana also produces cognitive disorientation and diminution of inhibitions, accompanied by freely flowing ideas and images; many users find this effect pleasant and identify it as a source of creative energy.

126

However, these same effects distort judgment and reduce reaction time, making it dangerous to drive an automobile after smoking pot. Similarly, users should not make important decisions while intoxicated with marijuana, as the capacity to appreciate how impaired one's judgment is, is itself often impaired.

After conferring an initial burst of energy, marijuana leaves smokers feeling tired and sleepy. However, while most users calm down and "loosen up" when they smoke marijuana, a substantial number of users become tense and withdrawn and even evince paranoid episodes; others become so anxious that they feel panicky. People encountering these latter effects, which are classified as dysphoric rather than euphoric, generally do not continue smoking marijuana. They would rather avoid repeating these unpleasant experiences. If they do try marijuana again in the future, typically their reaction is dysphoric again. Marijuana can precipitate panic attacks that continue to occur, even if the drug is never again used.

Some people find smoking marijuana extremely pleasurable. These are the people who may become addicted to the drug, smoking several times every day, sometimes beginning shortly after waking in the morning and continuing until they go to sleep at night.

Most researchers think that regular consumption of marijuana creates a low-level physical dependence and that abrupt cessation of its use engenders only a mild physical withdrawal. However, unlike many other drugs of abuse that are cleared from the body in a few hours, THC, because it is stored in fat cells, may still be found in the bloodstream for many weeks. This means that course of physical withdrawal from THC is slow and hard to appreciate. Many people who discontinue use of THC fail to notice any physical discomfort. Therefore, what drives continuing and out-of-control use of the drug is recurrent craving rather than physical dependence. When regular marijuana smokers find their supplies of the drug interrupted, they become uneasy and nervous. They become preoccupied with renewing their consumption of the drug and often are unable to think about or concentrate on anything else until they can satisfy their urge to get high.

The effects of regular use of marijuana, like the effects of acute exposure to it, are also highly individualized. Some people can smoke every day while continuing to work, interact socially, and enjoy ordinary recreational activities. Others descend into a nearly continual torpor, in which their energy is sapped and their initiative is disrupted. These users find it difficult to hold a job or to undertake any sustained effort. They live in a cloud of marijuana smoke, unable to accomplish little apart from lighting their next joint (marijuana cigarette).

GATEWAY DRUG?

Marijuana is often regarded as a gateway substance to other drugs of abuse. Because it is relatively easy to obtain on the street, is relatively inexpensive, and is perceived as relatively risk free, marijuana is often the first illegal drug to which a person is exposed. Because its effects are relatively mild, and, like the effects of most other psychoactive drugs, these effects diminish, sometimes markedly, over time, people who use marijuana frequently resort to trying stronger psychoactive drugs in order to renew their experience of a high. For example, a marijuana smoker whose constant use has blunted the effects of THC may experiment with cocaine or heroin, the use of which generally leads to addiction.

Marijuana is also known as the universal mixer. People getting high on other drugs, including heroin, cocaine, amphetamines, and alcohol, often smoke pot at the same time, to intensify or at least add an element of novelty to their total drug experience.

The variation in marijuana's effects is one of the major reasons that so much acrimony and dissension surrounds the question of whether the drug poses a serious threat to mental health. Objective evaluation requires that we recognize that, for some people, marijuana is life-disrupting and therefore extremely dangerous while, for others, it is a relatively mild and harmless recreational indulgence. This all needs to be taken with the caveat that one of marijuana's signal effects is impaired insight—in other words, users are unaware of the severity of their impairment. Therefore, motor and cognitive performance are typically significantly impaired, but users do not recognize that fact.

The life impact of smoking marijuana corresponds in part to the age at which it is first regularly used. Adolescents who begin habitual consumption of marijuana before the routines of work and social interaction have become well established are more frequently derailed by their encounter with the drug; it seems to drain their energy and distract them from experiencing and learning from other activities. In contrast, marijuana use in adults who have well-established lives can result in less disruption. The "amotivational syndrome," wherein chronic marijuana users have been noted to exhibit apathy, dullness, impairment in the ability to concentrate and remember things, as well as loss of interest in personal appearance and the pursuit of conventional goals, is commonly mentioned in discussions of marijuana use. However, well-controlled clinical studies have failed to provide strong evidence that these effects are in fact a direct consequence of the drug's use. Many adolescents who never smoke or use drugs exhibit this syndrome for varying periods of time and then outgrow it.

Recently it has been discovered that cannabinoids are produced naturally in the brain, as part of what is called an endocannabinoid system. These internally produced cannabinoids play a part in brain functioning, including the regulation of mood, appetite, and pain. In fact, pharmaceutical companies are now investigating the therapeutic implications of endocannabinoids for the treatment of addiction as well as of obesity and pain.

Regarded from the standpoint of evolutionary biology, the existence of endocannabinoids and of endorphins, or opioids produced by the brain itself (see Chapter 11), suggests that the vulnerability to drug abuse is a "natural" consequence of genes that contribute in some as-yet undetermined way to survival. If we accept this notion, we cannot think of addicts as different from individuals who suffer from other illnesses in which physiology is disturbed. For example, consider diabetes, which is a disorder characterized by either the pancreas producing insufficient insulin or the disruption of insulin's effects in the body. Some researchers have speculated that persons whose brains do not produce adequate amounts of endocannabinoids, or in whom the actions of endocannabinoids are disrupted, are susceptible to regular marijuana use as a means of compensating the shortfall. If this is the case, it becomes increasingly difficult to justify the stigma directed toward people who enjoy smoking marijuana, especially when we consider that cigarette smoking and social drinking are not stigmatized to the same extent.

In the 1960s, the use of *any* marijuana by the Flower Power Generation met disapproval from their elders. The term "unsanctioned use" became popular, because there was not sufficient evidence that the amounts most youths were consuming would lead to tissue damage or mental illness (i.e., that the use constituted "hazardous use"). Meanwhile the older generation was consuming the socially "accepted" drugs of alcohol and cigarettes in hazardous or even "harmful" amounts (amounts known to cause organ damage or psychopathology). In the 1980s, the media initially presented a history of marijuana use by politicians while they had been in college as grounds for disqualification for major public office. Subsequently, the recreational marijuana use among this generation became the topic of satire; eventually it was quietly accepted by their contemporaries and most of the public as a "lifestyle choice."

Because marijuana is effective at reducing nausea, it has been advanced as a possible medication for combating the side effects of chemotherapy. Consider these common arguments in the debate as whether to legalize marijuana:

Argument 1: The difficulty of establishing the purity of marijuana and the presence of so many compounds in it makes it undesirable as a pharmaceutical.

Response: Some researchers believe that instead of smoking the plant, we should try to identify the active elements of marijuana and separate them for uses approved by the Food and Drug Administration.

Argument 2: The potential for overuse and possible brain toxicity from chronic use of marijuana, along with the availability of other, perhaps safer medications, should override any decisions to legalize it. Moreover, the so-called gateway role of using marijuana should give policymakers pause when considering legalization.

Response: Some researchers point out that the use of "alternative medicine" is now in vogue. Natural compounds should be used for medical reasons. For example, St. John's Wort is a natural compound used for depression throughout Europe. Also, both alcohol and tobacco are legal to use, despite their detrimental health effects.

THE CASE OF JOHN T.

In high school, John always wished he could make friends. But he never quite seemed to be able to "fit in." On the surface he was no different from the other kids—it was just that he *felt* he did not belong. He had old and used clothes that were not fashionable, he was desperately shy and introverted, and he was reluctant to participate in any extracurricular activities because he had so much work to do at home after the school day ended. His father was a quadriplegic on disability, as a result of an automobile accident sustained after he had had "a little too much to drink" after work. His father was always angry and domineering, and he used John as a "gopher" when John was not at school. To support her family, his stolid mother worked from early morning to dusk at a bakery in the small town in Indiana where John grew up. She, too would give him chores to do on his return from school.

The family house was small and disorderly, and John's room contained little more than a twin bed, a bureau, and an old, broken desk. John was never very good at his studies, mainly because his mind was always elsewhere. During class, he sat near the back of the room and drew pictures, finding it almost impossible to absorb the discussions going on around him. Most of the teachers had given up on John and seemed to just "look through him." Mrs. Smith, who taught John in first grade, had tried to help;

but, after getting very little support from John's parents, it seemed futile to put much effort into the shy introverted child, who always scraped through and never caused anyone any problems. John tried out for school team sports, but felt guilty leaving his father alone after school. Although it seemed that he just didn't have the coordination, strength, or speed necessary to qualify as a participant, the big problem was that his mind was on all his obligations at home. Nothing, not even sports, could really make him happy. He tried joining the chess club, imagining himself a potential champion player. But, although he mastered the rules of the game, he could scarcely concentrate long enough to finish a game, let alone to develop winning strategies. This all added to his perceptions that he was just "no good at anything." His one companion was his dog, Red, a mixed breed Irish terrier, a source of pride and affection. In nice weather, John found himself walking down the highway with Red and exploring the nearby woodlands.

Unsuccessful at his efforts to form associations with other students, John progressively withdrew from the world around him. When a car driven by a drunken driver hit Red, he carried the dog to the veterinarian. The veterinarian was able to save Red and turned him over to John to be nursed back to health. While helping his dog to recover, John formed the idea that he was cut out to become a physician, and he resolved that, someday, he would "get his act together," qualify for entrance to medical school, and graduate as a doctor.

Carl, a new boy who moved into the neighborhood, was also quiet and not very successful academically. John and Carl became friends and, after school, Carl introduced John to drinking beer. Finally, one day, Carl decided to invite John to turn on to marijuana. John knew nothing about pot, except that it was supposed to make people "feel funny." But, almost immediately, John liked the effects of the drug. When he smoked marijuana with Carl, he felt calm and secure. He felt as if he were in his own world, a world where he didn't have to face other people. He also felt "cool" when they would smoke together, like a kind of outlaw or artist. Marijuana seemed to stimulate his imagination and lead him to more and more often think about and talk with Carl about his plan to become a physician. John and Carl began turning on to pot every day. Because money was tight around his household, John started to do odd jobs and also would borrow money from Carl to get the funds for his "habit."

When John graduated high school, his mother helped him secure a job at a local dog kennel. John fed the dogs, cleaned the cages, and watched over them while he was on duty. The owner was rarely around, so he was able to smoke pot while at work, and he began doing so regularly. With his earnings from the job, money was more available, and he was able to pay back the money borrowed from Carl.

He rented a small apartment, in a dilapidated rural building that was little more than a shack. But John liked being on his own. He would get up, smoke a joint, walk to work, smoke intermittently throughout the day, then return home and light up again, continuing to smoke marijuana until he was overcome by sleepiness. Carl would visit him a couple of times a week. But, usually, John kept to himself, reading magazines, watching television, and dreaming about the day he would "get it together" and enter medical school. He would fantasize about women, but his desperate shyness would prevent him from even talking to women who brought their pets to the dog kennel.

While at work, John met Trevor, a middle-aged man who came by every week to furnish the kennel with supplies. Trevor was also an inveterate pot smoker and had connections to buy the drug in quantity, at a good price. John had what he thought was a great idea: He could get a quarter pound of pot from Trevor and sell it at a profit through Carl's friends. He tried out this scheme, and, he was delighted when it worked out well. He made a profit. Using marijuana regularly made him more sociable. John could face others, and his ability to sell the weed he brought "wholesale" to his "customers" at a "retail price" surprised even himself. Life wasn't half bad if you were providing a service to others and could have all the weed you needed! He even considered asking out one of his "clients," but could not work up the nerve to do so.

He decided to continue in this business and determined to save money for medical school. Unfortunately, with the advent of his new supply, his own pot smoking increased dramatically. Now, he would roll big joints and smoke them almost continuously. Most of the money he made started "going up in smoke." But he didn't seem to mind. He walked around, almost in a trance. He was almost always tired, and his life was confined to spending his days at the kennel and spending his nights at home in a cloud of marijuana smoke. Now, more than ever, he still dreamed of turning himself around, going to college, and, eventually, graduating from medical school. However, he slowly realized that, like his dad, he now had become "paralyzed" in his life, with pot rather than paraplegia. He became progressively more depressed, and his feelings of guilt and worthlessness were soon overwhelming. He stopped visiting his family once Red died. And his parents had enough concerns without John weighing them down with his worries. His mother tried to reach out, but John avoided letting her find out how limited his life had become. He resigned himself to pornography for his sexual release and that made him feel all the more guilty. His "pot buddies" were his only contacts outside of work.

PATTERNS OF USE

As children grow into adolescents, entering puberty and beginning to experience independence from their parents, marijuana is often the first illegal drug they try. The greater their use of marijuana, the greater the chances that they will try and become addicted to other, more dangerous drugs, such as cocaine. The distribution of marijuana use in a given population, therefore, is one predictor of addiction to other drugs.

Recently marijuana use has been declining in young adults, but for the first time, rates among girls are higher than those among boys. It is possible, therefore, that the gender-related differences found in alcoholism may also be applicable to marijuana and other drugs of abuse.

INTOXICATION

As mentioned, the subjective effects of marijuana are somewhat different among people. These differences are determined by the dose consumed, the method of ingestion, the setting in which it is consumed, the user's expectations, and the individual's vulnerability to the drug's undesirable psychological effects.

Typically, intoxication of marijuana smokers begins with a "high," or euphoria, which is best understood as a sense of well-being and contentment. This euphoria is often followed by drowsiness or sedation. Smokers' perception of time is altered, and they may experience distortions in both hearing and vision. The subjective effects include a feeling of isolation from others. Actual hallucinations are rare among marijuana users, although individuals prone to hallucinations due to underlying mental illness may experience an exacerbation of their typical hallucinatory experiences. Impaired mental functions are observed in a number of cognitive and performance tasks. These include impaired memory, distorted time sense, and worsened reaction time as well as impairment in forming concepts, learning, perception, coordination, and the ability to pay attention.

After users smoke one or two joints, the judgment and physical coordination required to drive an automobile safely is impaired. Users remain impaired for four to eight hours, a period that long outlasts the high, or the subjective effects, of the drug. Because marijuana smokers are unaware of these persistent impairments in their ability to drive, they are at greater risk of becoming involved in traffic accidents. The impairments in perception and coordination produced by drinking alcohol are additive to those produced by smoking marijuana. Regular marijuana smokers, who have become tolerant to some of the drug's effects, tend to perform better on performance tests than inexperienced marijuana smokers. But even they are unable to gauge accurately how impaired their performance actually is.

At higher doses of marijuana, the distortions in perception can induce panic reactions or mild paranoia. With extremely high doses of marijuana, psychosis, characterized by loss of the sense of self and of reality, has been reported. However, such severe effects of marijuana are extremely uncommon in the United States, where the drug is not particularly potent. They are more common in countries in which there is heavy use of stronger preparations of marijuana, such as in the Caribbean and the Indian subcontinent. It is unclear whether any hallucinatory experiences are attributable to marijuana or are simply brought out by the drug in a person who is on the verge of developing them without the marijuana use.

Physical signs of marijuana intoxication include red eyes and rapid heartbeat. Although increased appetite is often attributed to marijuana smoking, this phenomenon has not been consistently confirmed in controlled studies.

PHARMACOLOGY

Marijuana is the common name for the plant *Cannabis sativa*. Other names for the dried, crushed, flowering buds and leaves include: weed, grass, pot, hashish, bhang, kif, and ganja. The highest concentrations of the psychoactive cannabinoids are found in the flowering tops of female plants. In use, the plant is cut, hung upside down to dry, chopped, and then rolled into marijuana cigarettes. The primary psychoactive constituent of marijuana is (-)-delta-9-tetrahydrocannabinol (delta^9-THC), commonly called THC. However, the cannabis plant contains at least 400 chemicals. Other chemical compounds in marijuana smoke, like certain components in cigarette smoke, may be carcinogenic.

ABSORPTION, DISTRIBUTION, METABOLISM, AND EXCRETION

As noted, THC is the main psychoactive ingredient in marijuana smoke. Most of the other 60 cannabinoids present in the plant are inactive or only weakly active, but they may interact with THC to increase or decrease its potency. The amount of psychoactive chemicals that reaches the bloodstream varies with the THC content of the marijuana smoked.

ENDOCANNABINOID SYSTEM

It was recently discovered that chemicals similar to THC occur naturally in the brain, produced by the so-called endocannaboid system. Endogenous cannabinoids—those that occur naturally—play a part in the way the body works and specifically affect the way the brain functions. The effects of these naturally occurring cannabinoids help regulate such things as moods, the appetite for food, and the response to pain.

After cannabinoid receptors were discovered in various organs, the pharmaceutical industry launched a program to find out if related compounds could be synthesized that would bind to these receptors to block the actions of the endocannabinoids. Such drugs could be used as medications for various illnesses, including obesity, pain, and the treatment of psychiatric problems related to addiction.

There are striking parallels between THC and other cannabinoids and heroin and other opioids. The endogenous opioid system in the brain, which produces naturally occurring opiates, has many similarities with the brain's endocannabinoid system. Moreover, there is also some evidence for endogenous benzodiazepines. It is not a far leap to view catecholamine neurotransmitters, namely dopamine and norepinephrine, as atavistic remnants of compounds derived from the coca plant.

These discoveries underline the grand sweep of evolution and how receptors for psychoactive drugs are remnants of biological structures that existed in the animal and plant kingdoms before human beings appeared. Because some people have genes that make them more prone to abuse these drugs than other people, from the postulates of evolution, these genes must make some as-yet-undetermined contribution to the survival and reproduction of those in whom they occur. Again, once we recognize the natural, genetically determined vulnerability to becoming addicted to psychoactive drugs, it becomes clearer than ever that we should think of addicted persons in the same way as we think of people who suffer from any other physical illness. Put another way, when we recognize the underlying genetic components of the disease of addiction, it is impossible to attach a stigma to people who suffer from addiction, a stigma that is not, of course, attached to people with other diseases.

MEDICAL COMPLICATIONS

As explained earlier, in scientific and popular accounts of the effects of smoking marijuana regularly, a so-called amotivational syndrome has frequently been described. This syndrome is characterized by apathy, dullness, and impaired judgment, concentration, and memory, as well as loss of interest in personal appearance and the pursuit of conventional goals. However, well-controlled scientific studies have not produced good evidence that this syndrome, where it exists, is actually a result of using marijuana.

There has been some evidence of harm to the reproductive system, immune system, and lungs as a result of regular marijuana smoking. The discovery of naturally occurring cannabinoids makes these problems easier to understand. For example, there is new evidence showing that naturally produced cannabinoids may contribute to the development of the fetus early in pregnancy. If this is true, pregnant women should be careful about avoiding the use of marijuana, because externally introduced cannabinoids would then be presumed to have an undetermined effect on the fetus.

NOTE ON TOBACCO

The cases of emphysema patients who are told by their physicians that they are going to die if they do not stop smoking clearly show how addiction and medical illness overlap. Consider the patient who cannot stop smoking, although he has been encouraged by his physician to do so for several years. The physician has even threatened not to see the patient again if he continues to smoke. Nevertheless, the physician follows the patient religiously and meticulously manages his lung disease with bronchodilators and antibiotics. Eventually, more and more heroic measures requiring hospitalization are needed, until the patient is unable to get around without a tank of oxygen on his hip. The patient continues to smoke until the day he dies; near the end, puffs from cigarettes almost alternate with puffs of oxygen delivered by a nasal cannula prescribed by the physician. This patient exposes himself and others to great danger, as the fire from the cigarettes is brought in close proximity to the combustible oxygen—both of which the patient perceives as essential in some way to his life.

As a young medical student, Dr. Martin was shocked and exasperated to see one of his patients smoking compulsively through his tracheotomy opening. The opening was a result of surgery performed a few months earlier to remove from the patient's windpipe life-threatening cancer caused by decades of chain-smoking. It was then that Dr. Martin realized just how irresistible addiction to nicotine in cigarettes can be.

Recent advances in pharmacological replacement of nicotine and the use of agents that activate the same nicotinic receptors as are activated with smoking hold considerable promise in treatment of chronic smokers. Moreover, smoking and abuse of other drugs typically occur in tandem, and addiction psychiatrists are beginning to pay greater attention to smoking cessation as part and parcel of recovery from drugs of abuse and alcohol.

PART IV

Gaining Understanding: Treating Behavioral Addictions

CHAPTER 14

What Are Behavioral Addictions?

THERE IS NO single explanation of why, although the opportunities to engage in activities that form the basis for behavioral addictions are widely available and widely indulged, some people form these addictions while others do not. Everyone must eat to live, but not everyone develops overeating or obesity; sexual relations are a common part of a healthy life, but relatively few people develop problematic hypersexuality; and there are many more occasions to gamble than ever before in history, but relatively few succumb to pathological gambling.

A case can be made that gambling, a form of risk taking, is a variant of a natural drive: curiosity and exploration. Once one accepts this idea, pathological gambling appears very similar to the other behavioral addictions. Thus all the behavioral addictions can be understood as human drives gone awry.

The drive disorders underlying behavioral addictions, like the drive disorders that underlie psychoactive drug addictions, are complex and multifaceted, and take different forms in different people. For one thing, the life situations that give rise to addictive behaviors vary widely. Further, in some people, these problematic behaviors continue inexorably until users die or become severely incapacitated as a result of the damaging effects of the behaviors. Other people can decrease or stop these behaviors completely. Because of the diversity in the ways behavioral addictions manifest themselves, they are best understood as a result of many different factors interacting over time.

The salient fact that most of the people who engage in behaviors related to natural needs do *not* become addicted to them leads us to try to identify the factors that make some people vulnerable to developing behavioral addictions.

A variety of biological and psychological factors probably predispose a person to lose control over behaviors that to most other people simply represent one part of a balanced life. These factors (which correspond with similar factors that arise in connection with substance abuse addictions) include:

- A greater "need" to engage in these behaviors in order to be sated
- The pattern a person follows in carrying out the activities involved in a behavioral addiction
- Rapid adaptation of the brain to regular engagement in the given complement of behaviors
- Personality traits that incline a person to engage in the activity (e.g., thrill seeking or antisocial traits)
- High vulnerability to the associated brain changes and emotional effects of engaging in these activities

Just as in drug addictions, certain emotional difficulties have been seen as increasing a person's vulnerability to becoming overwhelmed by a behavioral addiction. These include emotional distress caused by: various mental disorders, such as depression, anxiety, attention deficit disorder, or psychosis; medical illnesses, such as those creating chronic pain or other disabilities; and a severely stressful life experience, such becoming the victim of a crime, a sexual assault, or financial disaster or engaging in a military battle. Certain people seem to begin to engage in addictive behaviors when they attempt to cope with or numb their emotional problems. However, susceptibility to experiencing heightened stress when faced with extreme challenges may arise from the same causes as behavioral addiction itself, so that this heightened stress may not, in fact, be the reason a person becomes an addict.

Social factors, especially among family members, also contribute to a person's vulnerability to developing a behavioral addiction. Peer pressure is also very important. Finally, the lack of availability of alternative activities, including educational, recreational, and occupational opportunities, also increases the likelihood that a person will succumb to these behavioral addictions. The odds of succumbing are also increased by exposure, during early development, to others who suffer from these addictions and who serve as role models. This exposure can also lead to gambling, overeating, and sexual acting out, and, ultimately, to addictive patterns in one or more of these behaviors. For example: Growing up in a family in which all adversity or causes for celebration are seen as excuses or opportunities to eat can teach a young person that overeating is a normal and desirable "coping mechanism." Similarly, a father who compulsively engages in short-term relationships with all sorts of women, in order to find solace from an empty life, without ever finding satisfaction, provides a model for problematic hypersexuality that his son may emulate. An even more dangerous scenario is if the father actually involves his son in his sexual conquests or exposes him to sexual exploitation by others. Nevertheless, as with drug addiction, simple exposure and sampling do not lead to addiction in resilient people.

The typical course of behavioral addiction begins by repeated *exposure* of a vulnerable individual to given situations in a particular social context. Casual involvement in these activities progresses to addiction when the desire to engage in them becomes *compulsive*, or irresistible. As people lose control of their decision to gamble or overeat, they narrow their life focus. Eventually, as the behavior becomes all-consuming, social, psychiatric, and medical complications can develop. At each stage of the behavioral addiction, the interactions among the person, his behavioral repertoire, and the environment are altered. For example, the behavior of a teen "making out" on a date differs dramatically from masturbating in front of a computer screen until one's penis is raw and bleeding or searching out prostitutes and having sexual relations with one or more at the same time without protection from sexually transmitted diseases. Similarly, gambling in Las Vegas while attending a professional conference is different from betting the family's food money on the horses and borrowing from loan sharks at exorbitant rates of interest to try to "get it back."

The stages in the development of behavioral addictions and drug addictions are strikingly similar. However, less is known about the speed of the development of behavioral addictions and their severity in comparison with what we know about drug addictions. One reason for this is that we have learned a great deal about drug addictions from animal studies, whereas related animal models of behavioral addictions are only now being developed. Nevertheless, we do know that one of the factors affecting the speed of the progression and the severity of behavioral addictions is the availability of opportunities for engaging in the behavior in question. For example, some evidence suggests that increased availability of opportunities to gamble is associated with higher prevalence of problematic gambling. The current increase in childhood obesity to some degree reflects the ready availability of high-fat and caloric junk foods and their advertisements to youngsters. The effects on human relationships and ultimately on sexual intimacy within the marital relationship that are caused by flooding the entertainment and advertising media with sexually provocative material and the exposure of young children to this material are of considerable concern but are not yet fully understood.

Often months or years can pass between a person's initial exposure to certain activities and the time when engagement in these activities becomes an uncontrollable urge. For example, the serious complications caused by gambling typically occur years after initially playing at low stakes. And, in the past, classic sexual addiction did not develop until the person was sexually initiated and had some instruction from others and also was mature enough to have mastered the courting behaviors required to engage a partner. Today, however, a casual computer surfer, searching the Internet for pornography, no longer requires a willing partner to satisfy sexual urges and can develop into a full-blown addict after only a few months. Thus, whereas sexual addiction formerly progressed at the tempo of alcoholism, the speed of its development is now comparable to the speed of developing an addiction to cocaine, a much more reinforcing drug than alcohol. Therefore, with the availability of computer technology and the Internet, the onset of serious behavior problems after first engaging in problematic sexual activities is much faster. For this reason, computer pornography has been touted as the "cocaine of sexual addiction."

A fundamental concept that unites behavioral and drug addictions seems to operate through the basic principles of learning and memory: The greater the intensity of one's involvement in a behavior owing to its reinforcement value, the more engrained in the wiring of the brain it becomes (i.e., the "better" it is learned and the more difficult it is to forget). Computer presentation of information can be extremely rapid and highly repetitive; people watching the computer screen are forced to become intensely involved in the process. Together, these factors increase the likelihood of engaging in computer time at the expense of other behaviors that are necessary for a balanced life. The time spent viewing the screens reinforces, or encourages the person to search out, more and more lurid pornographic sites. Moreover, because computers and the Internet have become easily accessible, one need not "go without" these stimuli because of geography or other reasons.

Just as people often use several addictive drugs simultaneously or use different drugs serially, switching from one out-of-control and self-destructive behavior to another is quite common. Also, behavioral addictions may occur together in combination with each other and with drug addictions. It is not uncommon for problematic hypersexuality (so-called sexual addiction), pathological gambling, or drug addiction to trigger each other, and many pathological gamblers or sex addicts have drug addictions as well. Such combinations of drug and behavioral addictions strongly suggest that the similarities among addictions are more important than their differences.

For behavioral addictions that emerge from activities that are part of normal life—for example, sexual relations and eating—legal sanctions play a much smaller part than they do in relation to those that are illegal in some jurisdictions, as gambling is. There is no compelling analogy for gateway behaviors, as there is for gateway legal drugs that lead to an addiction to more "dangerous" drugs. Thus, intervening or preventing behavioral addictions does not follow the same pattern as intervening to stop drug abuse. Clearly, mentoring youngsters to ensure that they are leading a balanced life is not easy, especially if their lives are in turmoil for reasons that are not under their control. When a life is in turmoil, any activity that transports one from the here and now can become a source of comfort and will tend to be repeated over and over again.

While the gateway concept of progressing from softer drugs to harder ones and the parallels between drug addictions and behavioral ones suggest that interventions directed at drug prevention *may* influence behavioral addictions, this has not been established. However, the common factors shared by drug and behavioral addictions suggest that the same factors that make people vulnerable to becoming addicted to a certain behavior also make them vulnerable to addiction to drugs. These overlapping features also suggest that similar diagnostic criteria and treatment strategies should be applied to behavioral addictions as to the abuse of drugs.

Young people typically begin to lose control over the behaviors that serve to comfort them during a tumultuous adolescence. During this period of their lives, when they are developing into adults, they are confronted with the challenges of learning about human intimacy and sexuality, beginning productive work, and, in general, exploring and facing the challenges of life. They are also beginning to reconcile themselves to the idea that their family lives may not necessarily be representative of the lives of "normal" families and that some changes must be made if they are going to cope successfully with what life throws at them. During this crucial life period, addictive behaviors, such as sexual addiction, compulsive thrill seeking, and becoming a workaholic, interfere with meeting these challenges in ways similar to addictive substance abuse.

In order to achieve a better understanding of behavioral addictions, we now present case studies of addictive Internet activity and addictive sexual activity.

THE CASE OF MARILYN B.

Marilyn had grown up in a small New Jersey town, where she was the oldest of eight children. Her mother always seemed to be pregnant or busy with one of the younger children. Marilyn soon found that the only way to get noticed was to become a "mother" to her younger siblings. Her father was always working at two jobs to help make ends meet, and, when he came home, everything had to be "in order," as he was "not to be disturbed." Once or twice a month, Marilyn's father would go out with his friends on a bender and come home "as sweet as can be." Marilyn imagined that it was during these periods that her mother became pregnant yet again. Marilyn had little time to do anything, as she became responsible for another newborn every other year. She married early to get away from home, attended a junior college for two years, became a legal secretary, and lived in Newark for over 10 years. She and her husband drifted apart, as he wanted to start a family, and she couldn't face the prospect of yet another baby to take care of. Unhappy and dissatisfied with her life, she decided to get a divorce and move to New York, where she moved to various apartments around town, unable to settle down and get far enough away from home and her family. Finally, she transplanted herself to San Francisco, and continued to live alone, as she had for a long time.

As a young woman, Marilyn had been a pretty, pixieish brunette, with a good figure and a winning smile. Since adolescence, she had been subject to bouts with depression. But no one, except her closest girlfriends, was allowed to see that side of her. As she entered her forties, she put on a substantial amount of weight. Now, in her mid-forties, she was obese, and the chief indulgence in her lonely life was eating.

Eating, however, even splurging on her favorite junk food daily, wasn't working to dispel the depression that had become a more serious, nearly constant problem in recent years. She tried psychotherapy, which she really couldn't afford, but found it to be of no help and gave it up. One of her therapists prescribed medications, including antidepressants and tranquilizers, which she continued to take. The tranquilizers helped her to sleep. But she remained depressed. What she really needed, she told herself, was a companion in her life, a man to share her world with—one who would love her for who she was and would place no demands on her.

She tried going to dance clubs in the evenings after work. But, even though she made an effort to be friendly and appear upbeat, she was too shy to initiate many conversations, and few people seemed interested in initiating a conversation with her. She saw classified ads in the paper for and finally resorted to calling "love lines," commercial social contact services, that charged men, but invited women to call free of charge. She spent hours on the phone talking to dozens of men. Usually, these men would end up telling her they weren't interested in meeting a woman as overweight as she admitted to being. Several times, however, she arranged to meet men she had spoken to. Once was for coffee. Twice she ended up paying for her own dinner. She continued talking to one of the men on the telephone occasionally, but saw none of the men again.

Although not naturally inclined to spend time using her home computer, she was connected to the Internet and had an e-mail account. From her activities at work, she had become accustomed to sitting at a keyboard and looking at a monitor. Growing bored with the telephone social connections, still depressed, and still overeating and gaining weight, she decided to follow a friend's suggestion and log onto some Internet chat rooms, places intended for single people who were looking for companionship from the opposite sex.

It didn't take long for Marilyn to become fascinated with the kaleidoscope of personalities she encountered online and what she regarded as the potential for partnerships this variety offered. Within a couple of weeks after entering her first chat rooms, she found herself daydreaming at work, anticipating going back to take up conversations where she had left off and to search for new men to cultivate. She would hurry home, and, bringing her take-out dinner over to the desk, log on and begin chatting while she ate. Later, she would pour a big diet cola and tear open a large bag of cookies, eating while pondering clever things to say or questions to ask.

In the ensuing months, Marilyn led an increasingly divided life. She went to work in the morning, did her job, with minimal interaction with her co-workers, and cashed her paycheck every two weeks. But in the evenings and, often, late into the night, she settled into her desk chair at home and entered a world of silent voices, an exchange of typed messages, that had become more real and important to her than anything that happened during the day. When Marilyn had started chatting on the Internet, she told herself that it was "just for fun." She had heard horror stories about women who were robbed, raped, and even killed after agreeing to meet strangers encountered online. She certainly had no intention of joining their number. But you could tell a lot about a person after an extended exchange of messages, Marilyn thought. Some of the men she chatted with wanted to meet her. That was natural, Marilyn believed. She was an interesting person, wasn't she? She wouldn't agree to meet just anyone she had chatted with online. In fact, there were a number of men she absolutely would never want to meet. But there were also a few who sounded intelligent, and fun, and they had made her curious to put faces and voices to the soundless words that appeared on her computer screen. Moreover, they seemed to be interested in her.

SEX ADDICTION: PROBLEMATIC HYPERSEXUALITY

A debate continues as to whether problematic hypersexuality—that is, sexual conduct that is excessive and persists despite the difficulties it engenders for the person engaging in it—should be regarded as a true addiction. We think that problematic sexuality should be understood as an addiction that can be treated successfully with a pharmacopsychosocial approach. The compelling similarities of problematic sexuality to the addictions we have discussed are twofold: (1) the term "problematic hypersexuality," by definition, refers to sexual behavior that is out of control and self-destructive, and (2) because it is a long-term problem that is subject to frequent relapses after treatment.

The majority of people who suffer from sexual addictions are men. This may be because these behaviors are less socially accepted in women and hence are kept concealed. These addictions usually begin to evidence themselves before the age of 18 and peak between the ages of 20 and 30. Like gambling addictions, which take diverse forms, including standing in a trancelike state before a slot machine, excitedly putting money on a roulette table, buying lottery tickets, or visiting the racetrack daily, sexual addictions manifest themselves in a variety of ways, including:

- Fantasy sex, including compulsive masturbation and stalking
- Voyeuristic sex
- Exhibitionism
- Paying for sex
- Cybersex, including visiting pornographic web sites and sexual chat rooms
- Exploitative sex, in which primary sexual satisfaction derives from imposing sexual advances on vulnerable parties

THE CASE OF ALEX T.

In his own view, Alex had made a mess of his life with the help of his parents. He had grown up in a fundamentalist household. His minister father was strict beyond comprehension and his mother was so meek and mild that she couldn't protect the children from the "hell and brimstone" that was frequently accompanied by severe beatings to make them repent for carnal thoughts. If Alex had a dollar for every time he had been beaten bloody or had his mouth washed out with soap he would be a rich man!

Alex was a good student and athlete and managed to get a baseball scholarship to a small school in the Midwest. He became a heavy drinker during his college days when he seemed to be doing little else but drinking and finding coeds. After college, he tried to "settle down" and married the homecoming queen from school and started working in sales in Chicago. Nothing in his marriage seemed right to him, even though his very attractive young wife tried as hard as she could to bring him pleasure and to satisfy him. He avoided his aging parents and his family of origin as the memories were just too painful to bear. He felt he was stuck in a job he hated and living with a wife who had come to despise him. He started getting drunk almost every night, to try to escape from his depression and boredom. He discovered pornography on the Internet for the times when he was at home and was not drunk, but soon he began surfing the net at work. When he was in his early forties, one day, his boss caught him surfing and after a disciplinary action, he was asked to resign. He felt it was time for a "geographic cure" and he asked his wife for a divorce so he could get a new start in every way he could. He applied for and was hired as a top sales executive in a men's formal wear company in Philadelphia.

His new home seemed at first to agree with him. Alex was a short, athletic man who spoke in a soft, even voice, and had a relaxed, easy manner and a winning, understated sense of humor. Finally free from the constraints of a smothering marriage, he took a small but comfortable apartment in the center city and resolved to begin enjoying an active social and sexual life. After work, he began hanging out at Panache, the hottest dance club in town, notorious as an active, upscale singles scene, one block from where he lived. This sure beat anything he could find on the Internet as these women lived and breathed! He continued drinking heavily, starting every night at cocktail hour and finally staggering home at the 2 A.M. closing time. But his depression was gone. He was making a good living, was good at and enjoyed his work, which he found easy to do successfully, and got along with the other executives in the company. Best of all, he enjoyed his nightly forays in the singles world of the dance club.

Alex seemed to lead a charmed life when it came to mixing with women. He affected a serious, sincere bearing, softened by a self-deprecating sense of humor. Several nights a week, on average, he would bring a woman he had just met home with him to spend the night. At first, he convinced himself he was looking for the "right woman," someone he could form a partnership with. But, as time passed, he discovered that the thrill of finding a new woman gave him a rush of pleasure and an expansive feeling of euphoric triumph. It became clear to him that the experience of a fresh conquest was what he really wanted. The sex was not particularly satisfying—but what it lacked in quality he made up for in quantity! There were nights when he managed to score with two or three different women in sequence. His favorite was when he convinced two nubile creatures to come home with him, together. But once he had slept with a woman, he rarely called her again.

He became notorious for his persistence, and his male friends, also habitués at the club, observed him "operating" with ironic amusement. He would approach women who were complete strangers to him and, looking them straight in the eyes, begin quietly complementing them on some particular feature or aspect of their appearance, such as their hair, their eyes, or their lips. If the woman responded favorably, he would begin buying her drinks and continue to press his sexual intentions upon her. If the woman failed to respond, he would turn away, pick another woman nearby, and go into the same act. On successive nights, he would frequently return to the women who had turned him down before, gradually getting to know many of them, sometimes succeeding in changing their answer from "no" to "yes." No matter how many times he was successful at taking these women home, the nearly overwhelming surprise and gratification he felt not only did not subside, but seemed to intensify. His delight in "scoring" with new women became so strong, that he spent his days fantasizing about the encounters he would have in the night ahead. He would arrive at the club with the sense he was on a hunt or going into battle. Each night he set himself the same goal: Find a new woman and convince her to go to bed with him.

His drinking increased but did not seem to interfere with his work or his social success. However, he was starting to get a reputation as a libertine at the club, and had "run through" many of the regulars. The club offered a good supply of "fresh meat," as he described the women he met there to himself. But, nevertheless, it was becoming somewhat more difficult to form new liaisons. As a visitor to the club almost every night, he passed long hours, standing around, drinking with his male friends, intensely watching the crowds, searching for fresh targets for his sexual advances.

Liz, a tall, gangly redhead, thirty-two years old, one of the women he had picked up and slept with, had been a virgin until her encounter with Alex. She became obsessed with Alex, deciding that she was in love with him. She constantly approached him in the club and he, as gently as possibly, consistently rebuffed her advances. One day, she waited for him in the parking garage as he came out of work, declaring that they were meant for each other and that she couldn't live without him. Alarmed by this development, Alex made an effort to interest his friends in Liz, hoping Liz would transfer her affections to one of them and leave him alone. But his friends, aware that Liz kept following Alex around and had become a kind of stalker, were shy of falling into the trap he was laying for them. When Liz failed to turn up at the club for a couple of weeks, Alex was appalled to discover that, in despair over his refusal to continue their affair, she had attempted suicide by taking sleeping pills.

Alex decided that he had had enough novel sexual encounters to last him for a long time. He continued to go to Panache, but, he resolved that, instead of trolling the bar for women, he would spend his evenings carousing with his drinking buddies. He passed several nights without making any serious sexual advances to women and went home alone. But he found it hard to get to sleep and started "cruising" the Internet and masturbating in order to allow him to have a few hours of fitful sleep. And, during working hours, he found it difficult to concentrate on business. He kept seeing Liz in his mind, opening her bottle of pills, a look of despair distorting her features. He felt repelled by the image. But, at the same time, he felt a thrill pass over him as he thought about how this woman had succumbed so completely to his charms that she had been driven to attempt to take her own life. Within a few days, his decision to abandon his rakish ways forgotten, he allowed himself to be carried away by an irresistible desire to bring a new woman home to bed.

His drinking increased. When he woke up in the morning, he was more and more often unable to clearly recall the events of the previous night. When he found a woman sleeping in bed next to him, he sometimes couldn't remember her name. Each day, as he showered and dressed for work, he renewed his resolution to stop looking for new women. But each afternoon, as he sat at work, he was plagued by fantasies of fresh conquests. And each evening, as he went to the club, he gave in to the desire to try to pick up yet another woman. When he went home alone, which was now more and more frequent, he felt cross, anxious, and agitated and turned to the Internet.

It had been two weeks since Alex had made a successful proposition. He started arriving at the club early every night and staying until the final bell. One night, a half hour before closing, he stood unsteadily near the exit, a feeling of desperation rising inside him. He saw a small woman, a hunchback, her face slightly deformed. She was walking with difficulty around the bar and was obviously very intoxicated. His internal radar focused in on her. In seconds, he was standing by her side, romancing her with all his power. The woman, intoxicated and unused to male attentions, was overwhelmed, and she agreed to go home with him. When he woke up the next morning, groggy and hung-over, and saw the woman sleeping next to him, he ran to his bathroom and vomited.

CHAPTER 15

Pathological Gambling

GAMBLING IS ONE of the world's most ancient and widespread amusements. Gambling can be defined as wagering money on outcomes, usually of games of chance (i.e., card games and rolling dice) or of competitive activities (i.e., horse races and other sporting events). Artifacts related to games of chance dating from 3000 B.C. have been discovered in the ruins of the city of Babylon. The Romans of the early empire, around the time of Christ, bet on chariot races and on dice, and they were by no means the first people to do so.

The Russian novelist Feodor Dostoyevsky wrote a novel called *The Gambler* in 1866, mirroring the consequences of his own devastating losses in gambling. Sigmund Freud analyzed the meaning and role of gambling in the Russian's life in his 1928 essay "Dostoyevsky and Parricide," in which he theorized that the novelist's out-of-control gambling was related to traumatic childhood events, especially the loss of his father at a crucial stage in his development.

Beginning in the 1920s, organized gambling, which was illegal in most jurisdictions throughout the United States, became one of the major sources of revenue for organized crime. In particular, the "mob" was involved in the numbers game and "running a book" on horse racing and professional sports, such as football and basketball. This is highly reminiscent of the mob's role in providing access to other forms of illegal activities that have the potential for growing out of control: drinking alcohol during Prohibition, taking narcotics, and consorting with prostitutes.

Dr. Robert Custer established a treatment unit for compulsive gamblers at the Brecksville, Ohio, Veterans Administration Hospital in 1971. Gamblers Anonymous (GA) and Gam-Anon were created based on an adaptation of the principles of the 12-step movement.

During the last 30 years, most states have legalized some forms of organized gambling. Casinos, which offer a range of gambling games under one roof, typically including roulette, blackjack, baccarat, dice, and slot machines and gambling wheels, have opened in 35 states. Whereas government policies uniformly oppose and try to curtail drug use, state-run gambling, in the form of lotteries, have been instituted in 46 states as a way of raising revenue to supplement tax receipts. These revenues are being applied to pay for education in many jurisdictions, and it is difficult to argue against any activity that helps to educate our youngsters. This is not fundamentally different from the tremendous revenues the government generates through the sales of alcohol or tobacco products. Nor is it any different from what those who propose to legalize marijuana suggest might be possible from taxing the sales of cannabis products.

Often a legal license to participate in self-destructive activities is granted. If it is not, someone will, for a profit, offer the opportunity to participate in them illegally. Obviously, if the activities are legal, taxing them can raise revenues that can be channeled to areas society perceives as beneficial. What this says about human nature and the role of addiction in society is open to discussion. The underlying assumption that makes this notion ethically palatable is that the *majority* of those who participate in these activities do so for entertainment rather than because of pathological urges they cannot resist. Nevertheless, most people would not deny that those prone to addictions occupy a particularly vulnerable place in society. Their illnesses, even when they do not recognize them as such, should not be harnessed to fuel the engines of progress. Clearly one way to face this ethical dilemma head on is to channel some of the tax base provided by these potentially addictive activities into research and treatment facilities that address the ravages of the resulting illnesses. Unfortunately, this does not often happen. Rather society regards it as a stigma when the behavior becomes an addiction and looks the other way.

In the last 10 years, gambling has also exploded on the Internet. Partly because of the low start-up cost, hundreds of web sites now offer portals to online casinos, where people can use credit cards to place bets on electronic forms of the same games found in traditional brick-and-mortar casinos. Because computers are in people's homes and can be used any time of day, without the need to travel, this addictive behavior can be particularly hard to stop. Even when the behavior does stop, people can easily resume gambling the next time they feel the need to remove themselves from life events that they perceive as unmanageable.

EPIDEMIOLOGY

Partly as a consequence of these greatly expanded venues for gambling, it is estimated that 80 to 90 percent of adults gamble to some extent. Gambling, then, affects a substantially greater proportion of the population than drugs and alcohol do. In general, as the availability of gambling opportunities expands, so does the proportion of the population that develops problems associated with gambling. Therefore, as gambling has spread, compulsive gambling has been on the rise. It is now estimated that 1 to 2 percent of the adult population of the United States are compulsive or pathological gamblers, people we shall also refer to as gambling addicts. In addition, an estimated 2 to 4 percent of Americans have "problem gambling," a milder disorder that does not meet the criteria for pathological gambling. This term is analogous to the term "drug abuse," used to refer to drug use disorders that fall short of drug addiction.

According to epidemiological studies, the typical gambling addict is a married, white man in his thirties, with children, from a low socioeconomic class and with a high school education. However, more recently gambling addicts include increasing numbers of women, who have better-paying jobs than in the past; older people, who have more disposable income; and adolescents, who often have the use of their parents' credit cards. Today's youngsters are the first generation to be raised on the Internet at a time when gambling has become decriminalized. Current rates of gambling addiction in students in the sixth to tenth grade are about 6 percent, or almost six times the prevalence rates in adults.

High prevalence rates for gambling addiction have been documented in surveys of residents of drug and alcohol addiction programs and among psychiatric patients and jail and prison inmates (4 to 10 times higher than in the general population). The findings from community surveys also show an association between pathological gambling and drug, alcohol, and psychiatric disorders. Besides coexisting drug and alcohol abuse and dependence, anxiety and mood disorders, such as the manic phase of bipolar disorder, seem to be most frequently associated with gambling addiction.

THE CASE OF JOHN C.

John C. found it difficult to make and keep friends. He didn't know it, but what drove people away was his incessant talking. John just couldn't keep quiet. Ask him any question, and you opened the floodgates for an onrushing deluge of words, in which one subject seemed to lead seamlessly into another. Growing up, John had been the only child of an aging couple who had adopted him when he was a baby. They loved him desperately, but were not very energetic or sociable people, and John became the center of their limited lives. Everything he did was okay, and it was almost as if it was up to John to infuse a little excitement into the family. Whereas his childlike behavior was encouraged at home until his late teens, he was considered a dunce in school and belittled mercilessly by the jocks, who found him peculiar because of his diminutive stature and immature demeanor.

John had a small group of buddies who typically spent time after school playing computer games or poker. They would laugh and get really excited and have a lot of fun. John was rather good at poker, so he developed a modicum of respect among his buddies. No stakes were involved at first, other than matchsticks, and, when they moved up to pennies, no one lost or gained more than 10 or 15 cents during the afternoon. Everyone viewed it as good fun, and they would occasionally talk about their lives, but nothing terribly serious. When talk about members of the opposite sex came up, they guffawed and made adolescent jokes. It was a good time for John away from most of his peers who would ridicule him and from his parents who would indulge him. He was in his late teens when his parents died within one year of each other after serious illnesses. His life fell apart. He was devastated but had nowhere to turn for comfort. Most of his buddies were on their way to college, and their after-school gaming had petered out. With no financial means to go to college, he had no alternative but to start a dead-end job at the Newark Transit Authority and face a life that would offer little else but his job.

John and his coworkers sat at small desks adjacent to one another, looking back and forth from notepads and stacks of papers to their computer monitors, keying in information. Fortunately for those around him, the work required silent concentration, so John's coworkers were spared what would otherwise have been a nonstop and needy peroration.

But John could not keep his mind quiet, even if his mouth was closed. From nearly the moment he sat down in his desk chair in the morning, he began daydreaming about driving a sports car, over the speed limit, on a nearly empty highway. If he had that car, he thought, all his wishes would come true. For one thing, girls would hang all over him! The first question they asked was always: What kind of car do you drive? He felt a painful clenching as he remembered the recurring question and his answer: I don't own a car. It didn't help his cause that he was only 5′ 6″ tall, he realized, ruefully. But the lack of a car was the kiss of death.

When he started working for the transit authority, he used to repair to the neighborhood tavern after work, joining several of his co-workers in a few rounds of beers. But, unaccountably to him, these "friends" had grown offish, even sarcastic. They didn't seem to want him around. So, now, instead of going to the bar, he would typically pick up a burger, fries, and cola from McDonald's, head for his small, walkup apartment, strip down to his boxer shorts and undershirt, read his mail, which consisted of bills and junk mail, and watch television as he ate. He really was very lonely, and what kept him going was his rich fantasy life fueled by all the excitement he experienced on the Internet and television. He sometimes played computer games all night, as they offered him a distraction from his isolation.

One evening when he came home to his usual ritual, he tore open an envelope and found what looked like an oversized check, printed in red, white, and blue. It was not a check, of course. It was a voucher for a roundtrip bus ride to Atlantic City, priced at $15.00. However, if he could believe the offer, on arrival at the Bally Hotel Casino, he would be given a $20.00 roll of quarters to do with as he liked. That was $5.00 profit and a free trip! At least this would get him out doing something different.

The next Saturday, John stood on the floor of the Bally Hotel Casino. It was not as opulent as he had imagined casinos would be, after having seen the famous ones, like Monte Carlo, in the movies. The room had relatively low ceilings, was brightly, but not harshly, lit from recessed fixtures above, and the décor was what might be called "commercial hotel modern." But what impressed Bob was the *activity* all around him. Literally, as far as he could see, banks of slot machines stood, back to back, in long lines, broken by aisles. Some were not being used. Some small areas seemed almost deserted. But, overall, the place was alive with ardent slot machine users, seated at their chosen silver or gold machine, leaning forward, occasionally with a drink or a cigarette, either pressing a button or pulling the lever, and staring fixedly at the flashing, changing lights of the rectangular display before them. It was good to have living and breathing people around him outside of work—people who seemed so *involved* in what they were doing.

John walked across the floor and sat down in front of a machine with a sign advertising that it accepted 25¢ bets. In a few minutes, he had the hang of it. You put into a slot as many quarters as you liked. The machine registered your credit. Then, you chose from among a couple of options, including how much you were betting and the kind of bet you wanted to make, and touched a pressure sensitive box on the panel or, if you liked the old-fashioned feel of it, reached over to pull down the arm of the "one-armed bandit."

He lost his first few bets. Then he won one. Then he lost a few more. Then he won three in a row. After 15 minutes, he was down a little, but still, he considered, very much in the game! This brought back some pleasant memories from high school, when he was stacking up the matchsticks and his long-gone buddies were admiring his poker skills. His $20.00 ran out after a half an hour, so, without thinking about it too long, he decided to pull out four $5.00 bills from his wallet and insert them as well. How convenient, he thought, the machine even takes bills! You don't even have to get up for change. Over the next hour, he was, at one point, up over $15.00. But, eventually, he lost both the $15.00 and the $20.00 he had initially put into the machine. He sat back and looked at the machine in consternation. This could get expensive, he could see that now. He looked around him, eying the others working the slot machines, stretching, row on row, into the distance. The casino really had a system, he thought. All these suckers, throwing their money away. But, he had to admit, it was fun. Then, he had an idea. He had seen banks of 5¢ machines, a little further on in the room. Yes, no doubt the casino positioned them further back, so people like him would encounter the $1.00 and 25¢ machines first. But for a guy like him it really didn't matter whether the stakes were 5¢ or $5.00. It was the action and feel of the place and playing that was important—in fact, the less it cost, the longer he could play.

He fed some single dollar bills into a nickel machine. Already, he felt better. He could spend the afternoon here, have a good time, and maybe even make a profit! The jackpots, even for these 5¢ machines, paid pretty big money. A young girl in a skimpy outfit, resembling a one-piece black bathing suit with lace trim, fishnet stockings, and high heels, offered him a drink, gratis. He watched her swaying away to get the drink and decided that this place wasn't so bad, after all. He looked around him again. Most of the other players were older women, many were older men. But there was the occasional younger woman. Maybe with some big jackpots he would attract one of these pretty young things—they might be awed by his skills with the one-armed bandit and come to ask him for advice. His fantasies went wild—there were possibilities here, definite possibilities!

While at work, John's daydreams were now of playing the slot machines, winning a jackpot, as a pretty young girl watched, clasping her hands together in approving excitement. He still imagined himself in a sports car, but now it was a car he had bought with his winnings from the casino. He started taking the free bus to Atlantic City every Saturday and, then, both Saturday and Sunday. He was only giving up visits to McDonald's, computer games, and an occasional walk in the park. He kept no accounting of the money he was betting. He just had the feeling that he was slightly ahead, and when you added the fun he was having and the free drinks—he was making a killing. When he checked his bank balance at the end of the month, however, he found it was several hundred dollars less than he'd expected it would be. Well, there had been those visits to the dentist, which were only partly covered by his employee health insurance. And he had taken out Chinese food instead of McDonald's more than usual, which always cost more. So, though he acknowledged to himself that he had lost something at the casino, he concluded that the situation wasn't that bad. He had been going there for fun, after all. He deserved some fun. He hated those coldhearted creeps he worked with. Winning money wasn't the whole thing. Winning was just a nice, little extra that gambling offered you that other activities, like drinking with your friends, going to the movies, or eating out at fancy restaurants, just didn't. Any money you spent in those other ways was gone and gone for good. But you never knew—there was a reasonable chance that you'll actually *make* money when you gamble, even, possibly, a *lot* of money! And that bright red sports car and the fond glances from the women in the fishnet stockings . . .

But John did not make money. He began losing steadily. He traded off between the nickel and quarter machines, just "for variety," he told himself, but actually to get the feeling of putting more on the line and going for a bigger score. Along with hundreds, even thousands, of others, he had become a "regular." The casino staff, mostly attractive young men and women, were trained to recognize the regulars, greet them, converse briefly with them, and offer them drinks and an occasional voucher for a free meal. John liked the casino girls. They were, he fancied, genuinely friendly. And they wanted him to win. They always asked how he was doing, said they were sorry when he told them he was losing, and lit up when he said he was ahead. Well, why not, he thought. The money didn't come out of *their* pockets. They probably hated their bosses just as much as John was starting to hate the hidden, faceless men, who, he imagined, were luxuriating in one of the hotel's penthouse suites, drinking champagne, taking telephone calls about their daily take as a beautiful young girl rubbed their feet.

He was getting fed up with what he was starting to see as penny-ante stuff. If he could make some real bets, put up some real cash and go for some real money, he could show everybody and buy himself a new life.

GAMBLING ADDICTION: BEHAVIORAL CHARACTERISTICS

If gambling is so widely practiced, what makes the behavior an addiction?

First, and foremost, gambling involves staking something of value (typically money) on an event that is governed *predominantly* by chance. The more skill is involved in determining the winner, the less likely the activity should be regarded as gambling. For example, playing pool or bridge for money are competitions, not gambling. Wagering on others who play these games is gambling, although knowledge about the relative skills of the players does contribute somewhat to one's success.

Second, the activity that forms the basis of gambling addiction must be short term, so that the thrills, excitement, and related emotions have an immediate link in time to the action. For example, long-term financial investments in the stock market, undertaken following careful research, do not meet this standard; rapid trading does. Separating gambling for fun from gambling addiction requires an assessment of the amount of time spent in the activity and the relative value of what is wagered. For example, gambling pennies weekly in a game of poker does not qualify; nor does $5.00 blackjack for a multimillionaire, unless he spends so much time doing it that he has no more time for work or family.

Finally, the social context of gambling is also important. Playful and joyful gambling involves social exchange with friends. Losing the social banter and allowing the mechanics of gambling to become the most important thing can signal that gambling is becoming out of control and may be an addiction.

Although there are those who view pathological gambling as either an impulse control disorder or a compulsion, we believe that gambling addiction is a disease that is fundamentally similar to alcohol and drug addiction. Therefore, like other addictions, gambling addiction is best understood in terms of the biopsychosocial model of the causes of addiction. And, also like other addictions, gambling addiction can best be treated by implementing a holistic, pharmacopsychosocial treatment.

The experience of gambling addicts is characterized by the rush that attends placing wagers and by the fear of financial, legal, and psychological consequences of losing. The first signs of the disease of gambling addiction are excessive preoccupation with gambling and using gambling to escape depression or other psychological problems. Because gambling does nothing to alleviate the underlying causes of depression, the effort to combat depression with gambling tends to continue and increase over time. So does gambling addicts' self-loathing at their growing recognition that they should, but cannot, stop what they are doing.

The two symptoms of the disease of gambling addiction—gambling has become out of control and self-destructive—are the same symptoms we have observed in other addictions. Unsuccessful attempts to curtail the frequency of gambling and the amounts wagered, and feeling restless and depressed during efforts to do so, are an important warning signal. Often this progresses to lying to others about the amount being wagered, committing illegal acts to raise money for gambling, and sacrificing or risking personal relationships or employment or career opportunities. When present, these factors indicate that a person is, in fact, a gambling addict. Gambling addicts also often look to their family to bail them out (in spite of the gamblers' shortcomings), just as do people with other addictions. And as with other addictions, the family often relents, because of the fear of legal actions and other consequences of unpaid debts, without fully appreciating how likely it is that the addictive gambling will return. One symptom of gambling addiction that has no equivalent in drug or alcohol addiction is chasing one's losses—addicts return after a day of heavy losses to get even and recoup the losses.

NEUROADAPTATION?

Gambling addiction is a disorder that typically begins in adolescence when gambling ceases being fun and part of normal social activities. Gambling addicts tend to have high scores on psychological tests that measure impulsivity, and people with high levels of impulsivity in mid-adolescence tend to be more involved in problem gambling in late adolescence. These findings are supported by recent studies using brain scans (functional magnetic resonance imaging [fMRI]) that show abnormalities in the prefrontal cortex of the brains of pathological gamblers that resemble those found in drug addicts and alcoholics. These abnormalities suggest that these people have difficulty with decision making and planning because of their impulsivity. Such impairments interfere with their capacity to size up the long-term risks associated with actions they take for immediate gratification. The tendency to act impulsively seems to characterize most self-destructive activities. Gambling addiction progresses in a manner that suggests the process of neuroadaptation, or changes in the brain mediated by the physiological and chemical underpinnings of learning, is occurring.

The clinical course of gambling addiction is typically described in three phases, according to Custer: winning, losing, and desperation. Gambling addicts' careers usually begin with wins based on skills that make them feel special, as people who can succeed by playing games while others have to work for a living. Wins are greatly dramatized, losses are forgotten and may even be denied. The losing phase begins with a losing streak that is a natural part of gambling, but that is perceived by gambling addicts as a wound to their extraordinarily high opinion of themselves and of their gambling skills. Now there arises the need to beat the house or get even for the loss. They begin to gamble less cautiously and effectively, and the losses mount. Lying to cover losses and deterioration of bank accounts go hand in hand. Gambling addicts' lives transform to little more than urgent solitary gambling and continually searching for money to repay debts. As debts mount, gambling addicts may be arrested and prosecuted. They are overwhelmed with depression, irritability, mood swings, and escape fantasies, which may culminate with a suicide attempt. Family members of gambling addicts suffer along with them. They may have the same difficulties in confronting the illness of their loved one as do the families of other addicts.

It is important to recognize the cascading and complicated collection of behaviors that evolve into gambling addiction, a fundamental distortion in decision making, that involves the capacity to ascertain the risk associated with immediate gratification. The underlying sign of a problem is difficult to recognize: The brain function for this erroneous way of thinking is, of course, unseen.

Pathological gamblers are addicted to the aroused state they experience while gaming. Some gambling addicts have likened this state to the high experienced after having used a stimulant like cocaine. While involved in a bet, gambling addicts are liberated from the worries of daily living and the dysphoric affects that are part and parcel of their lives when they are not gambling. Women who become pathological gamblers seem to have a more rapidly progressive disorder than men; however, they are less likely to commit criminal acts and go into debt. Women also have higher rates of co-occurring anxiety and depression than men, and women are more aware that their gambling serves to reduce distress from painful life experiences and losses. However, many of these differences may be related to differential availability of gambling venues. In the early 1990s, the male to female ratio for the rates of gambling was 2 to 1 in population surveys; in more recent surveys, the ratios approach 1 to 1.

As noted, the latest scientific studies of gambling addicts using brain imaging techniques suggest that the reward circuits we identified as operative in drug and alcohol addiction are also involved in gambling addicts. These imaging studies suggest similar subtle dysfunctions in the frontal regions of the brain that are involved in attention, decision making, and planning in behavioral and alcohol and drug addicts. In addition, parts of the brain comparable to the parts of the brain activated in drug addicts are activated when gambling addicts are exposed to visual cues that engender anticipation of the chance to gamble. There is also some evidence for similar neurochemical disturbances of the reward circuits of the brain in drug, alcohol, and gambling addicts, disturbances that have been dubbed the reward deficiency syndrome.

Tolerance and Dependence

As people begin to gamble regularly, they soon find that they need to spend increasing amounts of money on the games in order to achieve the desired excitement and to escape from anxiety or depression. A related aspect of this phenomenon is the need to spend an increasingly greater proportion of time in gambling pursuits or in thinking about or trying to arrange these activities. This is possible only if gambling addicts begin to neglect the other activities of a balanced life. Thus, gambling attains greater salience in their behavioral repertoire. As gamblers are taking from their family, both in terms of the time they spend away from home and the monetary losses sustained, they begin to hide the extent of involvement in gambling. Gambling addicts commit fraud, forgery, theft, or embezzlement to procure funds, so that they can win back their losses and repay family or the business from which they have "borrowed" to fuel the gambling addiction. Marital and family relationships are usually the first to be affected by gambling addiction. For this very reason, however, these relationships are also the most powerful motivators for recovery. Ultimately, the greater the gambling addict's preoccupation with gambling, the more he or she moves to the margins of society. The consequences of this marginalization are increasing involvement with drugs and alcohol, criminality, unhealthy sexuality, and neglect of physical and emotional health.

WITHDRAWAL

Pathological gamblers slowly recognize the devastating consequences of their addiction on their family and on the other aspects of their life. When gambling addicts try to stop or cut down involvement in gambling or related pursuits, they often are overcome by intense irritability and restlessness. At a meeting of Gamblers Anonymous, most members describe having had these or similar experiences, including insomnia, headaches, weakness, shaking, sweating, or breathing problems, and gastrointestinal symptoms, such as heartburn, "butterflies," diarrhea, poor appetite, and, finally, heart palpitations. What is striking, however, is how quickly such symptoms abate once gamblers begin gambling again. However, the guilt pathological gamblers feel for being so "weak" that they cannot stop is the price they usually pay for this relief.

Although the symptoms that follow cessation of gambling do not include the potential risk of withdrawal seizures or delirium that occurs with discontinuation of central nervous system depressant drugs, they match many of the symptoms that generally characterize drug abstinence syndromes.

CHAPTER 16

Food

As WE HAVE seen, the neurotransmitter dopamine is released in the reward circuits of the brain when people take psychoactive drugs and when they engage in sexual activity. Likewise, dopamine is released when we eat and when we anticipate eating. The release of this neurotransmitter when consuming or expecting to consume food is a survival mechanism that reinforces the desire to eat. Unfortunately, the release of dopamine engenders a complex set of behaviors that can go awry. When something goes wrong, and eating becomes disproportionately important, even the most important thing in a person's life, eating can become irresistible and self-destructive. That is, eating—which is to say, "overeating"—can become a behavioral addiction.

Typically, hunger augments the reward value of food, whereas satiety reduces it. Consider how good the first bite of a favorite food tastes and how even the best meal can make you feel stuffed once you have eaten your fill. Note also that if the food does not appeal to you, you may need to be extremely hungry to consider eating it. There is a common saying for this aspect of the appetite for food: "Hunger makes the best chef." Hence, one way to conceptualize healthy eating is by the accuracy with which a person can perceive, interpret, and strike a balance between hunger and satiety when seeking and consuming food. In contrast, pathological eating occurs when hunger and satiety are inaccurately tuned, so that the person eats so little or so much that his ability to function is compromised or the balance of his life is upset by the effort he expends pursuing the satisfaction of his urge to eat.

Of course, these definitions must be applied in relation to the availability, palatability, and social significance of food. For example, if people are starving, it is realistic for them to devote all of their energies to finding food. In contrast, if a large array of favorite foods is available at a banquet table, most healthy eaters overeat in the sense that they eat more than satisfying their caloric requirements would require. By surveying of the amounts of food and drink consumed at the wedding feasts of various nationalities, we can recognize how appetites can vary in presumably healthy people. Concern is appropriate when there is a mismatch between food availability and the drive to consume it, that is, when there is hunger in the midst of plenty (anorexia nervosa) or an inability to feel sated when food is not in short supply (bingeing). In other words, a red light should go on when food consumption or food restriction repeatedly and irresistibly manifests itself in a self-destructive manner. The two elements of *loss of control* and *consuming food to one's detriment* are analogous to drug addictions and other behavioral addictions, such as gambling.

Eating disorders comprise anorexia nervosa and bulimia. Almost 95 percent of those afflicted with eating disorders are women. For reasons that are not well understood, men, who suffer in large numbers from addictions, including overeating and obesity, only very rarely develop the eating disorders anorexia nervosa and bulimia. Madison Avenue and the movie business are sometimes blamed for the prevalence of eating disorders in women, because they blanket the media with representations of very slender, young women. According to this theory, exposure to images of beautiful women causes many women to feel inadequate and to compromise their health and well-being by compulsively trying to lose weight. However, the ideals of beauty have always been high; almost by definition, remarkable beauty is uncommon and, for most women, unattainable. The increasing incidence of eating disorders among women therefore cannot be blamed on the advertising or entertainment industries, since beauty has always been elusive. We must therefore look deeper if we are to understand why eating disorders afflict so many women and why their frequency is on the rise.

We define "food addicts" to include any person who suffers from the eating disorders anorexia nervosa or bulimia nervosa. Anorexics focus on food restriction, and bulimics focus on bingeing and purging. What anorexics and bulimics have in common is an excessive preoccupation with weight and body image and the behavioral components of food

consumption and elimination. However, often both anorexic and bu-
limic patterns are present in the same person at the same time, and the
person frequently switches from food restriction to bingeing and purging in the course of the illness.

As we have said, the disease of eating disorders can be well understood in terms of the same biological, psychological, and social factors
that underlie addictions. Over 25 percent of patients with eating disorders actually report a history of alcohol or drug abuse. Eating disorders
are typically long-term problems, subject to continual relapses, which
tend to worsen over time. Again, eating disorders are characterized by
compulsive, or out-of-control, behavior that threatens a person's social
interactions, health, and even life. On the biological level, bingeing involves the brain's reward systems, setting up a pattern of biochemical
changes that, like the biochemical changes that occur in the alcoholic or
drug addict, reinforce the disorder. Eating food, like drinking or gambling, causes a surge of dopamine, which functions as a reward mechanism. Abstention from food punishes compulsive eaters with the
discomforts of withdrawal. On the psychological level, when addicted
people abstain from food, binge on and purge food, or simply binge on
food, they enjoy a sense of well-being and relief from unpleasant feelings, such as depression.

One important difference between eating disorders and alcoholism
and drug addiction is that, unlike alcohol and drugs, food cannot be
given up entirely. This means that people suffering from an eating addiction must relearn patterns of food consumption in order to manage
their intake of food and avoid a relapse.

Anorexia nervosa may occur when a person's body weight is less
than 85 percent of the normal weight for age and height. It is characterized by a morbid fear of gaining weight or becoming fat, a distorted
body image, and an exaggerated importance placed on body image. In
women, anorexia is often attended by amenorrhea, which is defined as
missing the menstrual cycle for three consecutive months. Anorexics
achieve weight reduction by reducing food intake, purging (which includes vomiting and using laxatives and diuretics), and excessive exercise. If amphetamines and other stimulants are initially used to control
appetite and weight, they often become substance abuse problems in
themselves.

Bulimia nervosa may occur in persons with normal body weight. It is
characterized by recurrent episodes of binge eating, often of high-calorie
sweets that are consumed surreptitiously. Weight control is achieved by
using the same strategies that anorexics employ.

HARDWIRING THE BRAIN

One of the most surprising features of eating disorders is how the excessive consumption of food and the restriction of food intake, apparently opposing behaviors, can both become hardwired in the brain. Both of these patterns of behavior can be used to manage life stresses and can, in this way, become so consuming and salient that they assume compulsive and self-destructive proportions. The brain stimulation produced by either overeating or food restriction involves neural pathways related to those activated by taking drugs of abuse. And because the clinical profiles of people suffering from eating disorders and drug addiction greatly resemble each other, the diagnostic criteria for substance use disorders promulgated by the American Psychiatric Association in *DSM-IV* can easily be adapted to apply to eating disorders.

People suffering from eating disorders, like those suffering from drug or alcohol addiction, tend to come from families in which family members have higher than average rates of addictions and of other, related psychiatric illnesses. To a certain extent, these addictive behaviors are acquired through *environmental factors*, for example, the observation of close family members and identification with aspects of the behavior of these relatives. However, substantial *genetic factors* also contribute to all types of addictive disorders and with other psychiatric illnesses as well. We still do not know exactly which components of addiction are learned and which are passed on through the genes. But it is well accepted that one gene alone is unlikely to explain the genetic contribution to such complex disorders. Instead, most scientists are convinced that the actions of multiple genes, interacting with each other, blend to determine the development of addictive behaviors. Moreover, unlike eye color or blood type, the expression of these genetically inherited addictive characteristics is probably related to how the individual adapts to the environment. Therefore, as with other addictive disorders, whether people develop eating disorders depends not only on the information encrypted within their genes but also on what they learn and experience within the family and among their friends.

When we ask people who suffer from either drug or behavioral addictions how they understand their disorder, all addicts use very similar terms to describe their problems. For example, they use the term "craving" to describe both the longing for food and for drugs. Likewise, the preoccupation with weight or food, shared by those who suffer from anorexia nervosa, bulimia nervosa, or morbid obesity, is strongly analogous to the preoccupation with alcohol or drugs that characterizes alcoholics or drug addicts.

Addicts, including food addicts, rationalize or deny their addictions in order to enable them to cope with the pain of being engulfed by their addiction and the feeling that their lives are careening out of control. As discussed earlier, denial, often termed a psychological defense mechanism, consists of a series of cognitive distortions unconsciously employed by addicts to avoid facing their greatest fear: the loss of control over their destiny. Thus, in order to rationalize her behavior, the young woman with anorexia nervosa may take refuge in the delusion that she is fat, even though she is seen by others as skin and bones. Similarly, the anorexic who exercises excessively claims that her exercise proves that she is healthy and energetic, while others recognize that she is drained and debilitated.

Concealing addiction-related activities is an important way of saving face for addicts, as admitting how their addiction consumes their lives would severely compromise their self-esteem. The attempt to hide the problem leads to secretiveness, a common coping mechanism in both drug and behavioral addictions. Associates, friends, and family often recognize how disturbed an addict's behavior has become, even though the addict is trying to avoid confronting the problem and is doing her best to make sure that no one notices that she is in trouble. As with other kinds of addicts, food restriction addicts or overeaters often are the last to become aware that there is a real problem and that their behavior is totally out of control.

Depression, anxiety, social isolation, poor performance at work and play, and impaired social relationships are common complications of eating addictions, as they are of other addictions. Of course, as is the case in people suffering from other addictions, it is possible that some of these impairments may have been present even before the out-of-control eating behaviors began. These impairments, which include mood swings, shortened attention span, thrill seeking, poor judgment, inability to control one's impulses, becoming angry easily, feelings of hopelessness, avoiding novel situations, and preoccupation with order and tidiness, may therefore either precede or be consequent to an eating disorder. On one hand, such impairments may be compensatory defenses from a life in turmoil. In this case, these behaviors could correctly be seen as causal risk factors for the development of eating disorders. On the other hand, these behavioral impairments might have also resulted from subtle damage to the brain caused by food addiction and associated behaviors, specifically, metabolic or toxic neuropsychiatric complications, similar to those observed in alcoholics and drug addicts. Nevertheless, what is clinically most important is that these brain impairments, regardless of their origin, tend to compromise both patients' recognition of their addiction and their ability to seek solutions for controlling eating and weight problems.

PLEASURE AND PAIN

Because the pathological behaviors that define eating disorders provide pleasure or relieve painful emotional states, they are initially regarded as beneficial by addicts. Only after these behaviors have continued for a period of time do they become problematic for addicts and their loved ones. For example, the chubby, intense, and perfectionistic daughter, who could never satisfy a demanding mother, may initially have been soothed by her mastery over hunger, and she may even have received faint praise from her mother for having lost weight and looking "slim." These "positive" effects encourage the daughter to continue practicing food restriction in order to receive the associated reward. However, there will be instances when she cannot resist her hunger. When this occurs, she gorges herself—that is, she eats in an out-of-control manner. Because of this loss of control, she feels self-loathing and concludes that she was "weak" and will become "obese." Even more damaging is her fear that she will lose her mother's "love" if she should stray from being a "perfect" daughter in looks and behavior. The unfortunate truth, however, is that her mother's love is very tenuous, at best. She eventually learns that she can remedy the self-hatred that she feels after periods of uncontrolled overeating by inducing vomiting or using laxatives or diuretics. As these self-destructive behaviors begin to displace other important aspects of the daughter's daily life and fantasies, the associated complications destroy any possible benefits. At this stage of the illness, the eating addiction tends to compound the problems for which food restriction or bingeing initially provided some relief.

A major challenge in treating people who are struggling to recover from eating addiction is to enable them to unravel the motivations that underlie their behavior. The psychiatrist or therapist must help patients understand:

- Why they initially perceived the behaviors associated with the eating disorder to be beneficial
- That these perceived benefits were not, in fact, real
- That there are better ways to achieve relief from discomfort than food restriction, bingeing, purging, or overeating

Subsequently, patients must be helped to understand that their problematic eating-related behaviors are very detrimental to both physical and emotional health.

However, focusing prematurely on the conflicts that overeating and food restriction were used to cover up is often destined to failure. Food addicts usually cannot accomplish the psychological work necessary to overcome an eating disorder while they are actively engaging in the pathological behaviors for which they are seeking treatment. Therefore, addictive overeaters or restrictors need to be supervised and supported in a structured, therapeutic environment to enable them to stop engaging in these pathological behaviors. Only after physiological stabilization is achieved will patients be able to clearly examine the psychological conflicts that underlie the addictive condition.

The optimal period of monitoring abstinence from pathological eating behaviors is typically measured in weeks rather than days. This monitoring is best accomplished in an inpatient or residential treatment facility with experienced staff, including nurses, counselors, a nutritionist, and a recreational therapist in attendance. However, because of the high costs of inpatient care and the limitations of medical insurance coverage, treatment often must be carried out on an outpatient basis, unless patients have severe medical complications or are suicide risks.

These issues pertaining to the choice of inpatient versus outpatient care are similar to those presented in earlier chapters regarding choosing care for drug and alcohol addiction. We recommended that the alcoholic or drug addict undergo a period of abstinence as an inpatient, if possible, before beginning intense psychotherapeutic treatment. Often the use of appropriate psychiatric medications for treatment of accompanying disorders, such as depression, anxiety, mood swings, or even psychosis, can make people suffering from eating addiction more amenable to psychosocial and nutritional interventions.

OBESITY

Overweight and obesity are the second leading causes of preventable death in the United States today. The problem is even more widespread than it appears to be, because obesity is a significant problem for many people who are not included in epidemiological surveys. The emotional suffering associated with obesity is often more disturbing to the obese person than the physical consequences. On a daily basis, obese people face a social stigma and discrimination because of their appearance. Most of us know of youngsters who were tormented with name-calling by their classmates. These are the youngsters who were never picked for the team in sports or were not asked for a date to the dance because they were overweight. Also, it is not unusual for adults to be discriminated against in the workplace and not to be hired for certain positions because of their "undesirable" appearance. The economic impact and health care costs associated with this form of discrimination are impossible to calculate, but they should not be overlooked.

The National Institutes of Health (NIH) defines "overweight" as a body mass index (BMI) of above 25 and defines "obesity" as a BMI of above 30. BMI is calculated as weight in kilograms divided by height in meters squared. To estimate BMI using pounds and inches, we apply the formula: (weight in pounds/height in inches^2) × 704.5. As a practical yardstick, obesity is about 30 pounds overweight, equivalent to a weight of 220 pounds in a person who is 6 foot tall and to 185 pounds in a person who is 5 foot 6 inches. In adults with a BMI of 25 to 35, excess fat in the abdomen, out of proportion to total body fat and reflected in an increased waist circumference, increases risk for morbidity above and beyond body weight alone.

For tables showing the BMI risk factors and other tables pertaining to obesity, see the web site: www.nhlbisupport.com/bmi/bmicalc.htm.

Researchers have found that several factors can contribute to the likelihood of becoming overweight or obese. What people weigh is determined primarily by the balance between what they eat and their level of physical activity. All other things being equal, if the caloric content of the diet exceeds the energy burned by physical activity, there will be weight gain. Weight loss will be the result if the obverse is true. A number of factors can influence diet and physical activity, including personal characteristics, environment, sociocultural attitudes, and financial resources. Heredity also plays a significant role in determining how susceptible people are to becoming overweight or obese. This is because genes can influence the energy balance of the body, that is, how calories are burned for energy and how fat is stored.

The biomedical perspective, typically utilized by doctors, emphasizes the importance of calorie and fat metabolism and exercise. However, this limited perspective fails to adequately address the fundamental question of *why* the people are consuming food in excess of what they need to meet the bodily requirements. Doctors usually can effectively treat overweight people who are "motivated" to lose weight by prescribing weight-loss diets and exercise in the short term. However, obese patients who are not "motivated" are typically referred by their primary physician to nutritionists or bariatric surgeons. It is important that patients do not consider such referrals to mark abandonment by the doctor because he or she believes that the situation is "hopeless." Moreover, the doctor should give some thought to whether psychiatric referral is required.

Because of the primary physician's long-term relationship with patients, often they are in a good position to increase patients' motivation to seek psychiatric treatment for obesity. Here the primary physician's role is similar to the physician's role in referring patients to drug or alcohol addiction programs. To motivate patients to seek additional care, the physician should describe the dangers accompanying obesity and outline the strategy for clinically assisted weight reduction. To encourage patients and provide hope for successful weight loss, the physician should review prior attempts to lose weight and explain how the new treatment plan will be different from previous, unsuccessful treatments. Because motivating addicts to accept change is exceedingly difficult, this job usually has been regarded as the province of the psychotherapist. However, our contention is that, as the parallels between obesity and alcohol and drug addiction are better recognized, the fundamental role of the addiction psychiatrist in obesity treatment will become apparent. As anyone who has worked with addicts who are obsessed and careening out of control will tell you, it is impossible to foist the desire to change on anyone.

A purely biomedical perspective on obesity does not fully address the difficulty that overweight and obese people have in controlling their appetites. That is, these people cannot achieve a feeling of being satiated and are still hungry even after ingesting a normal amount of food. A major tenet of this book is that the addiction of overeating and obesity is precipitated by the same factors that give rise to alcohol, drug, and other behavioral addictions. When a person has an appetite that is out of control, he or she should be considered an addict and treated for addiction. Overeaters Anonymous, an organization that advocates the addiction model for obesity, can provide obese patients with help and support analogous to the other 12-step self-help programs. Nevertheless, the holistic, pharmacopsychosocial approach we advocate, involving professionals who understand the biomedical foundations of obesity, can increase the likelihood of success over what it would be when relying on a 12-step program alone. As is the case with treating other addictions, the best results are achieved when patients participating in self-help programs are also carefully evaluated by a psychiatrist and when treatment addresses the biopsychosocial foundations of the out-of-control behavior.

The NIH convened an expert panel on the Identification, Evaluation, and Treatment of Overweight and Obesity in Adults to compare the evidence published in the scientific literature. The panel concluded that the treatment for overweight should be differentiated from the treatment for obesity and recommended treatment of overweight only in individuals with two or more risk factors or a high waist circumference. According to the NIH panel, the treatment for overweight patients should focus on reducing the intake of food and increasing physical activity, in order to achieve moderate weight loss and, most critically, to prevent progression to obesity. However, the panel regarded the treatment of obesity as mandatory in all cases; that treatment should focus on producing substantial and prolonged weight loss and on avoiding what might be called the pendulum syndrome, when patients repeatedly lose and regain lost weight. Experience reveals that lost weight will usually be regained unless a weight maintenance program, consisting of dietary therapy, physical activity, and behavior therapy, is continued indefinitely. However, unlike the treatment options for alcoholism, which may include total abstinence as well as the possibility of "controlled drinking" (which we now know is not particularly effective), with eating addiction the only option is controlling food intake, rather than eliminating food intake entirely. This fact underlines the difficulties of treating behavioral addictions derived from a drive that must be fulfilled for physical health.

The necessity of treating obesity is supported by the fact that obesity increases morbidity and mortality. Conversely, weight loss in overweight and obese people reduces risk factors for cardiovascular disease by reducing blood pressure, reducing "bad" (low-density lipoprotein) cholesterol and serum triglycerides, and increasing "good" (high-density lipoprotein) cholesterol. Weight loss also reduces blood glucose levels in overweight and obese persons with and without diabetes mellitus and improves control of glucose levels in some patients with type 2 diabetes.

Effective treatment options for overweight and obese patients include:

- Low-calorie diets and low-fat diets
- Increasing physical activity with exercise
- Behavior therapy techniques
- Pharmacotherapy
- Surgery to reduce stomach size and slow the absorption of food

Experience proves that these approaches work best when two or more are utilized in combination. Pharmacotherapy and surgery are usually reserved for patients who suffer from morbid (life-threatening) obesity or who have severe manifestations of the medical complications just listed.

As is the case in treating alcohol and drug addicts, insufficient emphasis has been placed on the necessity of treating obese patients with co-occurring psychiatric disorders, especially depression, anxiety, and drug addiction. These emotional disorders are often overlooked because, as suggested by many old adages, "fat" is commonly equated with "jolly." Determining which came first, the obesity or the psychiatric illness—the proverbial chicken or the egg enigma—is not easy and may, in fact, have become a moot point by the time the need for treatment is recognized. However, psychiatric symptoms often worsen with the practitioner's futile attempts to control an obese person's pain or anxiety. Many of the musculoskeletal complications of obesity are accompanied by severe pain that further limits the person's capacity to maintain physical activity, and reduced activity is frequently accompanied by more spare time to eat. Back pain and other musculoskeletal pains are often exacerbated by anxiety that something is severely wrong with one's body. Treatment with pain medications and with low doses of antianxiety medications temporarily helps patients feel better. Caution must be exercised in utilizing these pharmacological interventions, however, because, as we have discussed previously, such treatments can sometimes increase depression and reduce activity levels. Most significantly, opioids, used to control pain, often increase appetite and lead to additional weight gain.

Patients who are overweight or obese often have other cardiovascular risk factors, such as cigarette smoking, high blood pressure, high "bad" cholesterol, low "good" cholesterol, diabetes, and a family history of premature heart disease. Doctors have found that patients with two or more of these factors require clinical intervention, because such patients are at a high risk for physical complications and even death.

Heavy cigarette smoking presents a particularly thorny therapeutic dilemma. Many well-documented health benefits accompany smoking cessation. However, about 80 percent of those who quit smoking gain an average of over 5 pounds, and in 10 to 15 percent of people who quit smoking, weight gain approaches 30 pounds. To make matters worse, weight gain that accompanies smoking cessation is usually very resistant to most dietary, behavioral, or physical activity interventions, perhaps because the anorexic and antidepressant effects of nicotine derived from cigarettes are some of the reasons that the person began smoking in the first place. In addition, obese people who smoke may have a particularly severe form of addiction that may not respond to commonly used weight-control strategies.

There is now a global industry devoted to publicizing and marketing diets of all kinds, some supported by only a modicum of scientific evidence. However, most practitioners would concur that particular emphasis must be placed on the obese person's *motivation* to lose weight, which is probably the most important determinant of treatment success or failure. Motivation is what enables people to reduce their food intake, increase physical activity, and abandon their tendency to seek satisfaction for all their needs—emotional, physical, and/or spiritual—through a myopic focus on "food for all occasions." Psychologists and physicians typically assess motivation by:

- Determining why the patient is seeking to reduce his or her weight
- Evaluating previous successful and unsuccessful weight-loss attempts
- Assessing available support from family, friends, and work associates
- Determining the patient's understanding of the causes of obesity and how obesity is injurious to health
- Evaluating the patient's attitude toward and capacity to engage in physical activity
- Determining the amount of time the patient has available for weight loss intervention
- Assessing financial considerations

Of course, a patient's motivation is greatly diminished by a complicating or concurrent depression, alcoholism, or drug addiction.

Motivation to overcome eating addictions can be nurtured by many of the same strategies useful for increasing motivation to recover from the other addictions discussed in this book. Cognitive and behavioral therapy (CBT) strategies, based on learning principles, are used to help patients reduce food intake and increase physical activity, both of which are essential for weight loss and weight maintenance. Specific CBT strategies include self-monitoring of both eating habits and physical activity, stress management, stimulus control, problem solving, contingency management, cognitive restructuring, and social support. For-profit organizations, such as Weight Watchers, as well as nonprofit groups, such as Overeaters Anonymous, both recognize that motivation is essential to achieve weight control. Both kinds of organizations emphasize peer support as the foundation for change. Interactions with others who are seeking to achieve the same goal of weight loss are invaluable in aiding addicts in their journey of recovery. Often considerable time is spent discussing how to change psychosocial issues that serve as a "stimulus to graze" rather than on the obesity per se. Unfortunately, the all-or-nothing approach of some self-help groups often excludes the valuable, additional help that can be afforded by medical interventions, such as diet, pharmacotherapy for concurrent psychiatric problems, and identifying which individuals are candidates for weight-loss surgery.

Just as in the treatment of alcohol and drug addictions, the enlightened approach we advocate in treating food addictions involves an integrated pharmacopsychosocial treatment approach. For example, bariatric surgeons have found that for surgery to prove effective, an integrated program must be in place to provide guidance on diet, physical activity, and behavioral and social support, both prior to and after weight-loss surgery. Once again, obesity is no different from other addictions in that the pharmacopsychosocial approach to management offers the best chance for long-term success.

ANOREXIA NERVOSA

Anorexia nervosa is an eating disorder characterized by an intense fear of becoming obese, a fear that does not diminish as weight loss progresses during the course of the illness. This fear, often completely unrealistic, sometimes progresses to a psychotic delusion, so that, regardless of what others say, anorexics cannot be dissuaded from it. However, the anorexics' perceptions of what is obese or slim are significantly distorted. Therefore, they not only fear becoming obese, but they also feel that they actually are obese and see themselves as fat when they look in the mirror, even though they may appear deathly thin to others. Anorexics also exaggerate the importance of slimness, confusing "slimness" with "attractiveness." A consequence of these distorted perceptions is an obsession with maintaining a pathologically low weight and an *active* refusal by anorexics to maintain their body weight at or above the low end of the range of normal for age, height, and body frame ("ideal" body weight).

The *DSM-IV* defines the low end of the normal range as 85 percent of ideal body weight or the failure to put on enough weight during adolescence to maintain this minimal weight for a growing body frame. The definition of ideal weight, based on insurance company tables, has recently been lowered in recognition of the obesity epidemic in America and the health risks associated with being overweight. (In an earlier edition of the *DSM*, the weight below which the doctor should consider patients as meeting criteria for anorexia nervosa was 75 percent of ideal body weight. The change in the standard underscores the fact that the weight that defines anorexia nervosa is somewhat arbitrary and should not be the primary consideration in the definition.)

The major problem experienced by anorexics is a *distorted self-image*, not how they appear to others or how much they actually weigh. Anorexics are fundamentally dissatisfied with themselves, equating their self-worth with superficial aspects of appearance. This syndrome is expressed in the famous pop culture saying from Fernando Lamas on the television show *Saturday Night Live*, "It's not important that you feel good. What's important is that you look good!" It should be emphasized that the standard that anorectic patients set for themselves can never be achieved because they harbor a distorted self-image. As a result, they set for themselves even more stringent weight goals than the impossible goals set by Madison Avenue. In any case, as the goal is approached, an even more unreasonable goal replaces the previous target. The outcome is predictable: pathological thinness or emaciation. The anorexic's pattern of thought is: If losing 10 pounds is good, losing 20 is even better, and losing 30 is better still.

Scientists have studied the self-image of anorexics and the social standard for the "ideal" female figure. They have discovered that, over the last century, the standard of an attractive body shape has changed, from a voluptuous ideal, to a slender, almost boyish figure endowed with large breasts. Unfortunately, few women can achieve this new standard. People's body weight and shape are largely determined by their genes. Women and men face a serious problem if they cannot feel comfortable in their own skin. This problem is aggravated when a person's personal standards make him or her even more self-critical than the new societal standards would dictate.

We have seen how a basic dissatisfaction with oneself is a fundamental component of many addictive disorders. In people suffering from an eating disorder, mastering hunger provides a way of using food to make the chaotic world more "predictable." This mechanism of taking control gives them a surge of satisfaction, the same way as taking drugs produces a high or as gambling produces a sense of excitement. Ultimately, all addictions involve the denial that a problem exists, so that addicts are often the last to recognize how self-destructive their behavior has become. In the most severe cases of eating disorders, a loss of contact with reality results in a pathological denial of the serious consequences of excessively low body weight. Death can occur as a result.

Two variants of anorexia nervosa are described in the *DSM-IV*: a restricting type and a binge-eating, purging type. Both types of the disorder are characterized predominantly by starvation in order to lose weight, in spite of severe hunger. Weight loss is typically accomplished by reducing food intake and greatly limiting intake of high-carbohydrate and fat-containing foods. Demanding physical exercise becomes an obsession, with the goal of augmenting the weight lost by dieting. In the bingeing/purging type, the efforts to lose weight through starvation and exercise are complemented with regular episodes of bingeing and purging, including self-induced vomiting and misuse of laxatives, diuretics, and enemas.

When weight loss is so extreme that it becomes noticeable to others, patients are often *taken* to see their doctors by family members. As we have noted, these patients rarely recognize that there is a problem requiring intervention. In women who have reached puberty, loss of their menstrual periods for at least three consecutive menstrual cycles may provide an objective sign of starvation and the severity of weight loss. This interruption in menstrual cycles offers an evolutionary advantage by helping women avoid pregnancy when food is in short supply. A healthy pregnancy would not result when women are severely malnourished, and the delivered child would probably not survive.

In severe anorexics, starvation can also lower body temperature, cause swelling of the abdomen and extremities, lower blood pressure and heart rate, and decrease concentrations of electrolytes in the blood, so that their hearts may even stop beating. To cope with severe hunger, some anorexics engage in binge eating, become intoxicated with various drugs of abuse, and hoard or conceal food. Their ambivalence about food and eating is sometimes manifested in the practice of preparing elaborate meals for others without participating in their consumption.

Anorexic young women have delayed development of sexuality during adolescence compared with their peers, and, as they mature, they seem to have greatly diminished interest in sexual relations. They often obsessively pursue cleanliness and are troubled by guilt over their inability to attain the high standards they set for themselves. Severe depression is a common and predictable outcome for them. In some long-term follow-up studies, the death rate resulting from complications of anorexia has found to be as high as 20 percent.

BULIMIA NERVOSA

The other type of eating disorder characterized by a disturbed body image is bulimia nervosa. Bulimia consists of repeated episodes of binge eating that are perceived as pleasurable but are accompanied by intense feelings of guilt, as the patients recognize that their pattern of binge eating is severely pathological. Most bulimics are within the normal weight range for their age, height, and body frame; at times they can even become overweight as their weight fluctuates between slim, normal, and chubby. They are intensely preoccupied with their sexual attractiveness and how they appear to others and, as a result, are often obsessed with fashion and beauty and other narcissistic concerns. They also frequently use diet pills, because of their desperation to achieve an alluring figure despite their intense urges to gorge themselves.

However, their difficulties in forming mature relationships render their apparent preoccupation with sexuality superficial and unsatisfying. These women also commonly abuse drugs and alcohol to help tolerate unpleasant affects associated with their lifestyle, which is characterized by a combination of a low self-image and a need to please. Typically, they have few ego strengths that allow them to take satisfaction from any accomplishments. These young women fear that they will be unable to stop ingesting voluminous amounts of junk food. Their eating binges are accompanied by self-deprecating thoughts and severe depression. Suicidal ideation may follow. It is no coincidence that the term "bingeing" has been applied to episodes of severe intoxication with drugs of abuse as well as to bouts of excessive eating. The feature that characterizes these episodes in eating addiction, as in other addictive disorders, is a loss of control and an inability to stop, despite recognizing that the binges are harmful.

Eating binges are often planned, as are "drunks," visits to the casino to gamble, or calling on prostitutes for sex. Planning for eating binges requires extensive and ritualized shopping to obtain the foods to be consumed during the episode. That food is generally high in calories, sweet, and of a texture that allows rapid eating or gulping down with little chewing. Tremendous shame accompanies these binges, and, therefore, eating is carried out in isolation, without the presence of "prying eyes." Often bulimics are unwilling to stop bingeing, even after they have exhausted their "stash" of food, and try to obtain more food. Eventually they are forced to stop eating by abdominal pain, sleepiness, interruption by a friend or family member, or self-induced vomiting.

Self-induced vomiting, in particular, is conducted in secret, because of the taboos and disgust associated with the smell and sight of undigested stomach contents. Vomiting decreases the pain or discomfort of abdominal distention, so that food addicts can either resume eating or, if exhaustion supervenes, stop for rest. Vomiting may serve also to "salve" the guilt associated with consuming tremendous amounts of food in a person obsessed with maintaining a slender body image. In bulimics who describe bingeing as intensely pleasurable, vomiting may represent a form of "atonement" for the sin of experiencing the pleasure of eating. Oscillations between pleasure and intense self-criticism, culminating in depression, is a syndrome common to all the addictive disorders discussed in this book.

Bulimia nervosa is seldom as severely incapacitating as anorexia nervosa, except in those who begin to spend significant proportions of the day in binge eating and self-induced vomiting. Electrolyte imbalance and dehydration are common complications of vomiting episodes. In less severe cases, the usual course of bulimia consists of a repeating cycle, alternating intermittent periods of bingeing, starvation, and normal eating.

SUMMARY AND COMPARISON
OF THE EATING DISORDERS

The diseases of eating addiction can best be understood in terms of the biopsychosocial factors that underlie all addictions. The commonality of these addictions is underscored by the fact that over 25 percent of patients who suffer from eating disorders have also abused alcohol or other drugs. Eating disorders are characterized by compulsive, or out-of-control, behavior that threatens a person's social interactions, health, and even life. On the psychological level, abstaining from food, bingeing on and purging food, or simply bingeing on food creates a feeling of well-being and relief from unpleasant feelings, such as depression, in addicts. On the biological level, bingeing, chronic hunger, or chronic overeating marshals the brain's reward systems, setting up a pattern of biochemical changes that serve to reinforce the addiction. Eating food causes a surge of dopamine, which functions as a reward mechanism, while hunger punishes compulsive eaters with the discomforts of withdrawal. However, in food restrictors, hunger itself is experienced as rewarding through various other neurochemical mechanisms while the feeling of fullness creates discomfort.

Like other addictions, eating disorders are typically long-term problems that are subject to continual relapses and tend to worsen over time. Anorexia nervosa and bulimia nervosa, eating disorders characterized by a preoccupation with body image, usually begin in adolescence or early adult life. Overeating to the point of obesity can begin throughout life, from childhood to middle age, as is apparent from the current epidemic of childhood obesity.

As we have seen, an important difference between eating disorders and other addictions is that, unlike alcohol and drugs, food cannot be given up entirely. This means that people suffering from an eating addiction must *relearn patterns of food consumption in order to manage their intake of food and avoid a relapse*. This is particularly difficult, as can be appreciated by the demonstrated shortcomings of controlled drinking for treatment of alcoholism. In addition, sufferers must begin to understand ways of relieving feelings of guilt, inadequacy, depression, and anxiety that foster the overwhelming preoccupation with overeating or food restriction.

To recapitulate: Anorexia nervosa may be present when a person's body weight is less than 85 percent of the normal weight for age and height. It is characterized by a morbid fear of gaining weight or becoming fat, a distorted body image, and exaggerated emphasis on body image. Weight reduction is achieved by reducing food intake, purging (which includes vomiting, laxatives, and diuretics), and excessive exercise. One difference between bulimia and anorexia is that bulimia may occur in persons with normal body weight. Bulimia is characterized by recurrent episodes of binge eating, often of high-calorie sweets, eaten surreptitiously. Bulimics achieve weight control by utilizing the same methods as anorexics. And, as is the case for anorexics, amphetamines and other stimulants, initially used to control appetite and weight, can become substance abuse problems in themselves.

EPIDEMIOLOGY

In surveys of young women, binge eating was reported by more than 30 percent of respondents. An estimated 25 percent of adolescents have engaged in self-induced purging as a means of weight control following overeating. However, relatively few of these people actually meet clinical diagnostic criteria for full-blown eating disorders. Again, the syndrome is analogous to alcohol and other drug addictions and other behavioral addictions. Many young people try drinking, cigarettes, or smoking pot, or experiment with gambling and sexuality, but relatively few develop substantial clinical difficulties with the use of these substances or the indulgence in these behaviors.

An estimated 1 percent of teenage girls develop anorexia nervosa, while up to 5 percent develop bulimia nervosa. Almost 95 percent of those suffering from eating disorders that involve preoccupation with eating habits and body weight are women. As we said earlier, men, who do suffer in large numbers from other addictions, including obesity, only rarely develop eating disorders that are characterized by preoccupation with food and weight control.

Anorexia typically begins in early adolescence, at the time most girls experience puberty, and bulimia typically begins in the late teens. These disorders rarely develop in middle age. Childhood obesity has become a raging epidemic in the developed world. One reaction to the increased prevalence of eating disorders, in adults or children, is a focus on weight "control." In addition, an emphasis on "sleek is sexy" seems to arise from social factors in our culture, fueled by the powerful entertainment and advertising industries.

Eating disorders are often precipitated by stress that attends a significant loss, such as the death of a relative, or the sudden independence associated with going away to college. About a third of obese people acknowledge having episodes of bingeing in addition to chronic overeating. Interestingly, unlike the disorders of weight restriction, binge eating is not almost exclusively a disorder of women, and more than a third of those with binge eating disorders are men.

Nearly 100 million adults in the United States are overweight or obese, and their numbers continue to grow at an alarming rate. Being overweight or obese substantially raises the risk of complications owing to high blood pressure, high cholesterol or triglycerides, diabetes, heart disease, stroke, gallstones, arthritis, interrupted breathing during sleep (sleep apnea), and various cancers. An estimated 65 percent of U.S. adults over 20 years old are either overweight or obese. Obesity appears to be most prevalent among minorities, especially in African and Hispanic Americans.

Because of the medical complications associated with obesity, its epidemic has significantly affected medical practice in the United States. Obesity increases the incidence of type 2 diabetes mellitus, with its deleterious consequences. Treatment of diabetes accounts for 15 percent of all health care costs in the United States. There is currently a minimum estimate of 150 million cases of diabetes worldwide, and, because of overeating, the prevalence of diabetes is increasing by about 50 percent per decade in developed nations. Therefore, even though most people regard addiction as synonymous with out-of-control drug and alcohol abuse, drugs and alcohol represent only the tip of the iceberg of addiction in our society and throughout the world. Overeating threatens the public health in a way that no other problem has ever done in the past.

NEUROADAPTATION: TOLERANCE, DEPENDENCE, AND WITHDRAWAL?

One of the profound developments in our understanding of drug and alcohol addiction has been recognition of the role of learning in addiction, independent of the pharmacological actions of the drugs of abuse. As our concept of addiction has expanded to include non-drug, or behavioral, addictions, such as eating disorders, the role of learning has also come to the fore. As a person eats more and more, regular overeating can become habitual, to the point that attempting to reduce food intake may elicit pangs of hunger, even though the person is overweight and does not really need to eat for survival. The bodily system that controls appetite progressively takes less account of hunger as the motivation for eating, and satiety is more difficult to attain with a "normal"-size meal.

In general, people who eat a lot do not seem to enjoy all parts of their meal to the same degree. The first bite or two may be highly pleasurable but, thereafter, eating seems motivated less and less by the desire to satisfy hunger. Instead, food is simply gulped down by habit. One of the benefits of this form of eating for the obese person is that eating takes attention away from the unpleasant aspects of life.

Changes in the way food is metabolized occur as more and more food begins to be regularly ingested. For example, when the stomach wall is stretched by habitual overeating, more food is required to fill the stomach cavity sufficiently so that the brain is signaled with the information that satiety has been attained. Rapidly gulping down food may not leave enough time for the brain to direct the person to stop eating because the stomach is full. In addition, the brain circuits that provide the pleasure and reward of eating food, that signal hunger, and that signal that satiety has been attained all become modified by neurochemical alterations in the brain that are associated with learning. These changes at the neuronal level are very similar to the changes that occur with chronic consumption of alcohol or other drugs of abuse or compulsive behaviors, such as gambling.

Food restriction represents the flip side of overeating. The associated hunger, which persists in anorexics even in the most severe forms of this illness, is not pleasurable. However, hunger does provide a certain satisfaction, or even "pleasure," consequential to exercising control over one's bodily urges. This pleasure may be particularly rewarding when one's life feels out of control because of the stresses of adolescence and early adulthood. When the potential reward value of hunger is compounded with the satisfaction of being able to master hunger and thereby accommodate society's high standard of beauty—perhaps even to surpass them if one tries "extra hard"—it becomes understandable why a young woman may continue to starve herself to emaciation.

Once again, the reward value of starvation and the perception of favorable changes in one's body shape and weight, together with a distortion of what is deemed to be the "ideal" body, facilitate learning the behaviors that are associated with food restriction, bingeing, and purging. These learned behaviors eventually produce changes in the reward circuits of the brain that are mediated by reinforcement, changes that are analogous to the brain alterations that occur in other addictive disorders.

Thus, people who binge, purge, or simply don't eat much food get a reward from the dopamine system. Tolerance and dependence in eating disorders can be understood in terms of the modifications of neural circuits that support the drive of hunger and the recognition of satiety when hunger is satisfied. The difficulties that attend the attempt to stop engaging in these pathological eating patterns is analogous to the withdrawal experienced as a result of abstinence from drugs of abuse. Clearly, there is no "pharmacological" component of withdrawal from eating addiction, because there is no drug to remove from the central nervous system. Consequently, there is no acute withdrawal syndrome, characterized by symptoms such as seizures or other physiological changes that signal evacuation of receptors occupied by the drug in question at its site of action in the brain. Nevertheless, the craving and the intense urge to engage in the learned behavior is very similar to the protracted withdrawal syndrome observed in alcohol and drug addiction. Finally, just as in alcohol and drug addiction, these elements of protracted withdrawal may result in a relapse to eating disorders. And just as in the treatment of alcohol and drug addiction, treatment of food addiction must involve extinction of cue-elicited stimuli that could precipitate a relapse to food restriction, bingeing, purging, or chronic overeating. This requirement for treatment provides the foundation for the cognitive, behavioral, and self-help approaches that must be used by food addicts if they want to stay healthy over the course of their lives.

PART V

Recovery as an Ongoing Process: Control Is Never Complete

CHAPTER 17

Criteria for Treatment Success

THERE IS NO single, objective standard for treatment success. A traditional model defines success as sustained abstinence from using an addictive drug or engaging in addictive behavior. Sustained remission is frequently considered to be abstinence lasting for more than one year. But no exact formula can substitute for clinical judgment in determining when patients have achieved what should be regarded as sufficient stability in abstinence that allows them to move successfully into aftercare. This is where the importance of having a detailed treatment plan in place becomes paramount. Only by assessing whether the goals of the treatment plan have been met can the doctor or therapist recommend advancing to aftercare treatment.

Costly and time-consuming treatment for addiction cannot continue indefinitely. In fact, the goal of treatment is to enable formerly addicted people to succeed in overcoming their problem with addiction and to reenter the "real world" of work and the normal enjoyments of life. One of the critical decisions for addiction treatment providers is at what point regular therapy or treatment can become less frequent and when it can be discontinued completely. The term "aftercare" is used to refer to the time when patients take charge of their own lives, putting into action the recovery skills they have learned in intensive treatment (either inpatient or outpatient) while still maintaining the safety net of access to physicians, therapists, and support groups, when and if their help becomes necessary.

This safety net and continuing, long-term pharmacopsychosocial aftercare, including medical care, psychotherapy, and social support, is at least as important to long-term success as the initial treatment program itself. Instead of abruptly discontinuing treatment sessions, gradual tapering off of the frequency of these sessions is more effective in enabling patients to make a successful transition to an independent life. Aftercare sessions generally occur about once a week for an hour or so. They may continue for six months or longer.

Aftercare is vital to the continuing struggle to stay drug free, when patients are no longer sheltered from the day-to-day challenges of life, as they had been in a relatively sheltered treatment program. Those with most of the elements of their lives intact do better than those who have lost a great deal as a consequence of their addiction. In this respect, the problems associated with addiction are no different from other medical illnesses. Chronic illnesses are never cured—you learn to overcome them and make the most of life. Recovering from chronic illnesses, including addiction, is not a fix like taking out a gallbladder. This similarity is an added justification for regarding addiction in all its forms as bona fide diseases. The essence of recovery is recognizing that you cannot be "in control." But you can have a better life in recovery from your addiction. This is the hard fact that the treatment providers must convey to all recovering addicts.

CHAPTER 18

Entering a New Life

RETURN TO WORK and to the family home can be challenging and stressful, because patients have changed emotionally during treatment. Even those closest to recovering patients may not understand the magnitude of this change and what it may mean for their life together. Despite this challenge, family and friends are valuable allies during the extended recovery period. Patients who have nothing to which to return after treatment have less incentive to stay sober. Therefore, patients without family or other outside help may benefit from structured living situations, such as halfway houses, which can provide support, a sense of belonging, and a way to connect with others. All these things are of fundamental importance to recovery. In addition, halfway houses may be preferable for individuals whose families are present but are significantly dysfunctional. Nothing is worse for an addict than returning to the family home that is a magnet for relatives who are still actively using drugs or who are in turmoil and whose words and actions add to the distress that causes the addict to want to escape to a world of addiction.

One of the major misconceptions of addiction treatment and recovery is that it is essential to sustain major losses by reaching "rock bottom" before addicted people can be motivated to change their lives. This erroneous view holds that until addicts lose everything, they will not overcome their tendency to deny that they have a problem and the desire to eliminate drugs or addictive behaviors from their lives will never be of paramount importance. Such an idea is patently false, because the journey back is easier to make when there is something within sight to regain. Addicts who have sustained major losses have the most difficult journey to recovery, a journey they can make only if they acquire some hope of success. Therefore, we emphasize the importance of chaperoning patients through the stages of wanting to enter recovery *before* they lose their life supports. Ultimately, patients have the best chance for a successful recovery if they enter treatment and aftercare while they still have a family who cares, a job to go to, and a bank account that is not depleted.

DENIAL AND "SLIPS"

Denial is a recurring problem throughout the entire course of the disease of addiction, from the time of active addiction, through the time patients enter treatment. Denial is the reason that addicted people have such difficulty in accepting treatment. It is also the basis for relapse in most individuals, even those who have been stellar participants in treatment and in support programs thereafter. After several months of sobriety, it is not unusual for the urge to use drugs or go back to addictive behaviors to reassert itself again. The rationale in the recovering addict's mind is: "I am doing so well that one drink can't hurt," "Betting on the game in the office pool won't do any harm," or "Partying with the my old girlfriend only once won't be a problem." The urge to return to the use of drugs or addictive behaviors arises in a wide variety of contexts, including feelings that arise when patients are in the company of certain people or reenter certain environments, in recurrent dreams, and in challenges from friends who urge recovering individuals to "loosen up and join the party." Even the renewal of sexual contact with previous intimate partners can be a potent trigger.

In recovery vernacular, a return to drug use or addictive behaviors during long-term care is called a "slip." Most therapists and leaders of self-help groups recognize, however, that slips can be part of getting well, if they ultimately serve to strengthen patients' resolve to stay in recovery. It is the length and intensity of the slip that can cause concern.

It is essential not to respond to these slips in punitive terms. Those helping recovering addicts must instead ensure that the slip does not turn into out-of-control behavior, or a true relapse, by encouraging patients to return to a therapeutic situation or relationship, such as a short-term hospital stay, renewed contact with the sponsor, or renewing participation in an outpatient program. One reason it can be difficult to halt a slip is that patients have a strong impulse to keep slips secret.

They think, "Maybe no one will find out and my recovery will continue." This may be true, but only until the next slip; then these slips will tend to recur, separated by shorter intervals of "clean" time. Eventually the addicts lose awareness that they are trying to keep drug use or behavioral addiction secret. That is what marks a full-blown relapse. Obviously, the more serious a patient's addiction was to begin with, the greater the risk that slips will progress into relapses.

The best way to prevent slips is to understand that the disease of addiction is always hibernating, as it were, and remains part of a person's life. Therefore, all recovering addicts must maintain a strategy for managing their illness. In this respect, the disease of addiction is no different from most other chronic diseases, such as diabetes, hypertension, depression, and heart disease. The need to cope with an illness throughout one's life, while still living a fulfilling life, is certainly not confined to addiction. It makes sense for patients to exercise their recovery skills as regularly as they exercise their cardiovascular system. And just as it is sometimes easier to go running if you have others who jog with you, the communal sense of participating in self-help groups can be invaluable in sustaining the remission that addicts worked so hard to achieve.

As soon as addicts delude themselves into thinking that a "cure" is possible, trouble begins. Addicts must strive to live a full and balanced life while continuing to be aware of the fact that if they deviate from doing so, a slip is probably not far behind. In fact, believing that it is possible to leave something as all-encompassing as an addictive disorder completely behind is a kind of magical thinking. The goal is rather to understand the complexity of addiction and to develop the strength to cope with the unavoidable tendency to relapse.

CONTINUING RELATIONSHIP WITH PHYSICIAN OR THERAPIST

It makes sense for patients to mobilize all possible resources to assist in long-term recovery. One of the most important of these resources, we firmly believe, is an enduring relationship with a physician or a therapist. As with all illnesses, this contact with a treatment professional should be more frequent early on, but it needs to be continued through good times and bad. Unfortunately, there are simply not enough psychiatrists specializing in addiction to provide care for all recovering addicts.

Today, most of the leading departments of psychiatry in this country have training programs in addiction psychiatry that are approved by the Accreditation Council for Graduate Medical Education. Graduates of these programs are eligible to take the examinations of the American

Board of Psychiatry and Neurology Board to become certified in the subspecialty of addiction psychiatry. However, at this time, there are still relatively few of these psychiatrists. For this reason, medical schools attempt to provide all medical school graduates and those who are psychiatry specialists with at least some expertise in management of addictive disorders. Obviously, however, psychiatrists who are highly trained in the treatment of addiction will generally provide better care than can non-specialists or primary care providers who lack this training.

SHOULD RECOVERING ADDICTS
BECOME TREATMENT PROFESSIONALS?

As we have pointed out, we are far from the point in addiction treatment at which recovering addicts can all have access to such specialists. Many psychiatrists without formal training in addiction avoid treating these patients or continue to have false confidence that they can deliver excellent care for addictive disorders. Moreover, there are those other medical practitioners who believe they have gained sufficient expertise in addiction treatment because they have gone through recovery themselves. It must be emphasized that, although having experienced a recovery can increase a practitioner's empathy for and understanding of patients, it in no way takes the place of formal academic training. When asked about the relative merits of recovering versus non-recovering caregivers, we often point out that a physician does not have to have had cancer to become an oncologist, nor does a physician necessarily become a trained oncologist because he or she has had cancer. The same thing holds true for addiction treatment. However, a recovering physician who has attained specialization in addiction psychiatry can be very helpful, indeed, to his patients due to his unique combination of knowledge and experience.

Another reason why recovering physicians believe they can treat recovering addicts without adequate formal training may be their continuing misunderstanding that there is nothing psychiatrically wrong with addicts. We have seen, however, that addiction is a serious psychiatric disease. As such, it requires the same specialized care as any other serious disease.

The desire for patients to seek out those physicians who are in recovery themselves to provide treatment may derive from a feeling of inferiority. These patients think, "Only someone who has suffered from the same illness as I would make an effort to try to help a hopeless case as me!" Also, patients may feel they can trust recovering physicians more than other physicians, asking "Doctor, if you're not in recovery yourself, how can you really understand what I am going through?"

Most questions about the best direction for managing long-term recovery can be readily answered once we acknowledge that addiction is multifaceted and requires care in the pharmacopsychosocial domains and that this care should continue even when all of the recovering addicts' problems seem far behind them. This care should be under the watchful supervision of a practitioner with appropriate training and experience who understands the importance of treatment with the recovering patient and his social support system.

CHAPTER 19

Managing Long-Term Treatment

RECOVERY REQUIRES MAINTAINING HEALTH

Patients must continue to work at maintaining their health now that they are in recovery from their addiction(s). Furthermore, like anyone else, they may require medical care from time to time. The availability of quality general medical care, in addition to the ongoing relationship with members of the safety net specifically involved in addiction after-care, should be viewed as a vital part of recovery because the trigger for relapse is often the stress associated with a newly diagnosed illness or the worsening of an existing medical condition. Those in recovery are no different from other people in this regard. They must have a primary care physician who helps monitor their health and deals with the vaccinations, annual checkups, colds, and aches and pains that are part of a healthy life, as well as coping with more severe illnesses, should they occur.

Neglecting general health (not eating an appropriate diet and not getting regular exercise) was symptomatic of patients' lifestyles during active addiction and must be rectified during recovery. Typical examples of this self-neglect include the individual whose blood pressure is too high, whose muscles are flabby, and who has low exercise tolerance. Many recovering addicts are overweight due to poor diet or underweight because of malnutrition and have painful cavities because they neglected dental hygiene. Regular examinations, such as blood tests, cardiograms, Pap tests, and colonoscopy, often have been overlooked for a considerable time. Recovering addicts should have a doctor whom they can call on to help catch up on these neglected health maintenance activities. In addition, they need to be able to consult a doctor if, for example, they develop pains after a heavy meal that do not quiet down after taking a few over-the-counter digestive tablets—someone to examine and reassure them that they have not had a heart attack and that they will be all right without further medical testing. They also need a doctor who knows them well, will visit them in the hospital if admission is required for a serious medical emergency, and can manage their care after being discharged by the specialist. However, if primary care providers are to do all that is expected of them, they must know, and may need to be reminded, that these patients have an addiction and are in recovery.

HONESTY WITH THE PRIMARY CARE DOCTOR HELPS BOTH PATIENT AND DOCTOR

Failing to give the physician a *complete* medical history is irresponsible—unfair to the doctor but, more important, detrimental to the patient. Telling the doctor about the patient's addictions and associated psychiatric illnesses is part of giving a medical history, just like reporting a previous heart attack or a thyroid condition. People who are struggling with recovery from addiction may rationalize incomplete disclosure in various ways. Some common examples are "I won't get adequate treatment for pain if I hurt myself or have to have surgery." "I don't want my doctor to treat me differently from a regular patient." "He won't like me if he knows." "He won't understand what I am going through." "He'll think this is not a *real* problem that he can help me with and will abandon me." "I understand why I have to tell my therapist, but not my *medical* doctor—I don't want to appear weak in *his* eyes." "I don't want people outside of AA to know."

However, an accurate and complete medical history helps doctors to provide patients with high-quality healthcare. Knowing that a patient is in recovery from an addiction will alert the doctors to consider potential complications of these disorders that they might not think of normally, such as depression, liver disease, and sexually transmitted diseases. If doctors know that a patient is in recovery, they will think twice about prescribing a medicine that could possibly lead to a relapse. For example, cold medicines, which pose no particular danger to the average person, have been associated with relapse to active addiction in some people who are in recovery. Clearly, informed doctors will suggest that such patients avoid these over-the-counter medicines. They may also be able to recommend a cough syrup without alcohol or codeine, if they know a patient is in recovery. Doctors will approach complaints of aches and pains or difficulty sleeping in a way that will not put the patient at risk for relapsing.

THE PRIMARY CARE DOCTOR: PARTNER IN RECOVERY AND POINT MAN OF THE RECOVERY NET

It is ultimately the responsibility of *patients* to find a doctor who understands what it means to be in recovery from addiction, one whom the patient will entrust with his complete medical history and care. The patient may ask, "How do I know that my doctor is the right one for me?" Reliable physicians take the time and effort to understand patients' problems. Such doctors will be amenable to open discussion about the addiction and will use information from patients' confidential medical and psychiatric history to help. While there are those who would argue that doctors should be in recovery themselves in order to know enough about addiction to help, an equally compelling argument can be made on the contrary. For example, a recovering doctor may give advice that worked for him in his recovery without recognizing that the patient is a different person and may not need the same things from life as he does. Doctors should have experience treating patients with various forms of addiction, or else they must have the skill to recognize those aspects of the disease they do not understand. Whether doctors are in recovery themselves is really of secondary importance. Because addictions are so prevalent, any good physician will have seen plenty of patients who are suffering from addictions. Ultimately, nothing is more important than that doctors be sufficiently enlightened that they will consult with knowledgeable colleagues on how best to help a recovering addict, if needed.

It must be emphasized that one doctor will not be able to provide everything patients need to be successful in recovery. Primary medical care *and* pharmacopsychosocial treatment take a great deal of time and attention. An important part of the recovery journey is choosing the right team to become the recovery net. This is a team whose members can communicate with recovering addicts and with each other and thereby assist patients in utilizing the multiple layers of care that complex disorders like addictions require. It is especially important that the team selected stays a team rather than providing patients with discrepant and conflicting information. For example, the Alcoholics Anonymous home group should not tell patients not to take an antidepressant ("You need to be drug free to attain recovery!") or no longer welcome patients who take antidepressants ("You are not working your program."). If the psychiatrist has made a diagnosis of depression that he thinks would benefit from medication, the patient should be encouraged to take it. Similarly, the primary care doctor should not provide the patient with Valium for "nerves" or for "sleep" if a referral to a psychotherapist may be more appropriate to deal with recurring problems, such as marital issues or job stresses, which may be leading to anxiety and potentially to a relapse. Finally, the psychotherapist should be able to recognize when depression worsens to a degree that a patient may need his psychiatric medications reappraised and therefore to return to his psychiatrist. The psychotherapist needs to have the skill to make this referral, instead of simply telling the patient, "You are not doing your part in getting better!"

Good doctors can be trusted to maintain confidentiality about a medical history and should be relied on to manage medical problems as they arise. In addition, the physician to whom recovering addicts entrust their medical care will not view addiction as anything other than an illness that needs to be managed in the most appropriate manner and in the context of the rest of the patients' lives. A good doctor views a recovering addict not as simply an "addict" or an "alcoholic" but as a *person* who is struggling to recover from a disease called addiction.

If recovering addicts talk with others who are farther along on the road to recovery than they are, they may get some helpful advice about which physicians in the community are the best ones to see. If they listen carefully at self-help meetings, they also may hear about doctors who are potentially dangerous to addicts in recovery.

BEWARE OF THE QUICKLY DRAWN PEN AND THE EVER-READY PRESCRIPTION PAD

As noted, not all physicians have adequate training and experience with addictions, nor are they inclined to deal openly with patients with these disorders. Unfortunately, there are still many doctors who are quick to put pen to prescription pad in response to problems that should be managed with discussion and understanding. There are also doctors who would rather not know that a patient has an addiction, because of their own previous unpleasant experiences with addiction within their family or with other patients. Such doctors may provide ephemeral solutions with medications, drugs that are potentially harmful to those in recovery from addiction. It may be hard for doctors to come right out and tell a patient that a lasting resolution of what is ailing him cannot be achieved with "medicines" alone. Ultimately, it is the patient's responsibility to recognize what is happening when the pen and prescription pad come out too quickly and not go along with it. If recovering addicts do not question a prescription that they don't think will help their problem, they risk a relapse.

DENIAL IS INCOMPATIBLE WITH RECOVERY— HEALING REQUIRES ACCEPTANCE OF ADDICTION(S)

When recovering addicts do not provide doctors with information about their addiction(s), either they do not fully accept the fact that they have a significant illness, or they falsely believe that addiction somehow does not count as a "real" disease but rather is some shortcoming in their personalities. These attitudes are no different from denial, the defense mechanism most addicts use to protect their self-esteem, which we discussed in Chapter 18. Denial makes it difficult for recovering addicts to recognize and admit that they have a serious problem with addiction in the first place. It is also the major focus of the intervention convened by friends and family who cared about the addicts and convinced them to enter a treatment program. Addicts may be surprised to find that their struggle with denial is not over. Even though they have completed the requirements of a formal treatment program, they are not yet at the end of their journey toward recovery. Because they will still need the support of their entire recovery net, they must be forthright with each member of the team and not hide the fact that they may need assistance to continue on the path to recovery. If recovering addicts do not want denial to get in the way of continued healing, they will most likely have to continue dealing with it in psychotherapy, as discussed later.

RESPONSIBLE RECOVERY— THE BLAME GAME HELPS NO ONE

One of the major tenets of this book is that recovering addicts must take responsibility for their recovery. But they must do so without blaming themselves for having an illness. Nor should they blame a doctor, a spouse, a father, or others for their disease and life situation. Like all adults, addicts make the best decisions they can with the information available to them. If information is not available or understandable, adults seek advice to make their decisions. But mature adults do not rely on others to make their decisions for them and then blame these people if the results do not turn out as they had hoped.

Blame for unexpected outcomes is of particular concern when medications are prescribed for addicts. These include pain medications of the opioid class; stimulants; anxiolytic and sleep medications of the benzodiazepine, barbiturate, and related classes; cough syrups that contain alcohol or opioids; and older classes of antihistamines and decongestants. Some blood pressure or heart medications can worsen depression, and steroids used as anti-inflammatory agents often can cause mood swings, which may interfere with judgment. Fortunately, many of these medications now have safer, newer alternatives, which knowledgeable physicians can prescribe as needed.

Informed patients should know which medications may potentially be harmful, so that they can have an open and frank discussion with their doctor. Patients should remind the doctor again that they are addicts and cannot take medications that are "mood altering" or potentially addictive. A good doctor will appreciate this reminder and try another approach that will do no harm. If a doctor does not know what to do, he should tell the patient and offer a referral for consultation with someone who does know. Finally, almost any medication can have unpredictable side effects on the central nervous system. The doctor is responsible for discussing the most common side effects but should counsel addicts that they might have a more unusual response. Patients must inform the doctor of any side effects that occur, because they may also cause an altered mental state that could be a precursor to relapse. If both doctor and recovering addict are careful with any new medication that is prescribed, disappointment or harmful consequences are less likely.

DRUGS ARE NOT DANGEROUS—PEOPLE WHO TAKE DRUGS CAN MAKE THEM DANGEROUS

In and of itself, a medicine is not harmful. The potential for harm stems from the *process* of prescribing or taking a medication. Prescription of any medication may be justified under appropriate circumstances, even to a person who is addicted to this agent or a related drug. Consider the examples of treating withdrawal from alcohol with Valium or treating withdrawal from Valium with phenobarbital—both the benzodiazepine class of drugs, like Valium, and barbiturates, like phenobarbital, possess significant abuse liability. For this reason, most doctors would not recommend these medications for recovering addicts unless needed for treatment of withdrawal; subsequently, a concerted effort should be made to stop these medications when the acute withdrawal syndrome has subsided.

Medications with abuse liability should be used only with caution or avoided in individuals who are recovering from addiction(s). It must be noted that the finest, safest, and most appropriately prescribed medication can become a "drug of abuse" if patients do not take it as prescribed or if they take it whenever they wish and use it for other than therapeutic effects.

The recovering addict may rightly ask, "Why would I become addicted to medicines like Valium, Xanax, or Klonopin, which really help me feel better, if the doctor prescribes it to me?" There is very little scientific evidence that these benzodiazepine drugs actually improve any of the disturbing symptoms associated with addiction for which they are regularly prescribed—sleeplessness, panic or anxiety, racing thoughts, or depression—for more than a week or two. Most specialists do not recommend long-term use of medications like Valium for that reason, and especially not in patients who have alcohol or drug addictions. Some specialists in addiction psychiatry would even think twice about prescribing benzodiazepines to their patients who have a significant family (genetic) history of alcohol or drug addiction. It is not clearly established whether these recommendations to avoid benzodiazepines should apply equally to those with behavioral addictions. However, since drug and behavioral addictions co-occur so commonly (both in individuals and in their families) and overlapping brain mechanisms seem to be involved, it seems prudent to apply similar guidelines for behavioral addictions as those used for alcohol or drug dependence.

Importantly, benzodiazepine medications have never been formally evaluated in scientific studies in patients who suffer from drug or behavioral addictions. They have only been used in the treatment of alcohol withdrawal. Pharmacologically, benzodiazepines potentiate the natural inhibitory gamma-amino butyric acid (GABA) neurotransmitter circuits of the brain in a manner that is not much different from the way alcohol does. Therefore, patients should not fool themselves by saying "My doctor prescribed me the Valium; I don't abuse it." They should be made to understand that, if they take Valium, they are actually taking "alcohol in tablets," and should do so only for a very short time.

Another reasonable question the recovering addict may ask is: "What is the difference between a drug of abuse and a medicine?" If an individual who is addicted to heroin has shattered his leg in an automobile accident, intravenous morphine in very large doses, given by the orthopedic surgeon, is a necessary and safe "medicine." It is a harmful misconception to believe otherwise, as many laymen do. Unfortunately, even some doctors may have unjustified concerns about "addiction liability" when giving opioids to their addicted patients under such conditions; and if they do prescribe opioids, they may administer inadequate doses to treat the pain. People who suffer from addictions need to have their pain controlled, like everyone else, when they are injured or undergoing surgery. In fact, due to the tolerance they have acquired during chronic abuse, they may require even higher doses for pain control than do people who have no tolerance to opioids. However, morphine quickly becomes a drug of abuse when it is no longer being administered for the leg fracture. It is good medical practice for doctors to negotiate with patients the discontinuation of opioid treatment as soon as the pain associated with their injury is normally expected to have resolved. If patients are allowed to determine when they no longer need the opiates for *bona fide* pain control, they are more likely to take these drugs whenever they feel like it.

In a similar vein, most people use laxatives as suggested by their physician for genuine constipation. Laxatives can be very effective and helpful to most people who use them correctly. However, laxatives can become deadly in the hands of patients with anorexia nervosa, who may develop serious electrolyte imbalances and even cardiac arrest by overusing laxatives to help them lose weight. Note also that patients can obtain laxatives over the counter without prescription, just as they can get cough syrup, antihistamines, antinausea medications, and certain sleeping potions. These, too, can be harmful if used in excess, or even addictive. Moreover, what is perhaps less appreciated is that even over-the-counter medications could contribute to a relapse from the primary drug of abuse because of the mood-altering effects they may create in susceptible people.

Therefore, it is not "a prescription" that differentiates a drug of abuse from a medicine. If a patient does inform the doctor about his disease and his aspirations for recovery, and the doctor starts misprescribing because the patient claims he needs a certain drug: Whose fault is that? Savvy addicts can usually find what they feel they need by visiting as many doctors as it takes. There are also many clinical situations in which it is relatively easy to "overwhelm" an inexperienced and trusting (some might say naïve) physician. Frequently used examples in the emergency room in the wee hours of the morning include pain ("a kidney stone"), anxiety ("a panic attack"), or geographic necessity ("I'm from out of town, Doc, and I have run out of [lost, left at home, had stolen . . .] medicine that my family doctor told me not to stop without his approval."). Then, taking the medicine "as prescribed" becomes a farce.

Perhaps the most difficult situation for both patient and doctor is the management of chronic pain with opioids. As noted, there is very little controversy about the appropriate way to manage acute severe pain in anyone: Use as high a dose of morphine as it takes to make the patient comfortable. However, whether to use opioids for treatment of chronic pain to maintain a patient's functioning at an "acceptable" level presents a major conundrum, particularly in the recovering individual. Good doctors prefer to prescribe milder analgesics, such as aspirin or nonsteroidal analgesics, physical therapy, massage, weight loss, and stretching exercises, instead of highly addictive opioid medications. Examples of chronic conditions that often progress to treatment with opioids include chronic back pain from a ruptured disc, fibromyalgia, headaches, arthritis, pain from cancer that has been effectively treated, and pain for which the doctor cannot identify an actual cause, among many others. Certainly there are documented cases of return to a normal level of functioning in patients who suffer from these otherwise incapacitating conditions. Success most often occurs in well-monitored patients who work in collaboration with their doctors and combine other complementary treatment recommendations.

Unfortunately, far too many patients who are treated for chronic pain with opioids require increasingly higher doses, and even then the pain relief is not satisfactory. The difficulty, of course, is that the patient is the one who feels the pain—the doctor only knows about the severity of the pain by the patient's report. As the doses of opioids rise, the prescribing doctor rightfully becomes concerned about whether there is an addiction problem, not just chronic pain. When the doctor asks for consultation from an addiction psychiatrist, the patient claims to be taking the medications "only as prescribed by my doctor." Only with careful inquiry does it become clear that the patient's quality of life on the high dose of opioids is not what was hoped for, and the pain is less fully alleviated by the medication than desired. In many cases, as the dose of opioids increased, the patient started to take extra doses of medication for breakthrough pain during periods between doses when the pain became excruciating. Moreover, the patient may also be nodding out and no longer able to function normally. Under such circumstances, the "medication" has become a "drug." At this point, a patient often recognizes that he wants to be drug free. He is willing to try other ways of controlling his pain and to undergo detoxification. Retrospectively, the patient will admit that he had been taking the opioids for some time in an addictive manner without telling the doctor. Of course, once the doctor had started on this slippery slope of opioid prescription for chronic pain, he was unfortunately committed to continue increasing the dosage if the patient requested it.

Obviously, just because recovering addicts have an "excuse" to use them ("It is a prescribed medicine!"), any drugs obtained through lying to the doctor or withholding information will certainly not help them in the long run. Again, it is the responsibility of patients to enlighten, not manipulate, the doctor. Unfortunately, in the real world, all doctors must be alert to the possibility that they might be the target of manipulation.

MUTUAL TRUST, RESPECT, AND OPEN COMMUNICATION IN THE PHYSICIAN–PATIENT RELATIONSHIP

Prescribing any medicine, especially one that is potentially addictive (for which there is on occasion a bona fide need), to a person who is in recovery must only be done in a stable physician–patient relationship in which there is mutual trust, respect, and open communication. The primary care doctor, or a specialist with whom this doctor is in contact, should prescribe all medications that the recovering addict needs to take. Moreover, recovering addicts should be counseled to inform all doctors what other doctors are prescribing and what medications they are taking over the counter. Patients should be encouraged to use the same pharmacy, where the pharmacist knows their illnesses and can provide educational material about the risks associated with any medications prescribed. Patients who are familiar with a particular pharmacist will be more comfortable discussing concerns related to any addictive potential associated with medications. When patients need to travel, it may be possible to have prescriptions filled by another pharmacy in the same chain of pharmacies. These chain pharmacies have access to a common computer database so that the pharmacist can better advise patients if there are potential problems with dangerous interactions between a new medication and others they are taking. In fact, one of the advantages of having such health databases, especially the one attached to patients' medical insurance (confidentiality issues aside), is the ability to minimize the kind of misprescribing associated with "doctor shopping." However, the option of not using insurance or using an alias still remains in a free country. Freedom without responsibility is a two-edged sword, particularly for individuals with addictions!

As noted, no medications are *absolutely* contraindicated in addiction. In fact, there are situations when the use of some medications cannot be avoided. The important point is that all medications need to be administered with sufficient knowledge and *supervision* from an experienced doctor. For example, after abdominal surgery, it would be barbaric not to provide adequate opioid treatment for pain. However, the number of patients who relapse to active addiction after surgeries or accidents when they were given prescriptions for opioids *without adequate follow-up*, or when they took inappropriate over-the-counter medications, is testimony to how careful recovering addicts need to be. By responsibly prescribing addictive pain medications, physicians can prevent such a relapse, but only if patients collaborate. Patients must also know how these medications, as well as those that might be obtained over the counter, may ultimately harm them.

The good primary care physician should monitor prescriptions proactively and be meticulous in what medicines are prescribed, because of recovering addicts' risk for relapse. This policy will ensure doctors do not renew a pain pill prescription, whether provided by the primary care doctor or a specialist, for an indefinite period of time over the phone, without seeing patients in person and evaluating their clinical situation. However, the busier doctors become in their practice, the easier it is for them to overlook providing this intensive supervision—after all, doctors are not supposed to be police officers. Good family doctors will challenge recovering addicts once they recognize that patients may be a little too liberal with continuing "pain control" or "sleep medications" when postsurgical pain or sleeplessness should be resolving. Instead of continuing the potentially dangerous medicine(s), doctors can offer nonaddictive pain control so patients can get over the rough spot. Such physicians will encourage patients to reconnect with their recovery program with added vigor, both before and after the surgery. They may also refer a recovering addict to an addiction psychiatrist for detoxification if a patient is having undue difficulty stopping the pain or sleep pills when they should no longer be needed. All of these approaches are preferable to the alternative: relapse.

The currency of such conscientious oversight is the enduring physician–patient relationship, which is built on mutual trust and open communication and requires time to nurture. It is important, therefore, for recovering addicts to get started working with a primary care physician early in aftercare. Patients should *not* postpone finding a doctor until something serious happens. Sometimes, patients may already have a doctor whom they really like, but to whom they are reluctant to return, because they do not want to tell the doctor about their addiction. After all, these patients have already been dishonest with the doctor. Perhaps this was a doctor whom the patients visited for one problem or another when they were actively addicted and seeking prescriptions. In fact, this doctor may previously have provided pain or anxiety pills, based on false information the patients provided. Returning to this doctor may be embarrassing, and patients may have the impulse to avoid this situation. However, interestingly enough, perhaps one of the most therapeutic experiences recovering addicts can have, after being discharged from the treatment program, is to meet with a doctor they respect and like. Then patients can tell the doctor what happened and why they were hospitalized. Both the doctor and recovering addicts will learn from the experience; in particular, patients will be able to judge by the doctor's response whether he is the sort of physician they can work with in the future. The best intentions for recovery can be sabotaged by lack of communication with the doctor and going elsewhere instead of answering questions that may be uncomfortable. An important step to maintain recovery is for recovering addicts to have a solid relationship with a doctor.

RECOVERY IS MORE THAN ABSTINENCE

Healing addiction goes far beyond simply ceasing to engage in an addiction, although that is a vital first step. Actually, a lot of the people who have not been drinking for years are still not in recovery, according to the wisdom of Alcoholics Anonymous. (Remember that we use AA as our example because its traditions are so well established. The same arguments apply to the other peer, mutual support fellowships and their particular drug or behavioral addiction.) Some of these people are considered to be in a dry drunk. Through supreme self-control ("white-knuckling it"), they have managed to stop drinking, but they have not succeeded in overcoming their alcoholism or in managing the consequences of their drinking. For these people, drinking is the symptom of more deep-seated problems that need to be addressed for proper healing to occur. According to the teachings of AA, such nondrinking alcoholics are always very close to relapse and never feel comfortable in their sobriety.

Abstinent individuals need to attain "serenity and spirituality," which are the prerequisites to recovery, by truly embracing the 12 steps and the traditions of Alcoholics Anonymous. This may sound more like religious dogma or even hocus pocus than a scientifically defensible clinical treatment for addiction. However, innumerable members of AA insist that the teachings of the fellowship are a prescription for living that leads reliably to recovery. It is important to recognize that membership in AA is highly inclusive: Wanting to stop drinking is the sole criterion for acceptance into group meetings. AA is not based on any religious precepts; it is open to all people of all religious persuasions, even to atheists or agnostics. Moreover, the teachings of AA are compatible with many diverse cultures found throughout the world, and they can also be adapted to diverse philosophical leanings.

The essential principle of AA is that people are intrinsically good and trusting. Those who are not "good people" have been hurt in their formative years by family members or friends who should have known better or were not well themselves. Feeling good about yourself, trusting others, and understanding that the universe is *not* malevolent is one of the keys to living a satisfying life. Recovering addicts cannot accomplish this by changing others, making them as the addicts wish them to be, no matter how important the people may seem. Instead, patients must focus on changing *themselves*. They must acknowledge to themselves how they wish to live their lives differently. Moreover, because the control we often feel we have over all aspects of our life and environment is illusory at best, it is unnecessary to feel recriminations, to blame oneself, for everything that has gone wrong previously. If recovering addicts can be encouraged to take responsibility for living their lives in a more constructive way, recovery will take care of itself, in due course. Recovering addicts must also be taught to forgive those who have hurt them, because holding grudges wastes a great deal of energy that could be productively used in recovery.

To many people, these ideas may seem naïve and even childish, unrealistic in the modern world so filled with crime and violence, and difficult to accept. Nevertheless, the optimism expressed by these precepts certainly makes life more satisfying and surroundings less hostile. Most important, being more tolerant of others' shortcomings allows recovering addicts to be more accepting of themselves and of their addiction and, therefore, more amenable to recovery. Understanding (overcoming denial) and moving beyond the addiction may be difficult, but it is possible. The alternative is for patients to become victims or to eventually become more like those who have hurt them. Both of these conditions are quite incompatible with recovery.

Some recovering addicts may be uncomfortable with the religious overtones implied by the words "serenity" and "spirituality." These people are turning their backs on the considerable benefits of a life of recovery from addiction merely because they do not like the religious connotations of the 12 steps. Perhaps their experience in childhood with religion was overly punitive; perhaps they were raised to view religion as a crutch for those who did not know better. Patients must be helped to overcome the idea that the reason they became so ill was because they were "weak." This erroneous idea leads addicts to the belief that, if they had enough "willpower," they could overcome their addiction. When patients condemn themselves in this way, they reinforce self-loathing, which all too often begins a downward spiral away from healing and recovery.

The addiction psychiatrist should discuss such issues with patients who are struggling with the devastating complications of addiction and the notion of relinquishing themselves to a "higher power." The doctor should ask if they would feel "weak" if they had diabetes, pneumonia, heart disease, or some other similar life-threatening illness. "Certainly not," they invariably reply. "Those illnesses would be beyond my control." The lesson for recovering addicts is that they should not feel that they have contracted an addiction because of some moral shortcoming. The doctor might want to indicate to these patients that he is a physician, not a religious leader who advocates conversion. The goal is to help recovering addicts find a way of living that is fulfilling, one that they will find preferable to the life they lived while buried within the confines of addiction. The doctor should stress that most patients do not find doing this easy. He should explain that patients should not be frightened away from the 12 steps by any preconceived skepticism about the value of religion or of the obligation to worship. They should view the 12 steps as a way to feel better about themselves, not a religious construct designed to limit their self-determination. If they can make this readily available recovery network work for them, they should not be skittish about becoming part of the process of recovery it embodies. The physician can educate patients about how the fellowship should be conceptualized as distinct from religion and how it can provide the acceptance they may have been unable to find previously or the kind of support a family should have provided during their formative years but did not.

The concept of "serenity" can be thought of as a level of comfort recovering addicts feel inside themselves and about their role in the world beyond. It can also be conceptualized as accepting the uncertainties of life without abandoning responsibility for their own well-being. The way to serenity is through spirituality, which incorporates the now-popular notion of transcendence, that is, being able to believe in something greater than yourself. Life is much easier if you acknowledge that you are not responsible for everything that happens in the world! Patients must be encouraged to move beyond the feeling that they are controlling the universe. Instead of being mired in guilt and shame, they must give themselves time and energy for joy and pleasure. Life is much too complex to believe one person can take responsibility for everything. Obviously, this does not mean that recovering addicts should relinquish all responsibility; it merely means that they recognize what is and what is not within their power to change. In some ways spirituality can be viewed as the obverse of the narcissistic tendencies that encapsulated the "Me Generation" of recent years.

Striving for serenity through spirituality is highly compatible with the importance of lifestyle in the causation and treatment of a variety of diseases with which we as a society are struggling. This is a venerable precept in medicine, one that physicians have recently learned to accept again since the pervasive focus on technology in the mid-twentieth century. Alcoholics Anonymous (and mutual help fellowships for other addictions) offers tremendously important clinical tools for doctors to use as the underpinnings for all they are attempting to help patients accomplish through the pharmacopsychosocial approach to treatment.

A common misconception among certain members of the fellowship is that if patients are unsuccessful in attaining the goals of AA at first, they must try and try again to "work the program" until they "get it." To many, this seems like hitting your head against a wall until you gain enlightenment. What is the likelihood that enlightenment will be achieved? In other words, some individuals can attain the serenity and spirituality that lead to recovery and develop a level of comfort in their lives by peer support alone. Most, however, can benefit from work with a professional therapist or counselor to overcome the mistrust and low self-esteem that present barriers to embracing *anything* outside themselves. Furthermore, members of peer mutual support fellowships who suffer co-occurring psychiatric disorders in addition to addiction(s) should have these disorders addressed by an experienced psychiatrist, one who can determine whether psychiatric medication is necessary in addition to psychotherapy. No matter how effective peer support is—and the tenet of this book is that it can be extremely helpful—it may not be sufficient for everyone who is afflicted with addictions. There is often a fine line between not "working your program" and not being able to do so because of a co-occurring psychiatric illness. Complementary psychiatric treatment is advisable for all those individuals who have severe co-occurring disorders in addition to addiction(s) or in whom trust and self-esteem are so depleted by previous psychological trauma that they may not be able to effectively use the support provided by their peers.

PHARMACOPSYCHOSOCIAL TREATMENT KNITS A STRONG RECOVERY SAFETY NET

Earlier we mentioned the need for a team of professionals to manage the multiple layers of addiction aftercare and to assist recovering addicts in their efforts toward continued recovery. Recovering addicts may not understand why they need a psychotherapist or an addiction psychiatrist in addition to a primary care provider. After all, the patients will be attending peer support meetings that are intended to facilitate and guide their journey to recovery. Next we explain why psychotherapy and other psychiatric care received from professionals other than the primary care physician is significantly different from, but definitely complementary to, the mutual support that patients receive at 12-step meetings.

Talk therapy, in either an individual or a group setting within a dependable and supportive relationship with a trained professional therapist who has expertise in treating addiction, can often help people struggling with recovery to begin to accept and ultimately thrive in a 12-step fellowship as well as elsewhere in life. In addition, appropriately prescribed medications for depression, mood swings, post-traumatic stress disorder, panic attacks, poor impulse control, and other conditions can often help this process along. Talk therapy can be performed by a psychiatrist, psychologist, social worker, mental health nurse practitioner, and various certified counselors, including pastoral counselors or clergy, but medications are typically only prescribed by physicians. Mental health nurse practitioners can prescribe psychiatric and other medications under a physician's supervision, although the physician does not necessarily have to have formal training in psychiatry. In addition, there have been legislative initiatives in some states to provide prescriptive authority to doctoral-level psychologists who have not completed medical school.

The managed healthcare system has reduced the incentive for psychiatrists to provide psychotherapy. This is understandable, because it is more profitable for managed care companies to assign psychotherapeutic tasks to healthcare workers who have lower hourly fees. Of course, the argument proffered by such for-profit organizations is that nonphysician therapists have better honed psychotherapy skills because that is all they do. However, nonphysician psychotherapists do not have the medical training to complement their psychotherapy skills, as psychiatrists do. The multidimensional skill set of psychiatrists can be essential for management of the often complex addiction patient population. Although addiction psychiatrists are perhaps best trained to provide the spectrum of care required by addicted patients—the pharmacopsychosocial treatment approach—recent financial pressures have relegated most psychiatrists to the role of medication managers, while other psychotherapist clinicians interact with patients in more depth.

Fortunately, the smoothly integrated team of the professionals just mentioned can deliver acceptable pharmacopsychosocial treatment for addictions. Of course, the key to effectiveness of these teams is communication among the professional members—something not always easy to accomplish within the time constraints of managed care and the energy many recovering addicts require. For example, a highly experienced psychologist could work effectively with a primary care physician who would prescribe any needed psychotropic medications; a counselor may combine forces with a psychiatrist; or a social worker may collaborate with an addiction psychiatrist. However, most professionals who treat addictions would agree that prescription of relevant psychotropic medications to this challenging population of patients is probably best accomplished by a knowledgeable psychiatrist who understands addiction as well as the challenges of recovery.

Another viable alternative for treatment teams that do not include a psychiatrist with expertise in treating addictions is to request a consultation when unusual problems present themselves. No matter how desirable a combination of clinicians seems on the surface, it is feasible only if permitted by the insurance provider, which is devoted to cutting costs and may reject the need for added input. Thus, patients with co-occurring diagnoses often are not allowed to fully address all the issues that need to be overcome for a healthy recovery. They may be required to pay for some treatment on their own. Unfortunately, most patients who seek treatment for addiction are not only at the end of their rope with respect to their physical and emotional health, but are also financially depleted and unable to pay for treatment out of their own pockets. There is considerable evidence from health economists that the policy of insurance corporations to restrict addiction treatment is penny wise and pound foolish for society as a whole. Nevertheless, this discrimination is likely to continue, unless current attempts to legally rectify the unfair treatment of this vulnerable population of patients are successful.

In addition to financial obstacles, there are other reasons that make involvement of professionals in the aftercare of addictions difficult to maintain. Many people who are in recovery continue to mistrust professionals and may therefore avoid physicians altogether. Even if they see their doctor, often such patients are not forthcoming about their "secret." Recovering addicts should be encouraged to ask themselves, "Why am I reluctant to tell my doctor, whom I have entrusted with my life, that I am in recovery from an addiction?" Earlier we discussed the concerns often voiced by most patients, which are related in one way or another to patients not wanting others to know that they are "different." Many patients have convinced themselves that the only way to be certain that the secret that they are "addicts" will not get out is to not tell *anyone*. A concern for confidentiality is explicitly stated in 12-step meetings. However, confidentiality is no less important in the physician–patient relationship. It is vital that patients understand that confidentiality has been a tradition of the medical profession since its inception. Moreover, medical records are protected by law; these rules are strictly enforced for records related to all mental illnesses, and particularly so for alcohol or drug addiction. Therefore, concerns expressed by some people in recovery about whether their doctor can be trusted to maintain confidentiality are not really justified. Their reservations about divulging that they are in recovery probably reflect the vulnerability they would feel with complete disclosure of intimate secrets that are inter-twined with the history of their addiction(s). Additionally, patients must be counseled to consider whether their lack of comfort about their self-worth and whether they truly "belong" among "healthy" (nonad-dicted) people could also be contributing to why they cannot let down their guard with doctors or others outside of the peer support recovery fellowship.

PEER MUTUAL SUPPORT FELLOWSHIP: A SAFE HAVEN IN THE STORM OF ADDICTION

What's in a name? Sometimes a great deal. A combination of shame about addiction and lack of trust is probably why the members of com-mon 12-step mutual support fellowships typically use the cognomen "Anonymous," which connotes the safety of nameless membership. To create the name of a given 12-step group, the name of the specific addic-tion from which the participants are attempting to recover is added to this term. The familiar and comforting ritual of introducing yourself— "Hello, I'm Mike R., and I'm an alcoholic or addict"—is customary at the start of the meetings of all the 12-step fellowships. Although this overture seems directed to fellow members, it is equally meant to be self-affirming and empowering for speakers. They are addicts, and that is not something they have to hide. Not surprisingly, learning to become comfortable with the person you are is a major thrust of all these mutual support fellowships. Participants probably will experience tremendous reassurance, almost a cocoon-like feeling, when fellow members pledge not to divulge their personal "secrets" to others outside the fellowship. One common way of putting this is "What is said here stays here." The opportunity to honestly recount your life journey and what you believe you have learned as a result can be incredibly cathartic and the first step to finally forgiving yourself. Not surprisingly, those who listen to such stories no longer feel as alone as they had prior to learning that their own experiences are not unique and that everyone present is convinced that there is a way out. The empathy and acceptance offered by peers is transformative and may be the beginning of learning to accept the self. Shared compassion and understanding also constitute a vital part of these meetings and are believed to be the means to recovery.

The fellowship receives a new member without question or reserva-tion; the sole criterion for membership is the desire to stop engaging in an addiction and a willingness to share life experiences in an atmosphere that is conducive to trust and self-disclosure. Feeling accepted within a peer mutual support fellowship is essential for addicts to relearn how to feel good about themselves and to trust that others will respect them once they know them. Unfortunately, this favorable supportive experience may be as short-lived as the duration of the meetings or other activities in which the members participate with their peers.

What happens to the newly discovered self-esteem outside of the meetings, when 12-step fellowship participants are at home with family, at work with colleagues, or at play with nonaddicted friends? Most of those who are struggling to achieve recovery from addiction(s) feel a significant need to reenter, as an equal partner, the world of those who are healthy and have never been addicted and to be accepted by them. But they are hampered by their attitude that, although they are in recovery, they are not fully "worthy" of acceptance by those who have never been addicted. This self-deprecation is subtle. It can, however, gnaw away at recovery. Such a feeling of "unworthiness" is experienced, for example, when refusal of the offer of a beer at a party is followed by quizzical looks from the host. It also arises when recovering addicts apply for the annual renewal of a professional license or for malpractice insurance. They must answer that they have been convicted of drug offenses, or have lost their license to practice, or are on probation because of an addiction. Finally, the sense of moral inferiority wells up within recovering addicts when family members mention their former addiction(s) in an accusatory manner. These may arise in the context of arguments about issues that are now only distantly related to the disease, such as why there is not enough money in the family coffers to live in a better house or buy a new car. Often these arguments are about subjects that recovering addicts no longer regard as particularly timely or important. Nevertheless, the bitter truth stings.

RECOVERY REQUIRES SELF-EXAMINATION— WITH HELP FROM OTHERS WHO CARE ABOUT THE RECOVERING ADDICT

Two fundamental issues—lack of trust and enduring shame—contribute to and may also be consequences of most cases of addiction. Both suspicion and a feeling of humiliation will probably persist for a considerable time after recovering addicts have completed their formal treatment program. This will probably be true even if patients succeed in staying "clean and sober" or stop engaging in behavioral addictions. The members of the treatment team must work to resolve these feelings if recovering addicts are to regain and maintain their health.

What do we mean by "lack of trust and enduring shame"? Why do we believe these will become the significant issues patients must confront during recovery? As we have discussed, lack of trust as well as shame about being afflicted with addiction(s) may explain patients' reluctance to let others, even primary care doctors, find out that they are in recovery. We are not suggesting that recovering addicts should wear their addiction on their sleeves and discuss it with everyone. After all, recovering addicts are entitled to privacy, like everyone else. However, the fact that a patient is having difficulty trusting the doctor could reflect broader concerns that may influence many of the other close relationships in his life.

The difficulty in confiding in others may stem from previous hurt patients have suffered at the hands of people who occupied positions of trust in their past. Remembering or reexperiencing these prior hurts may make patients feel wary or unsafe. In fact, patients may greatly fear that similar transgressions may recur, without warning, in future interactions with others with whom they wish to become close and to whom they would like to reveal their true feelings. The attempt to avoid remembering this hurt, which may have constituted a psychological "trauma," may have contributed to patients' becoming addicts initially. However, even after patients have completed a formal treatment program and have succeeded in staying clean and sober or not engaging in behavioral addictions, these disturbing feelings may have not yet subsided. Unfortunately, failing to adequately address such deep-seated emotions in a 12-step program or in psychotherapy with a professional is associated with a poor prognosis and relapse. In the same vein, the fact that patients believe that a competent doctor will not respect them for who they are, simply because they have an addiction or other psychiatric disorder, signals that they do not feel good about themselves. Even after successfully graduating from a treatment program, recovering addicts probably still do not like who they see in the mirror every morning. This fundamental shame about the sort of people they think they are ("drunks" or "addicts") may make it difficult for recovering addicts to believe that anyone could genuinely care about them.

Therefore, it is probably a pleasant surprise and a great relief to be able to participate in the supportive atmosphere of 12-step meetings, which are populated by others who have been through similar struggles. They allow participants to experience genuine caring and perhaps even a glimmer of hope that they are *worthy* of recovery.

The fellowship of 12-step meetings certainly relieves patients' feelings of isolation and nonacceptance. However, feeling whole and accepted in 12-step mutual support meetings is one thing. Being accepted as a healthy member of society, instead of being regarded as "rehabilitated addicts," is another matter entirely. Similarly, believing that you are in recovery is one thing; feeling that you have *overcome* the issues that led you to your addiction and to your "mistakes" is quite another. Most of these feelings of inferiority, which continue well into recovery, reflect the profound stigma associated with addiction and other mental illnesses in our society. The support and caring that people afflicted with other illnesses receive is usually not forthcoming; even when this support is available, it is usually difficult for recovering addicts to accept. For example, people who have survived a life-threatening illness, such as a heart attack, usually feel relieved that they are alive and pleased that their family and friends sent flowers to their hospital room. In contrast, those afflicted with addiction(s) typically feel worthless, berate themselves incessantly for being addicts and for having hurt others, and feel that others will not accept them. Therefore, out of shame, they hide the fact that they are in treatment from their friends and even their family. So, in addition to the self-flagellation associated with buying in to the societal stigma associated with addiction, people starting the long journey to recovery may also have a sense of emptiness, of feeling that something within them is missing that keeps them from being complete. Most people in recovery share this general feeling, but its exact flavor is unique to each person. Such feelings may have contributed to their addiction in the first place and are probably still with them, even now that they are starting recovery and have been accepted by peers in 12-step meetings. Fortunately, the mistrust recovering addicts feel in early recovery diminishes as they become actively involved in a peer mutual support fellowship, begin to feel that they are regaining control over their lives, and start to make amends to others. Along with an increased ability to trust others, people in recovery will begin to trust themselves more and be less ashamed of who they really are. As this trust grows, patients may also find that they are able to venture beyond the healing 12-step "cocoon."

PROFESSIONAL GUIDANCE ON THE JOURNEY FROM ACTIVE ADDICTION TO RECOVERY

At this point, it may be time for recovering addicts to begin psychotherapy with a professional who can assist them in examining the fundamental issues standing in the way of extended recovery. These therapy sessions should give recovering addicts the opportunity to delve more deeply into their personal history and motivations than they can in 12-step mutual support meetings. In 12-step meetings, each participant is one of many members working together to help each other. In psychotherapy, recovering addicts become the focus of the attention of a competent and caring professional and have the benefit of personal guidance on this difficult journey. Through interactions with the therapist, patients may actually reexperience and better understand relationships with important individuals from the past, including parents, siblings, and/or intimate partners, and how these relationships unconsciously shape current relationships with others. Along the way, recovering addicts may relive particularly painful events that even now influence how they experience the world and the decisions they make. With the help of hindsight, the psychotherapist, who brings an independent, objective perspective, can help patients to reframe these formative experiences.

Group therapy is a preferred type of psychotherapy to treat addiction, for many reasons:

- It is economical.
- It is suitable for helping individuals deal with problems in their relationships.
- Patients in recovery have the cognitive and reality-testing skills needed to benefit from the input of their peers.
- Perhaps most important, the dynamics of group therapy are already quite familiar to those who are simultaneously involved in a 12-step fellowship.

Group therapy provides the sense of mutual support experienced in 12-step meetings while offering a more in-depth personal self-examination analogous to that experienced in individual psychotherapy sessions. In group sessions facilitated by an experienced therapist, not only can patients explore feelings they may have related to the therapist, but they can also examine emotions evoked by other group members as well as the ways these group members remind patients of previous relationships. In addition, patients gain insight from the observations other group members may voice about them. This is vital information if patients wish to better understand how their addiction has affected loved ones and how they can become a better spouse, parent, child, or friend. Nevertheless, some people do better working with an individual therapist, sometimes in addition to group therapy with the same or even a different therapist.

Considerable effort is made in therapist-led groups to understand the meanings of interactions among group members and how they may represent a dysfunctional way of coping throughout life. A professional therapist guides group members in this process of self-examination by asking questions, offering observations, and identifying recurrent patterns of interacting between individual group members. Some of these interactions are quite painful, and powerful emotions can emerge. The therapist helps to interpret these emotions constructively and to contain them so that the group session remains safe for all. The therapist emphasizes the importance of understanding dyadic relationships among group members, particularly as they relate to the personal histories of each patient: How do these relationships resemble fundamental relationships in the patient's life, in terms of disappointments, unfulfilled expectations, or the fear and anger they evoke? Primal feelings may emerge that are directed at other group members, for no apparent reason other than they may be of the same gender or hair color as the person who abused a group member in childhood. The therapist allows participants to appreciate these powerful feelings for what they represent and protects group members from the outbursts.

The therapist must also help connect how such emotions may be influencing the alcohol, drug, or behavioral addiction of the angry person. Of course, the therapist is by no means exempt from being a lightning rod for the expressed emotions of group members, as he embodies and elicits powerful feelings pertaining to authority figures. These feelings, too, will be interpreted and reviewed in terms of how they relate to each member of the group. The major focus on confidentiality in therapist-led groups makes them effective for sharing very private feelings and nurturing the capacities of members to trust one another. However, group members never feel the same degree of safety as they do in individual psychotherapy.

Although feedback from others in the group represents an essential component of both peer support meetings and professional therapist-led groups, the therapeutic processes are distinctly different. Ultimately, 12-step meetings are a safe home where each member tries to support the others. In contrast, therapist-led group therapy is predominantly directed toward understanding why each patient is the way he is and how he can go about changing. Twelve-step programs are characterized by egalitarian peer support. The presence of a professional facilitator, who is clearly the therapist of everyone in the group, changes the fundamental dynamic of groups. In 12-step meetings, senior members tend to take leadership and mentor the novices. Thus, issues of concern to senior members typically cannot be addressed, because sustaining novices from relapse, potentially a life-saving activity, clearly has priority. (Some of the needs of the senior members are usually dealt with during one-on-one interactions with their sponsors, as discussed later.) In 12-step meetings, all participants typically are suffering from the same identified addiction. Therefore, participants are all on the same journey, mutually guiding each other, using the comfortably ritualized traditions of the fellowship. The emphasis in the 12-step tradition is change through belonging to a fellowship of like-minded individuals with similar goals. A thorough understanding of oneself is less of a consideration in these meetings than it is in psychotherapy. The goal in psychotherapy is to effect change by using insight into oneself to solve the many problems confronting a former addict.

PSYCHOTHERAPY WITH A PROFESSIONAL IS HIGHLY COMPATIBLE WITH A 12-STEP PROGRAM

In spite of the differences among 12-step groups, therapist-led groups, and individual psychotherapy, their primary goal of healing addiction is identical. Therefore, these approaches are complementary rather than mutually exclusive. Early in recovery, when the primary focus is to stay drug or alcohol free or not engage in behavioral addictions, 12-step meetings may work better than intensive individual psychotherapy. Patients are particularly fragile at this stage. Focusing on emotionally traumatic events as is done in individual psychotherapy may interfere with the relatively straightforward, and logically prior, goal of staying abstinent. Some have used the analogy of not attempting to build the second floor of a house before making sure that the foundation is properly constructed. However, to extend the analogy, having an architectural plan of what the house will look like is necessary before beginning to build. Accordingly, during the first month or two of abstinence, recovering addicts should consider preparing a treatment plan for the time when they will want to delve more deeply into the recovery process. Formulating such a treatment plan typically requires a combination of working with the 12-step group and the patients' sponsors and beginning to work with a professional therapist.

If recovering addicts have been diagnosed as suffering from a co-occurring psychiatric disorder that requires medication or have suffered severe psychological trauma, it may be particularly valuable to begin work with a professional very early in recovery. By using specialized cognitive behavioral techniques that have demonstrated efficacy in preventing a relapse, this professional may help recovering addicts to contain their urges and cravings. As stated earlier, it is generally not advisable to engage in more intensive, insight-oriented exploration of emotions and motivations until stable abstinence has been achieved.

A great change has occurred in the approach to addiction treatment over the last three decades. At one time psychiatrists or other professionals who supplied the elements of pharmacopsychosocial treatment

of addiction were not involved in providing a safety net for people in recovery. As far as successful members of any 12-step mutual support fellowship were concerned, these professionals were not even in the
picture. Moreover, psychiatrists would only work with a patient who
had a "real" psychiatric illness. This was not thought to include addiction, which was viewed at this time as just a "bad habit." Oddly enough,
however, psychiatrists did not view problematic hypersexuality, gambling, and other similar behaviors we discuss in this book as addictions.
They were therefore very willing to treat such patients with psychotherapy—unless, of course, alcohol or drugs were an important part of the
presentation.

In past decades, though recovering addicts usually had a primary care
doctor to manage regular medical needs, their main focus quickly became the self-help, mutual support program. If they happened to have
begun work with a psychiatrist before it was clear that the problem was
addiction, they were told, "We cannot work together unless you are
sober." Enlightened psychiatrists of this era might suggest, "Why don't
you go to AA?" Patients on the road to recovery tried to attend as many
12-step meetings as possible (in the vernacular, "90 meetings in 90
days"), and it was hoped that they could "connect" with the fellowship.

This connection was typically achieved with help from others they
met at meetings who were farther along on the path to recovery and
were willing to serve as temporary sponsors. These experienced members served as informal facilitators, allowing newly recovering members
to become more and more involved in the meetings. The temporary
sponsors encouraged new members to attend meetings and provided
some guidance outside of the meetings. There was no limit to how many
temporary sponsors might be acquired along the way, but the more
sponsors newcomers had, the greater would be the number of people
who were interested in their welfare and who would encourage them to
keep coming back to the meetings.

The more time spent at meetings, presumably the more comfortable
recovering addicts became with the notion that it was acceptable to have
the disease of addiction, and the more confident they became that the
meetings and the fellowship were the way to recovery. An important
goal was to identify one of the "temporary" sponsors who could commit
to becoming a "permanent" sponsor. This permanent sponsor would be
the person on whom the "novice in recovery" could rely to make a more
lasting and intense commitment, who stood ready for a call 24/7, whenever the urge for relapse might present itself. The relationship with this
sponsor became the basis for the 12 Steps of Recovery, a significant un-

dertaking that the sponsor agreed to commit to, perhaps because he identified with the novice as a peer in an earlier phase of recovery. Moreover, the sponsor likely perceived that it was very important to his own recovery to continue to give back to the fellowship via this relationship. In essence, this meant helping those who might still be floundering by providing them with direction.

This self-perpetuating and mutually supportive process, which epitomizes the 12-step tradition, has resulted in a tremendously powerful network of people helping people. Over the years, this movement has spread across the world. Although most would associate this process of self-help with addiction treatment, it has also been effectively adapted to helping people cope with other kinds of illnesses. The self-help fellowship provides many of the elements of psychotherapy, in which people help others to address fundamental problems of coping with life through talking and other forms of interpersonal communication. There is a reciprocal nature to this process. Both sponsors and novices benefit greatly, though perhaps in different ways. This "therapy" is based on passing along the "wisdom of the fellowship" from sponsor to novice. Although sponsors have no professional training as therapists, they do have experience with and some success in recovery. This sort of peer support fellowship has returned many people mired in addiction to healthy lives. Moreover, life in the fellowship can continue to blossom for years after participation is initiated, nourished by every person that a sponsor takes under his wing as the recovering addict regains balance in his own life.

You may ask, "If the 12-step peer support fellowship works so well, why bother with anything else?" There are those who do very well indeed by attending meetings only and drawing sustenance from those who share the journey toward recovery with them. However, there are many others who, although they continue to attend meetings, have little success. Still others stop attending because of frustration over their lack of progress. Unfortunately, the assumption in "orthodox" circles of the 12-step fellowship has been that such people were clearly "not working the program." Now most people recognize that some members who attend meetings are unsuccessful because they need more than can be provided in the self-help setting alone. Typically, these members are suffering from co-occurring psychiatric and medical illnesses. These patients need the assistance of one or more professionals who can provide the pharmacopsychosocial approach to addiction treatment. Today most psychiatrists now recognize the complementary and constructive role they can play in collaboration with the self-help fellowship. The self-help support network provides the foundation for the pharmacopsychosocial treatment strategies advocated in this book. Certainly nothing in the pharmacopsychosocial treatment of addiction should interfere with the self-help network. The mutual support and professional perspectives of treatment are intended to synergistically strengthen the process of recovery. In fact, successful members of 12-step groups have come to realize that their recovery might be enhanced by assistance from an experienced professional and that enlisting such assistance will in no way dilute what the fellowship offers. All the same, most 12-step members would recommend that recovering addicts should not wallow in "terminal uniqueness," claiming that they are unlike others in the mutual support meetings because all they really need is a psychiatrist to "fix the chemical imbalance." Despite initiating treatment with a psychiatrist, recovering addicts should never eliminate the 12-step program from the journey to recovery. They should continue to actively seek out the support of peers and nurture healing relationships with them in the 12-step tradition.

HOW DOES A PROFESSIONAL HELP RECOVERING ADDICTS UNDERSTAND THEMSELVES BETTER AND ENABLE THEM TO HEAL THEIR ADDICTION?

Psychologists and other therapists have written extensively about the psychodynamic foundations of trust and self-esteem and how disturbances of these emotions can become the basis for developing addictions. Exploring these issues specifically as they pertain to recovering addicts' lives is the essence of the work they will undertake with a psychotherapy professional. Lack of trust, regardless of its origins in a person's life, can lead to experiencing the world as a very frightening and painful place, a world in which the individual has very little perceived control over what will happen next. For obvious reasons, children in dysfunctional families are particularly vulnerable to such feelings of not having control. In such families, youngsters rarely have reliable allies to assist them in navigating the challenges of growing up and learning to function autonomously in the outside world. Within therapy, recovering addicts should explore whether and in what ways their early lives were out of control. In essence, during the corrective, positive experience of psychotherapy, recovering addicts learn how to form a supportive alliance with the therapist, an alliance in which they can explore the childhood lack of guidance or support. Did the individual undergo particularly painful experiences that even now seem to control life choices? Answering this question often requires understanding how the recovering addicts' family lived as they were growing up.

- How were decisions made?
- How did the parents argue?
- Was there violence?
- Was there drinking or drug use?
- Were the parents committed to each other and to the children, or was the future and integrity of the family uncertain?
- Who comforted them when they were sick or hurt, or were they forced to fend for themselves?
- Did they feel safe, or were they fearful?
- Was the world outside exciting or frightening to them?
- Were they loved and appreciated, or exploited?
- Were they abused? How did they learn to cope? Were they witness to devastation?
- Did they experience unpredictable violence that seems to have marred their entire lives?

In this unpredictable world, engaging in behaviors that focus all of the attention and energies away from the tumult of life can serve to numb the fear and *seem* to deliver addicts from facing their uncertainties. The capacity of certain thoughts or behaviors to cause addicts to dissociate, or to be released from the "here and now," can provide the foundation of many other addictive behaviors, as we understand them. Thus, dissociative behaviors seem to offer a modicum of control, compared to life without these behaviors. The therapist will help recovering addicts address the coping styles developed in response to the childhood experience of feeling powerless over the environment. Moreover, the therapist will help them recognize and understand that *the present is not the past* and that different behaviors are now in order. These painful experiences should not be denied. But neither should they be allowed to continue to control patients' lives.

ADDICTION AS A WAY TO COPE?

It is not long before youngsters learn that there are even "better" ways to remove themselves from the painful aspects of life. Take a drug, and you will feel high for a short time. Have sex or gamble, and time stops while you are engaging in these activities. Youngsters quickly learn that engaging in pathological drug-taking, sex, or gambling can be pleasurable. More important, the consequences of engaging in these behaviors are somewhat predictable. During these short interludes, people can stop worrying about all the travails of life with which they have been struggling. This ephemeral increase in control gained by engaging in focusing or dissociating behaviors is, therefore, reinforcing. The therapist will help recovering addicts unravel initial experiences with drugs or alcohol or other behaviors that represent the foundation of their addiction(s). Questions may include:

- How did it feel in the beginning, and how did it progress?
- What were they actually running from?
- Did some important person in their lives introduce them to this way of coping in order to take advantage of them?

Of course, some reputable clinicians, even now, believe that the problems associated with addictions are not the "cause" of addictive behavior and that therefore stopping the behaviors is all that is needed to achieve recovery. While this may well be true for some people, it is simply not the case for many who suffer from addictions. Many addicts recover for a short time and then relapse.

The degree of reinforcement individuals initially experience from addictive behaviors is unique, based on an interaction of genetic constitution, personal experience, and environment. Nevertheless, after the pathological behavior/or alcohol or drug self-administration are repeated over and over again, they can become hardwired in the brain via learning mechanisms. As the behaviors become incorporated into the behavioral repertoire, they may no longer elicit the desired effect for the duration or to the degree anticipated or desired. Soon addicts find it hard to resist engaging in these behaviors, in spite of the fact that the benefits diminish over time. Therefore, the behaviors that were previously perceived as beneficial, because they were so predictable, are now out of addicts' control, in much the same way as their distrust of the surroundings and their relationships were out of their control. "When and how did you come to the realization that your addiction was now out of control?" is a question that the therapist may help recovering addicts to answer. Other questions the therapist may help patients address include:

- What was the tipping point, when you discovered that what was initially reliable fun had become a problem that had caused you to refocus the priorities in your life?
- How did you decide that something had to change?
- Did this frenetic need to engage in the problem behaviors ever make you question whether it was possible to go on?

It is tremendously disheartening for addicts to recognize that the addictive behaviors they had chosen to provide themselves a time out from painful emotions and a frightening environment no longer help in coping, but only make things worse. Feeling unequal to the tasks of life may represent the origins of the fundamental shame and self-hatred people who are struggling with addictions of all kinds so often report. The shame is further compounded by the guilt they may feel in having neglected themselves and their responsibilities to the other people in their lives. For example, a man may feel profound guilt because he bought cocaine with money meant to buy food for the children. His justification for using the cocaine, as an attempt to ameliorate his despondency or because he was out of control due to his addiction, does little to alleviate his guilt.

DESPONDENCY DURING RECOVERY

The sense of shame truly hits home during aftercare, when recovering addicts no longer have the addictive behavior as a way of escaping the realities of their emotional condition. The unavoidable realization that they do not believe their lives can actually be changed results in deepening despondency. The degree of change necessary to reverse this downward spiral in their spirits can be exceedingly difficult to achieve on their own. And reaching out for help from others who have faced a similar situation in their lives may be more than recovering addicts can accomplish, in spite of trying to do so. Many people suffering from addictions never actually learned how to ask for help as they were growing up. There may not have been anyone in their families of origin from whom they could ask help. Without anyone to help recovering addicts, their desperation may manifest itself as clinical depression. And if not properly treated by a professional, such as a mental health care provider, with psychotherapy or with antidepressant medication, the depression can easily progress to suicidality. By using the pharmacopsychosocial approach, the psychiatrist can help recovering addicts see how their lives can actually change, once their depression is alleviated and they resolve no longer to resort to addiction to manage the challenges they are certain to face.

Most people find that destructive emotions, such as anger, fear, and self-hatred—those with which they coped by indulging their addiction(s)—are often difficult to recognize until they become overwhelming and are out of control. Specifically, they may realize that once these emotions have escalated, they are next to impossible to control by any means other than engaging in addictions. Learning to appreciate and recognize the links between the antecedents of these painful emotions and the experience of being flooded by them can be accomplished through the self-examination involved in various forms of psychotherapy. But intellectual understanding of this association is only the beginning. In order to attain healing, *knowing* must be translated into *feeling*.

WANTING TO DO THINGS DIFFERENTLY

The goal of all therapy is to learn to recognize what happened before things got out of control. Recovering addicts can achieve control over the destructive consequences of addiction by changing the way they respond to the triggers that previously functioned as behavioral antecedents of the addiction. This process is often called "behavior modification." Once recovering addicts can map out problematic behaviors, in terms of what preceded them and then what happened subsequent to engaging in them, they can determine what they need to do to change the destructive outcome. This is not always as easy as it may sound. Recovering addicts will probably have difficulty being objective. Moreover, some antecedents of behaviors are feelings, which are often difficult to put into words that can be used to modify behaviors and ultimately feelings. Returning to the destructive ways in which people have coped with life for many years is usually easier than making changes. For this reason, a professional therapist can be helpful by "holding up a mirror" for recovering addicts, so they can better understand how self-destructive their behavior has become.

SETTING PRIORITIES IN ORDER
TO DO THINGS DIFFERENTLY

Once recovering addicts have made the decision to change, they will recognize that change requires considerable effort and discipline. Patients must stay motivated to avail themselves of the other important aspects of psychotherapy. One of the fundamental components of psychotherapy is to help people identify what is truly important to them, that is, what does their "gut" and "moral compass" tell them? How have their addictions displaced their previous priorities in life with activities that left them lost and empty? Ultimately, recovering addicts themselves (not the therapist, who is simply there to help) will have to decide how to get back on track, by making some difficult choices. They may well have lost the skills to make such judgments over the course of their addiction(s). When people are addicted, getting drugs becomes more important than taking a child to school or planting flowers. All addictions disrupt priorities. They make addicts do things that they would not be caught dead doing otherwise. Abandoning your principles for a short-lived fix that is no longer even pleasurable is something that he previously could never have imagined doing. Nevertheless, throughout their addiction, addicts probably knew the difference between right and wrong. Addictions cannot destroy people's moral compass, what they were raised to believe is right and wrong. Violating this moral compass is often why recovering addicts are so down on themselves early in recovery.

If recovering addicts no longer devote all their energy to their addiction, significant amounts of time will become available to them. The newfound time can become a burden, because recovering addicts may not know how to use it. Therefore, during therapy, patients and therapist must attend to a fundamental but concrete task: determining how patients will fill the time they previously expended in the pursuit of self-destructive behaviors. Patients' time during formal treatment programs is highly structured by others who mandate that patients participate in "recovery activities." Once outside the treatment program, however, they are on their own.

The "empty" time could easily lead to a relapse, unless recovering addicts decide to devote themselves to rebuilding their lives and regaining their physical and emotional health. They must force themselves to engage in self-examination. This is not an easy thing to do without help, because it will likely lead to a painful understanding of the changes that must be made in order to attain full recovery. Unless this process is managed with skill, by a therapist, it may culminate in considerable self-flagellation and despondency, even relapse. As part of this process of self-understanding, patients must determine their own priorities, an undertaking that requires considerable effort early on and continues throughout recovery.

Identification of priorities could direct recovering addicts to make monumental decisions with broad ramifications, such as leaving a destructive marital relationship, finding a new job, or returning to school. These priorities could lead to more straightforward changes, such as spending more time with the people who really matter to them, like their families; or devoting time to exercise and more healthful eating; or learning yoga or other relaxation techniques. Other outcomes of careful self-examination may be to return to potentially beneficial traditions of childhood, such as religious worship, or to a simpler, rural life, escaping the "bright lights and big city," where addictions are more likely to overwhelm vulnerable people. Some addicts, particularly those who have relapsed over and over again, may decide that they are not yet ready to make any of these decisions. They may choose extended residential treatment, in order to have a self-enforced time away from regular life and help with returning to the fundamentals of living. While this may seem drastic, sometimes it is the only way to go.

HOW TO MAKE CHANGES
AFTER DETERMINING PRIORITIES

One word of caution: Recovering addicts should not make major life decisions right after the completion of their formal addiction treatment program. They should wait until completing six or more months of substantive recovery work before "beginning again." Of course, delaying these decisions should not preclude deciding immediately to move out of a crack house or leaving a physically abusive and violent spouse. Also, electing very long-term residential treatment in order to make a very major decision to concretely remove oneself from surroundings in which his addiction occurred should not be postponed. In addition, it is strongly recommended that recovering addicts not become involved in any new intimate relationships until their abstinence is better established and issues are less "raw." The usual wisdom is to wait a year or more.

Organized peer support meetings are very valuable for dealing with rites of passage into recovery. Many at these meetings have struggled with the same issues and are eager to share their views. However, as we keep stressing, everyone is somewhat different. The essence of treatment is that each recovering addict must learn and feel empowered to make his own decisions. They all should look within, instead of mimicking others without understanding their own priorities. Recovering addicts should not allow themselves to be swayed by the influence of others who do not really understand them or may not have their best interests at heart. A useful analogy is that the goal in treatment is to develop the keel to the boat, so patients can avoid slipping with the winds of life or the waves of adversity, and stay on course to recovery.

RECOVERY MEANS UNDERSTANDING
THE ROLE OF FUNDAMENTAL EMOTIONS
IN ADDICTION, SUCH AS TRUST AND SHAME

Interestingly, recent research suggests that there are biological causes for certain of the deleterious emotions, lack of trust and profound shame, that may trigger a relapse to active addiction in the early stages of recovery. As the mother offers her breast to the newborn for nourishment, release of the hormone oxytocin from her brain allows breast milk to flow. It has been surmised that oxytocin may thereby help to cement the mother-child bond. More recently, it has been reported that this hormone plays a vital role in mediating the brain changes necessary for formation of close social bonds of trust in both genders and in other situations, such as the marital dyad of intimacy and even trust in business associates.

Researchers have long suspected that abuse or neglect early in life can permanently alter people's brains, making them more prone to anxiety and depression, less able to handle stress, or even incapable of forming strong attachments with others. A natural consequence of these brain alterations is that the people do not trust that others can like them, and they begin to have considerable self-doubts and difficulties in liking themselves. They are haunted by the thought that something must be terribly wrong with them.

The molecular evidence to support the theory that some hormones are essential for normal, intimate relationships to develop was only recently discovered. For example, it was reported that children who started life neglected in Romanian orphanages showed long-term abnormalities in hormones, such as oxytocin and vasopressin, accompanied by other impairments in brain functioning. Both these hormones are fundamentally involved in social attachment and learning. They are necessary for children to develop the learning and memory capacities that they need to be able to recognize familiar persons by sight, smell, and other sensory modalities and the associated familiarity and sense of security and well-being. Complementary findings from studies of nonhuman primates show that early separation from the mother leads to depression and even increased self-administration of alcohol later in life as a means to cope with stress. Moreover, some research studies suggest that these nonhuman primates who self-administer excessive alcohol may respond to pharmacological treatment of their depression with antidepressants. Thus, hormonal or neurotransmitter abnormalities seem to underlie the lack of trust in relationships in various addictions, although this finding remains to be formally demonstrated. Nevertheless, this line of evidence does support the need to appropriately treat co-occurring psychiatric disorders if recovery is to be attained.

Experienced therapists would argue that trust and shame cannot be adequately addressed early in treatment, when patients are still quite fragile. At this time, the focus should be on maintaining stability and abstinence. Prematurely reexperiencing painful emotional memories might trigger relapse or enhance the despondency patients typically feel after realizing how difficult change will be. Therefore, in the early part of recovery, the therapist will work with recovering addicts in a highly supportive manner, so that they begin to feel safe within the therapeutic relationship. As we mentioned, the depths of mistrust and shame may be so profound that achieving this trust may require considerable time. Good therapists always encourage their patients to bring up their feelings and experiences from their 12-step meetings for further discussion. Doing this provides a useful bridge to the more intense goals recovering addicts wish to achieve from their individual therapy. By allowing them to share their impressions of how things are proceeding for them in the mutual support fellowship, the therapist can begin to help them identify what they may need from individual therapy to complement issues that were not addressed adequately by peers in the fellowship. Only when patients feel they can trust their psychotherapist will they be able to discuss the painful aspects of addiction, its precursors, and its consequences. The mechanics of staying abstinent are the topics of early sessions with the therapist. Ultimately, during aftercare, the traumatic events of recovering addicts' lives should become the focus of psychotherapy. Patients will increasingly be concerned with maintaining abstinence by having a tight bond with the 12-step group and their sponsors.

As we have repeatedly stressed, some recovering addicts have never enjoyed fulfilling relationships with the people in their lives. A large part of the psychotherapist's work is related to building an effective therapeutic relationship with patients. Through this relationship, recovering addicts will begin to better understand what went wrong in previous relationships as well as create a template (of sorts) for relationships they may develop now that they are in recovery.

Maintaining abstinence from drugs or alcohol or not engaging in behavioral addictions is only the first step on the road to recovery. The pharmacopsychosocial approach to healing addiction has as its ultimate goal to imbue the capacity to live a healthy and full life—a balance of love and work.

Glossary of Terms

AA See "Alcoholics Anonymous."

Abstinence Refraining from a desired activity, such as using drugs, drinking, gambling, or sexual activity.

Abuse A pattern of substance use or behavior that leads to distress or impairment but that is less severe than dependence or addiction.

Acute withdrawal syndrome After abrupt cessation of heavy drug or alcohol use, the body mechanisms that compensate for the depressing or stimulating effects of the addictive substances and the accompanying stress reaction.

Addiction A more severe form of dependence.

Affect The way a person's mood appears to other people.

Affective disorders Disorders of mood, for example, depression.

Agonist A drug that activates the physiological effects of a given receptor.

Alcohol The term applied to members of a group of chemical compounds and, in popular usage, to the specific compound ethyl alcohol, or ethanol. It is a clear, colorless liquid, with a burning taste and characteristic, agreeable odor. Ethanol is the alcohol in beverages, including beer, wine, and brandy.

Alcoholic A person who suffers the damaging effects of excessive and habitual alcohol consumption.

Alcoholics Anonymous (AA) A worldwide support group founded in 1935 to rehabilitate alcoholics by creating a network of peers who provide direction and mutual support. AA initiated the 12-step program.

Amotivational syndrome Apathy, passivity, lethargy, and the inability or unwillingness to concentrate.

Amphetamines A class of powerful stimulants that increase energy and decrease appetite, the regular use of which generally leads to addiction.

Analgesic A pharmaceutical agent that reduces or eliminates pain.

Anhedonia The inability to take pleasure in situations that ordinarily give rise to pleasurable feelings, a feature of major depression or excessive use of stimulants.

Antabuse The brand name of disulfiram, a medication used to discourage alcohol consumption by producing unpleasant effects, such as nausea, vomiting, and cardiovascular disturbances, when alcohol is ingested.

Barbiturates A group of drugs derived from barbituric acid that produce sedation and sleep and are used by drug users for their intoxicating effects. They now have little role in medicine.

Behavioral addiction A disorder in which a pattern of conduct, such as gambling or Internet activity, is engaged in compulsively and is continued despite significant adverse consequences.

Benzodiazepine Any of a class of sedative-hypnotics, such as Valium, Xanax, Ativan, and Librium. These are the so-called minor tranquilizers that are used in the treatment of anxiety, insomnia, and epilepsy. They are generally safer than the barbiturates and are now the preferred drug for treatment of these conditions. As a result of their widespread use, tranquilizer addiction has become a problem.

Binge A periodic, uncontrolled indulgence in an addictive substance or behavior.

Blood alcohol concentration The percentage of a person's blood that consists of alcohol.

Bulimia An eating disorder, found mainly in women, defined by binge eating followed by self-induced purging and vomiting or the use of laxatives, diuretics, or excessive exercise.

Buprenorphine   A mixed agonist (like morphine) and antagonist (like naltrexone) that is very effective for treatment of opioid dependence. Trade names are Subutex and Saboxone.

Chipping   The intermittent use of an addictive drug, to the extent of supporting a low-level dependence.

Clonidine   An antihypertensive drug that is also used to reduce the symptoms of opiate withdrawal.

Cocaine   A powerful, addictive stimulant extracted from the leaves of the coca plant.

Codeine   A narcotic, chemically related to morphine, naturally occurring in the opium poppy and often used in cough remedies.

Cognitive capacity (intelligence)   The ability to think, remember, and plan.

Cognitive impairment   A decrease in the ability to think, concentrate, and remember.

Cognitive therapy   A treatment approach that tries to change a person's thought patterns, to favorably alter his or her behavior or emotional state.

Cold turkey   The symptoms occasioned by the sudden discontinuation of the use of an addictive substance without medical treatment; acute withdrawal.

Comorbidity   The co-occurrence of more than one disease in the same person, either causally related or independent of one another.

Conditioning (Pavlovian and other)   A process of learning by which a subject comes to associate a behavior with a previously unrelated stimulus.

Contraindication   A factor that renders a medication or treatment modality unsafe or inadvisable.

Crack   A highly addictive form of cocaine that can be smoked, giving rise to a short-lived, intense rush.

Craving   A strong, nearly irresistible desire, particularly for an addictive substance or behavior.

Cross-tolerance   Tolerance to a drug developed as a result of repeated exposure to another drug with similar pharmacological activity.

Crystal meth   A highly addictive form of amphetamine, sold in the form of a crystalline powder that can be sniffed or injected.

Cue   A stimulus or pattern of stimuli that creates a craving to use an addictive drug or engage in addictive behavior.

Dementia   The deterioration of mental functioning, often caused by aging or Alzheimer's disease, but that also can be caused by prolonged, heavy use of alcohol and certain other drugs of abuse.

Denial   The failure of a person to acknowledge to himself the reality of a condition or circumstances apparent to other people; for example, the refusal of addicts to admit that they are addicts and that their addiction is causing harm to themselves and others.

Dependence, physical   A chronic need to ingest a drug in order to avert physical withdrawal symptoms.

Dependence, psychological   A craving to ingest a drug in order to avert psychological discomfort. Closely related to craving.

Depression   A mood disorder characterized by an inability to concentrate, insomnia, loss of appetite, anhedonia, feelings of extreme sadness, guilt, dejection, helplessness and hopelessness, and thoughts of death. Depression is caused by a biochemical disturbance in the brain.

Disulfiram   See "Antabuse."

Dopamine   A neurotransmitter, which when released in specific brain reward centers gives rise to feelings of pleasure, that is a critical component of the brain mechanism underlying addiction and learning.

Drive disorders   Disorders in brain chemistry arising from the disturbances of natural drives such as hunger or sex and that underlie the abuse of drugs.

Drug abuse   The repeated use of drugs, despite their deleterious consequences, but to a less severe degree than dependence or addiction.

Drug-seeking behavior   An irresistible preoccupation leading to a pattern of conduct in which people pursue the use of drugs despite the deleterious consequences of their actions.

DSM-IV   The most recent edition of the diagnostic manual of the American Psychiatric Association, a text revision published in 2000.

DTs   Short for "delirium tremens," a dangerous form of alcohol withdrawal, caused by the sudden cessation of the heavy, prolonged use of alcohol that is characterized by mental confusion, hallucinations, and alternating levels of consciousness.

Dual diagnosis   The diagnosis of a psychiatric disorder in a person suffering from an addictive disorder. See "Comorbidity."

Endocannabinoid system   Cannabinoids that are naturally produced by the brain or body to subserve physiological functions.

Endogenous   Occurring naturally in the brain or body.

Endogenous opioid   Opioids that are naturally produced by the brain or body and serve a normal physiological role.

Ethanol Ethyl alcohol, the intoxicating component of alcoholic drinks, made naturally from the fermentation of sugar, starch, or other carbohydrates. See "Alcohol."

Euphoria A pervasive feeling of mental and physical well-being, such as is induced by ingesting an addictive drug or engaging in addictive behavior or as an aspect of bipolar disorder.

Family therapy A therapy approach in which the members of the family of an addict take part. The focus is how the family system may become a source of treatment.

Fentanyl A powerful opioid, with abuse liability, used intravenously as a preoperative anesthetic.

Fetal alcohol syndrome A condition in infants, young children, and adults caused by prenatal exposure to alcohol. The syndrome is characterized by growth retardation, cranial and facial defects, central nervous system dysfunctions, and organ malformations.

Food and Drug Administration (FDA) The United States governmental agency responsible for making and enforcing legal controls over the evaluation, manufacture, licensing, and marketing of pharmaceutical products.

Freebasing Smoking cocaine, a severely addictive mode of ingestion of the drug.

Gambling Betting on an uncertain outcome, as of a contest, or playing a game of chance for stakes. Gambling often becomes the basis of a behavioral addiction.

Gateway drug A drug that is easily available, the use of which leads to the use of more dangerous drugs that are more difficult to obtain.

Genetic risk An inherited predisposition to develop a pathological condition, including addiction or other psychiatric disorders. The basis is the altered genetic code in a person that leads to a chemical imbalance.

Habituation Tolerance to and dependence on an addictive drug or behavior, such as alcohol or gambling. It is more of a learning phenomenon than tolerance and dependence.

Halcion (triazolam) A benzodiazepine that is frequently abused; it is prescribed as a hypnotic (i.e., a sleeping pill).

Hangover Headache and nausea as an aftereffect of consuming too much alcohol or central nervous system depressants.

Heroin Diacetylmorphine, a powerful, highly addictive opiate synthetically derived from opium.

Hippocampus   A complex neural structure consisting of gray matter and located on the floor of each lateral ventricle of the brain. Part of the limbic system, a group of brain structures that are intimately involved in motivation and emotion. It has a central role in the formation of memories.

Hypnotic   A medication that induces sleep.

Hypothalamus   The part of the brain that lies below the thalamus and that regulates bodily temperature, certain metabolic processes, and other autonomic activities, including the regulation of food intake. It is intimately involved in the regulation of drives.

Insufflation   Ingesting drugs in crystalline or powder form by sniffing or snorting them nasally.

Intravenous drug user   A drug user who injects drugs directly into the veins.

Librium   A brand of cholordiazepoxide, a benzodiazepine frequently used in the management of alcohol withdrawal.

Mania   A mood disorder characterized by unreasonable elation, excitability, excessive activity, reduced sleep, and/or poor judgment.

Marijuana   The flowering tops of the cannabis plant, which are dried, chopped, and smoked to release the psychoactive cannabinoid THC (tetrahydracannabinol).

Methadone   A powerful synthetic opioid, similar to morphine and heroin, but producing a much lower level of intoxication, for a prolonged period. Prescribed in clinics to prevent the use of heroin by addicts and as a form of maintenance treatment.

Methamphetamine, Meth   A powerful amphetamine with a high abuse potential.

Mood disorders   Disorders in emotional states often arising from dysregulation of brain chemistry.

Morphine   The primary narcotic constituent of opium, constituting about 10 percent of opium by weight.

Naltrexone   A long-lasting opioid antagonist that reverses the effects of heroin and in the treatment of heroin and alcohol addiction. Marketed under the trade name "ReVia" in an oral form and as a long-lasting depot injection under the trade name "Vivitrol."

Narcotic   As a medical term, it designates an addictive drug, usually an opioid, that relieves pain and produces intoxication. As a legal term, it includes stimulants, such as cocaine and methamphetamine, and psychoactive drugs, such as marijuana and LSD.

Negative reinforcer An undesirable effect that discourages an action or behavior and results in its discontinuation.

Neuroadaptation Brain alterations, such as occur with the regular use of an addictive drug or the repetition of behaviors, that can lead to tolerance, addiction, and withdrawal

Neuron Any of the impulse-conducting cells in the brain, spinal column, and nerves, consisting of a nucleated cell body with one or more dendrites and a single axon. Also called nerve cell. Neurons are the building blocks of the brain and nervous system.

Neuroscience A branch of the life sciences that deals with the anatomy, physiology, biochemistry, or molecular biology of nerves and nervous tissue and especially their relation to behavior and learning, memory, sensation, and communication.

Neurotransmitter A chemical substance, such as acetylcholine, norepinephrine, serotonin, and dopamine, that transmits nerve impulses across the synapses between nerve cells.

Nucleus accumbens Part of the brain that is vital in the reward system of the brain.

Obesity Morbidly overweight.

Opiate A drug derived from or chemically related to the narcotic constituents of opium, such as morphine, codeine, and heroin.

Opioid A drug with the characteristic effects of an opioid on the brain, including analgesia and intoxication, though not chemically derived from opiates.

Outpatient treatment Nonresidential treatment, to encourage the patient to be able to function in the context of real life.

Overdose The consumption of a dose of a drug so large that it produces a serious deleterious reaction, possibly death.

Panic attack A sudden, overwhelming fear, attended by physiological symptoms such as sweating, trembling, chest pain, palpitations, shortness of breath, and dizziness. Sometimes characterized as "lightheadedness."

Paranoia A psychiatric condition characterized by persistent delusions of persecution and suspicion that the motivations of others are malevolent.

PCP (phencyclidine) An illegal hallucinogen, often inducing hallucinations and violent behavior, that was originally developed as an animal tranquilizer. PCP acts at the excitatory glutamate receptors.

Pharmacotherapy   The treatment of disease, especially mental diseases, with medicines.

Physiological dependence   A metabolic equilibration of the body systems for an addictive substance, characterized by the development of a tolerance and the onset of withdrawal when the use of the substance is discontinued. Also called "physiological adaptation."

Prognosis   The expected outcome of the course of a disease.

Psychoanalysis   The method of investigating and treating emotional problems originated by Sigmund Freud. It includes the attempt to interpret "conflicts" that interfere with normal coping and is often dubbed the "talking cure."

Psychological dependence   The need to continue the administration of a drug or engage in a behavior, the abrupt cessation of which would result in emotional and mental preoccupation with the drug or behavior and persistent craving to resume it.

Psychopharmacology   The study of and use of medicines for the treatment of psychiatric disorders.

Psychosis   A severe psychiatric disorder marked by the loss of contact with reality and characterized by disruptions of perception, judgment, hallucinations, and delusions (false beliefs).

Psychotherapy   The treatment of mental and emotional disorders through the use of psychological techniques designed to encourage communication of conflicts and insight into problems, with the goal being relief of symptoms, changes in behavior leading to improved social and occupational functioning, and personality growth. Psychotherapy includes the techniques of psychoanalysis, cognitive behavioral therapy desensitization, relaxation, nondirective psychotherapy, reeducation, hypnosis, and others.

Psychotropic medication   A drug that affects the mind. These include neuroleptics, antipsychotics, antidepressants, stimulants, and anxiolytics.

Rationalization   Making excuses to justify behavior that would otherwise be regarded as unreasonable or harmful.

Reinforcement   An event, a circumstance, or a condition that increases the likelihood that a given behavioral response will recur.

Self-help (12-step) groups   Groups made up of recovering addicts, in which addicted people help support each other through the process of recovery.

Spirituality   Concern with things of the spirit and spiritual development. May or may not involve a conception of one's relationship with God.

SSRI   Selective serotonin reuptake inhibitor. A class of antidepressants, including Prozac, Celexa, and others.

Synapse   The dead space between neurons at which a nervous impulse passes from one neuron to another.

Thought disorders   Disorders of cognitive functioning (the form and content of thought) often produced by disturbances in brain chemistry and associated with psychosis or severe mood disorder.

Tolerance   The need for increased amounts of an addictive substance to achieve intoxication or the desired effect; markedly diminished effects with continued use of the same amount of a drug. "Inverse tolerance" or "sensitization" is a characteristic of stimulant abuse whereby specific effects of the drug are augmented with repeated exposure. Strongly related to learning.

Transdermal patch   A patch applied to the skin that releases a drug into the body.

Trigger   A formerly neutral stimulus that attains the ability to elicit drug cravings because of repeated associations with drug use.

Upper   A colloquial term for a stimulant; in contrast to "downer," a colloquial term for CNS depressants.

Withdrawal   Physiological changes manifested by discomfort and pain accompanying interruption in the use of an addictive substance or in the practice of an addictive behavior.

Helpful Web Sites

ADDICTION SUPPORT GROUPS: 12-STEP PROGRAMS

Al-Anon Family Group Headquarters
www.al-anon.org

Alcoholics Anonymous World Services, Inc.
www.aa.org

Cocaine Anonymous
www.ca.org

Gamblers Anonymous
www.gamblersanonymous.org

Narcotics Anonymous
www.na.org

Overeaters Anonymous
www.oa.org

ADDICTION SUPPORT GROUPS: ALTERNATIVES TO 12-STEP PROGRAMS

Rational Recovery Systems
www.rational.org/recovery

Secular Organization for Sobriety
www.sossobriety.org

SMART Recovery
www.smartrecovery.org

Women for Sobriety
www.womenforsobriety.org

234

GRASSROOTS AND PROFESSIONAL INFORMATION SOURCES

Academy for Eating Disorders
www.aedweb.org

American Academy of Addiction Psychiatry
www.aaap.org

American Medical Association Alliance, Inc.
www.ama-assn.org
Volunteer arm of the American Medical Association has information on alcohol, drug abuse, and nicotine dependence as a part of their health information for patients.

American Psychiatric Association
www.psych.org

Dual Recovery Anonymous
www.draonline.org

National Clearing House for Alcohol and Drug Information
www.ncadd.org

National Eating Disorders Association
www.nationaleatingdisorders.org

Partnership for a Drug-Free America
www.drugfreeamerica.org

Problem Gambling
www.problemgambling.org

Recovery Zone
www.recoveryzone.org
Provides name, address, telephone number of self-help organizations.

GOVERNMENT WEB SITES

Center for Disease Control and Prevention
www.cdc.gov

The Center for Mental Health Services
www.mentalhealth.sam/sa.gov

National Institutes of Health
www.nih.gov

National Institute on Alcohol Abuse and Alcoholism
www.niaaa.nih.gov

National Institute on Drug Abuse
www.nida.nih.gov

National Institute of Mental Health
www.nimh.nih.gov

APPENDIX C

Epidemiological Tables

**Prevalence of Substance Use in Last Month
(per 100 persons aged 12 years or older)**

Drug	*Prevalence (%)*
Alcohol	50.3
Binge drinker	22.8
Heavy drinker	6.9
Tobacco	29.2
An illicit drug	7.9
Marijuana	6.1
Cocaine	0.8
Crack	0.2
Methamphetamine	0.3
Hallucinogens	0.4
Ecstasy	0.2
Heroin	0.1
Nonmedical use of psychotherapeutic drugs	2.5
Pain relievers	1.8
Tranquilizers	0.7
Stimulants	0.5
Sedatives	0.1

Source: Adapted from Substance Abuse and Mental Health Services Administration (2005), *Overview of findings from the 2004 National Survey on Drug Use and Health* (Rockville, MD: Office of Applied Studies, NSDUH Series H-27, DHHS Publication No. SMA 05-4061).

Prevalence of Substance Use Disorders during the Previous Year (per 100 persons aged 12 years or older)

Substance Use Disorder	Prevalence (%)
Any substance use disorder	9.4
• Alcohol abuse or dependence, *no* illicit drug use disorder	6.4
• Illicit drug abuse or dependence, *no* alcohol use disorder	1.6
• Alcohol *and* illicit drug abuse or dependence	1.4
– Marijuana abuse or dependence	1.9
– Cocaine abuse or dependence	0.7
– Opioid abuse or dependence	0.6

Source: Adapted from Substance Abuse and Mental Health Services Administration (2005), *Overview of findings from the 2004 National Survey on Drug Use and Health* (Rockville, MD: Office of Applied Studies, NSDUH Series H-27, DHHS Publication No. SMA 05-4061).

Pharmacological Treatment of Withdrawal Syndromes from Substances of Abuse

Substance	Agent and Dosage	Other Treatment
Alcohol	Diazepam, 10-20 mg/1–2 hours (typical dosage required, 60 mg)	Thiamine, 100 mg intramuscularly or 50 mg twice daily by mouth, and multivitamin tablets for 3 days
Other CNS depressants	Phenobarbital, 120 mg/hour (typical dosage, 900-1500 mg)	
Stimulants	Not usually needed	Anxiolytics or neuroleptics acutely for agitation or toxic psychosis
Opioids	3–5 days of clonidine 0.1–0.3 mg every 4–6 hours (check blood pressure prior to each dose, hold for BP<90/60). Alternatively, methadone dosed at 10–20 mg by mouth every 12 hours initially or buprenorphine dosed at 4–12 mg under tongue daily initially; both taper over a 5–10-day period to reduce withdrawal symptoms (1 mg buprenorphine is equivalent to 5 mg methadone, 5 mg heroin, 15 mg morphine, 100 mg meperidine)	Ibuprofen for muscle cramps, loperamide for loose stools, and promethazine for nausea or vomiting

Substance	Agent and Dosage	Other Treatment
Nicotine and tobacco	Nicotine patch started at 7–21 mg per day based on addiction severity with slow taper over 3 months. Nicotine gum started at 2–4 mg every 1–3 hours based on addiction severity with slow taper over 3 months	Clonidine acutely can minimize withdrawal discomfort
Cannabinoids	Not usually needed	Anxiolytics or neuroleptics acutely for agitation or severe anxiety
Hallucinogens	Not usually needed	Anxiolytics or neuroleptics acutely for toxic psychosis

Pharmacological Maintenance Strategies for Substance Dependence after Detoxification Is Completed

Substance	Agent and Dosage
Alcohol	Disulfiram 125–500 mg daily; Naltrexone 25–100 mg daily; Acamprosate 666 mg three times per day; Topiramate 25–150 mg twice per day (not FDA approved)
Other CNS depressants	None approved or recommended
Stimulants	None approved or recommended
Opioids	Methadone by mouth at 30–140 mg per day; Buprenorphine 4–32 mg under the tongue (available as buprenorphine/naloxone [4/1] to prevent diversion)
Nicotine and tobacco	Antidepressants often used
Varenicline (Chantix)	1 mg by mouth twice per day × 12 weeks
Cannabinoids	None approved or recommended
Hallucinogens	None approved or recommended

Bibliography

American Psychiatric Association. (1994). *Diagnostic and statistical manual of mental disorders* (4th ed.). Washington, DC: American Psychiatric Association.

Budney, A. J., Hughes, J. R., Moore, B. A., & Vandrey, R. (2004). Review of the validity and significance of cannabis withdrawal syndrome. *American Journal of Psychiatry, 161,* 1967–1977.

Carnes, P. (1991). *Don't call it love: Recovering from sexual addiction.* New York: Bantam.

Dani, J. A., & Harris, R. A. (2005). Nicotine addiction and comorbidity with alcohol abuse and mental illness. *Nature Neuroscience, 8,* 1465–1470.

Gahlinger, P. (2004). *Illegal drugs: A complete guide to their history, chemistry, use, and abuse.* New York: Plume.

Kessler, R. C. (2004). The epidemiology of dual diagnosis. *Biological Psychiatry, 56,* 730–737.

Koob, G. F., & Le Moal, M. (2005). Plasticity of reward neurocircuitry and the "dark side" of drug addiction. *Nature Neuroscience, 8,* 1442–1444.

Kuhn, C., Swartzwelder, S., & Wilson, W. (2003). *Buzzed: The straight facts about the most used and abused drugs, from alcohol to ecstasy.* New York: Norton.

Lieber, C. S. (2003). Relationships between nutrition, alcohol use, and liver disease. *Alcohol Research & Health, 27,* 220–231.

Lukens, T. W., Wolf, S. J., Edlow, J. A., Shahabuddin, S., Allen, M. H., Currier, G. W., et al. (2006). Clinical policy: Critical issues in the diagnosis and management of the adult psychiatric patient in the emergency department. *Annals of Emergency Medicine, 47,* 79–99.

Martin, P. R., & Petry, N. M. (2005). Are non-substance-related addictions really addictions? *American Journal on Addictions, 14,* 1–7.

Marzuk, P. M. (1995). Fatal injuries after cocaine use as a leading cause of death among young adults in New York City. *New England Journal of Medicine, 332,* 1753.

McLellan, A. T., Lewis, D. C., O'Brien, C. P., & Kleber, H. D. (2000). Drug dependence, a chronic medical illness: Implications for treatment, insurance, and outcomes evaluation. *JAMA: The Journal of the American Medical Association, 284,* 1689–1695.

Naimi, T. S., Brewer, R. D., Mokdad, A., Denny, C., Serdula, M. K., & Marks, J. S. (2003). Binge drinking among US adults. *JAMA: The Journal of the American Medical Association, 289,* 70–75.

Nestler, E. J. (2005). Is there a common molecular pathway for addiction? *Nature Neuroscience, 8,* 1445–1449.

Nunes, E. V., & Levin, F. R. (2004). Treatment of depression in patients with alcohol or other drug dependence: A meta-analysis. *JAMA: The Journal of the American Medical Association, 291,* 1887–1896.

O'Brien, C. P. (2005). Anticraving medications for relapse prevention: A possible new class of psychoactive medications. *American Journal of Psychiatry, 162,* 1423–1431.

Peele, S., & Brodsky, A. (1991). *The truth about addiction and recovery.* New York: Simon & Schuster.

Perkinson, R. (2004). *Treating alcoholism: Helping your clients find the road to recovery.* Hoboken, NJ: John Wiley & Sons.

Vaillant G. E. (1996). A long-term follow-up of male alcohol abuse. *Archives of General Psychiatry, 53,* 243.

Volkow, N. D., Fowler, J. S., & Wang, G. J. (2004). The addicted human brain viewed in the light of imaging studies: Brain circuits and treatment strategies. *Neuropharmacology, 47,* 3–13.

Washton, A. M., & Zweben, J. E. (2006). Treating alcohol and drug problems in psychotherapy practice. New York: Guilford Press.

Ziedonis, D. M., Smelson, D., Rosenthal, R. N., Batki, S. L., Green, A. I., Henry, R. J., et al. (2005). Improving the care of individuals with schizophrenia and substance use disorders: Consensus recommendations. *Journal of Psychiatric Practice, 11,* 315–339.

Index

About the Authors

PETER R. MARTIN, M.D., is a professor of psychiatry and pharmacology at Vanderbilt University School of Medicine. He is also director of the Division of Addiction Medicine, the Addiction Psychiatry Training Program, and the Vanderbilt Addiction Center. Dr. Martin received his Honours B.Sc. in Molecular Genetics in 1971 and M.D., C.M. in 1975, both from McGill University and his M.Sc. (Pharmacology) from the University of Toronto in 1979. He was resident in internal medicine (1975–1976), fellow in clinical pharmacology (1976–1978), and resident in psychiatry (1978–1980) all at the University of Toronto. Subsequently he was a visiting scientist in the Section of Experimental Therapeutics, Laboratory of Clinical Science, National Institutes of Mental Health (1980–1983); chief of the Section of Clinical Science, Laboratory of Clinical Studies, National Institute on Alcohol Abuse and Alcoholism (1983–1986); and associate professor in the Departments of Psychiatry and Pharmacology at Vanderbilt University (1986–1992). Dr. Martin's research and scholarly interests include the molecular basis, diagnosis, and treatment of drug use disorders with an emphasis on substance-induced mental disorders, including investigations of the molecular biology of thiamine; magnetic resonance spectroscopy and functional magnetic resonance imaging to elucidate the pathogenesis of addiction and alcohol-induced brain damage; and the clinical pharmacology of addictive substances, including novel pharmacological treatments of addictive disorders. Dr. Martin is a fellow of the Royal College of Physicians (Canada), a distinguished fellow of the American Psychiatric Association, and a diplomate of the American Board of Psychiatry and Neurology in psychiatry with certification in the subspecialty of addiction psychiatry.

BENNETT ALAN WEINBERG, ESQ., AND BONNIE K. BEALER are prizewinning writers in science and medicine, celebrated for their facility in rendering complex ideas into rigorously accurate, clear, briskly written, and entertaining prose. Weinberg holds degrees in English and philosophy from Columbia University's Columbia College and Graduate School of the Arts, and in law from New York University School of Law. Bealer holds a degree in psychology from Temple University College of Arts and Sciences and has studied finance and computer science at the University of Pennsylvania's Wharton School.

Weinberg and Bealer collaborated to create the critically acclaimed *The World of Caffeine: The Science and Culture of the World's Most Popular Drug* (Routledge, 2001), the first book in any language to comprehensively treat the natural, cultural, and social history of the most popular drug on earth, from ancient Chinese medicinals to the colas and coffeehouses of today. This definitive academic reference book—yet a book that has been praised for its accessible style—has been published in successful Italian, Spanish, and Japanese translations. It was nominated for a 2002 James Beard Foundation Award and is the recipient of the André Simon Memorial Highly Commended Prize for 2001.

Weinberg and Bealer are also the authors of *The Caffeine Advantage: How to Sharpen Your Mind, Improve Your Physical Performance, and Achieve Your Goals—the Healthy Way* (Free Press, 2002), a health and self-help book written to educate the public about a substance in nearly universal use.